PRAISE FOR *SECURITY METRICS*

"Throw out the security religion and make informed

> —Mark Curphey
> ISBPM, Inc.
> "Connecting People, Process and Technology"

"I'm very excited that Jaquith has written a text on metrics, and expect this will be the standard reference for years to come."

> —Adam Shostack

"Andrew devotes an innumerable amount of time and effort to helping our profession out at SecurityMetrics.org. His book is wonderful, entertaining, and well thought-out. I found myself nodding my head in agreement more than a few times."

> —Alex Hutton
> CEO, Risk Management Insight

"Andrew has written a book that most people who work in information protection and those who manage and work with them should read, not because it is particularly informative about information protection, but because it is highly informative about the challenges of measuring protection programs effectively. While lots of books are out there about this or that aspect of security, from a security management standpoint, you cannot manage what you cannot measure, and Andrew puts his stake in the ground with this book about what you should measure and how to do it."

> —Dr. Fred Cohen
> CEO, Fred Cohen & Associates
> http://all.net/

"To paraphrase Lord Kelvin's famous quote, 'You cannot improve what you cannot measure.' Computer security has inhabited this sorry state for years, leaving too much room for snake oil, scare tactics, and plain old bull feathers. Andy's book helps to remedy this problem by sending a strong clear message that metrics are both necessary and possible. Buy this strikingly well-written book today and help put an end to security nonsense."

> —Gary McGraw, Ph.D.
> CTO, Cigital
> Author of *Software Security: Building Security In*

Security Metrics

Security Metrics

REPLACING FEAR, UNCERTAINTY, AND DOUBT

Andrew Jaquith

♦♦Addison-Wesley

Upper Saddle River, NJ · Boston · Indianapolis · San Francisco
New York · Toronto · Montreal · London · Munich · Paris · Madrid
Cape Town · Sydney · Tokyo · Singapore · Mexico City

The publisher offers excellent discounts on this book when ordered in quantity for bulk purchases or special sales, which may include electronic versions and/or custom covers and content particular to your business, training goals, marketing focus, and branding interests. For more information, please contact:

U.S. Corporate and Government Sales
800-382-3419
corpsales@pearsontechgroup.com

For sales outside the United States, please contact:

International Sales
international@pearsoned.com

 This Book Is Safari Enabled

The Safari® Enabled icon on the cover of your favorite technology book means the book is available through Safari Bookshelf. When you buy this book, you get free access to the online edition for 45 days.

Safari Bookshelf is an electronic reference library that lets you easily search thousands of technical books, find code samples, download chapters, and access technical information whenever and wherever you need it.

To gain 45-day Safari Enabled access to this book:

- Go to http://www.awprofessional.com/safarienabled
- Complete the brief registration form
- Enter the coupon code QID1-EUYC-MUTP-2QCE-X8SX

If you have difficulty registering on Safari Bookshelf or accessing the online edition, please e-mail customer-service@safaribooksonline.com.

Visit us on the Web: www.awprofessional.com

Library of Congress Cataloging-in-Publication Data:

Jaquith, Andrew.
  Security metrics : replacing fear, uncertainty, and doubt / Andrew Jaquith.
    p. cm.
  Includes bibliographical references and index.
  ISBN 0-321-34998-9 (pbk. : alk. paper) 1. Risk management. 2. Decision making. I. Title.
  HD61.J37 2007
  658.4'7015195—dc22

                            2006103239

ISBN 0-32-134998-9
Text printed in the United States on recycled paper at RR Donnelley, Crawfordsville, Indiana
First printing, March 2007

To dreamers and contrarians

Contents

Foreword

From Kelvin's "[W]hen you cannot express it in numbers, your knowledge is of a meagre and unsatisfactory kind" to Maxwell's "To measure is to know" to Galbraith's "Measurement motivates," there is little need to argue here on behalf of numbers. Doubtless you would not now be holding this book if you didn't have some faith in the proposition that security needs numbers.

But what kind of numbers? Ay, there's the rub. We need numbers that tell a story and, which is more, say something that allows us to steer for where we are going, not just log from whence we have come. We have to acknowledge the central creed of the statistician: all numbers have bias; the question is whether you can correct for it. As security practitioners we have to know our place: Security is a means, not an end. We have to share with preachers and teachers the understanding that the best must never be the enemy of the good. So let's begin by laying bare the bias of this essayist and this book alike.

In *The Book of Risk*, Borge reminds and instructs us, "The purpose of risk management is to improve the future, not to explain the past." The past is a beautiful thing, whether we read about it or stand reverentially in the graveyard, but it is not what we, or this book, can afford to fix our gaze upon. No, we have to manage risks, seeking that optimal set point between, on the one hand, accepting silly risks and, on the other, burning our entire fortune fleeing that which cannot be escaped. Borge goes further: "Risk management means taking deliberate action to shift the odds in your favor—increasing the odds of good outcomes and reducing the odds of bad outcomes." This is my job description, this is your job description, this is our job description: to shift the odds in our favor. Need we remind ourselves that our opponents understand this 'pert well?

Need we remind ourselves that our opponents pick the places where the odds are in their favor?

To change the odds we have to know what those odds are, and we have to be able to detect when the odds change under our influence. To do this, we need security metrics. The job description for those security metrics is this:

> *Security metrics are the servants of risk management, and risk management is about making decisions. Therefore, the only security metrics we are interested in are those that support decision making about risk for the purpose of managing that risk.*

If you want to argue with that, this book is not for you, and I know without asking that Andrew would agree. Neither he nor I want to waste time convincing folks who have no use for numbers that numbers are somehow cool; what Andrew does at length and I am doing in shorter form here is to say that there is no need for despair—quite the opposite: This is the that idea whose time has come. It is an idea whose time has come so much so that despair of life without it or indifference to life with it is not even a luxury that you cannot afford. So let me compliment you for your intuition that this idea is timely (and how), as well as that this is the author to read (double and how). You are right on both counts.

Understand that numbers are insufficient, but they are necessary. To be the raw material for decisions, they need to be well enough thought out that you know what they mean. We have to be careful with what we claim to be measuring, and we have to make sure that our readers have some understanding of what we are measuring on their behalf. Numbers can mislead if they are not understood. Numbers are much like security in that they are a means rather than an end. Numbers exhibit vulnerabilities like computer systems in that whether misuse is intentional or inadvertent matters little if misuse is at hand. Numbers, like the surgeon's scalpel, can harm or heal, but we need them. As Fred Mosteller put it, "It is easy to lie with statistics, but it is easier to lie without them."

In November 2003, the Computing Research Association convened an invitation-only workshop on what "Grand Challenges" in digital security the National Science Foundation should concentrate a decade of funding on. There were four:

- No further large-scale epidemics
- Effective tools with which to certify systems
- Achieving low/no skill as a requirement to be safe
- Quantitative information risk management on par with financial risk management

That last one is why we are here. We need to do for the security arena what the quants have done for the financial markets: We need to understand, quantify, measure, score, package, and trade digital security risks as effectively as all the other risks with which the financial services sector already deals.

Finance has a concept—namely, that of "value at risk" (VaR), which is a daily number summing up a bank's exposure to loss. VaR is not without its faults (and Andrew takes up this idea later), but the core idea is that there is a target for risk and a metric that says how far off the target you are. It was my privilege to sit through a full review of a leading bank's VaR calculation. At the end of the day, the top economist leans over the lectern and says to his peers, "Now, you may ask yourself why all this works. (Pregnant pause.) It works because there is *zero ambiguity* about which of you owns what risks." At that moment of epiphany, I realized that that is what separated his field from mine—in our field, there is nothing *but* ambiguity about who owns what risk. We will not achieve the meaningful equivalent of a VaR calculation, and we will not fulfill the NSF's Grand Challenge, unless and until we have a way to score the game.

For any game, without a way to score the play, you cannot improve your performance as a player. That is where we are today: no way to score the game and no way to improve our play. This is not just a failing; it is a risk in and of itself. If we cannot make headway on measuring, on scoring, on understanding our risks well enough to change the odds in our favor by backstopping decisions about risk, we will have created one of those vacuums that Nature abhors. If we cannot measure risk and predict its consequences, the public, acting through its legislatures, will simply assign all the risk to some unlucky player. If assigning the risk and liability does not kill the unlucky assignee, from that point forward new players will find a barrier to entry like no other. In plain terms, innovation in the digital sphere and in the Internet itself is what is at issue here. If we cannot find a way to measure the security problem, I am afraid our choices will become difficult.

Some would say that regulation, not measurement, is what is needed. Some would say that the answer is to somehow force more investment in security—that, if this is an arms race, the good guys can win, because at the end of the day, they can outspend the opposition. That may be true in the physical world, but it is a dangerous delusion to think it can work in the digital world. In the digital world, the defender's work factor is proportional to the sum of all the methods the attackers possess times the complexity of that which is to be defended. The attacker's work factor is the cost of creating new methods as fast as old ones must be retired while complexity ensures that the supply of new methods can never be exhausted.

This asymmetry does not allow an "Outspend Them" strategy. Writing on 23 October 2001, six weeks after 9/11, the then-Chief U.S. Economist for Morgan Stanley wrote in the *New York Times* (in paraphrase) that "The next ten years will be a referendum on whether we consume the entire productivity growth of the U.S. economy for increased security spending." Perhaps the U.S. or some other country could endure that, but if it does, security, whether that means us or armies, becomes a fundamental rate-limiting block to wealth creation. Being a block to wealth creation is a side effect that cannot be sustained by us or anybody else.

For these reasons, the canon of digital security is now that of cost effectiveness, and the analysis of cost effectiveness runs on the fuel of measurement: measurement of inputs and outputs, of states and rates, of befores and afters. There is no greater need in the digital security sphere than to have a set of definitions of what to measure and to measure against those definitions. This will produce no miracles; human nature ensures that: The insecurity a computing monoculture engenders is long since proven theoretically and long since demonstrated empirically, but those proofs have not caused much behavior change; the buying public still longs for a technical fix, and the sellers of technical fixes are glad they do. But we—all of us who practice in this space—must find a way to measure and thus manage the risks that are rising all 'round us. My friend, the Red Queen, told us to run faster and faster if we wanted to stay in the same place. Evidently we are not yet running fast enough, because we are not achieving stationarity.

It is my fervent hope that Andrew's book—this book—sets off a competitive frenzy to measure things, to fulfill that Grand Challenge of a quantitative information risk management that is as sophisticated as what our brothers and sisters in finance have constructed with the very computers that we are now trying to protect. A competition of that sort will be brutal to some, but I, for one, would rather compete in that sphere than endure competition based on the side effects of needless complexity—complexity crafted by knaves to make a trap for fools. I want to compete on my terms with those who would manage risk at the minimax of lowest marginal cost and highest achievable control, rather than compete with the legions of digital doom on their terms.

This is your chance, Dear Reader, to be present at the creation or at least to be a passive consumer. Andrew, by writing this book, has erased any chance you thought you had to say, "Can't be done" or even "No one is doing that." As soon as this ink dries, both of those excuses are terminated with extreme prejudice. We, you and I, cannot waste our time on wishful thinking. To go on from here we cannot use words; they do not say enough. If you want to be a hero, make *your* book as much a step function as this one is.

Daniel E. Geer, Jr., Sc.D.
Cambridge, Massachusetts
November 2006

Preface

WHAT THIS BOOK IS ABOUT

This book is about security metrics: how to quantify, classify, and measure information security operations in modern enterprise environments.

HOW THIS BOOK CAME TO BE

Every consultant worth his or her weight in receipts accumulates a small trove of metaphors, analogies, and witty expressions. These help explain or clarify those rarified things that consultants do and tend to lubricate the consulting process. Oh, and they also tend to be funny. One of my favorite bits—particularly relevant to the topic at hand—is this one:

> *No good deed goes unpunished.*

This simply means that with any worthwhile endeavor comes many unwitting (and often unwanted) consequences. So it is with the world of "security metrics." As you will see in the story I am about to tell you, my steadfast belief that security metrics ought to be a very! serious! field of study! has brought with it its own punishment.

Several years ago, several colleagues and I undertook a series of elaborate empirical studies on the subject of application security. We rigorously gathered and cleansed far-flung source material, aggregated and analyzed the resulting data, built an exotic mathematical model, and wrote a short research paper on the subject, complete with eye-catching charts and graphs. It was well received by customers and media alike. Some time later I was asked to present a condensed version of our findings on an Internet webcast run by an industry trade publication. In this case "webcast" meant a PowerPoint presentation accompanied by previously taped narration. The audience, as pitched to me by the sponsor, was to include "CSOs, technologists, and decision-makers."

That sounded great; I relished the opportunity to impress the bejeezus out of the vast numbers of grand globetrotters promised by the publication. In addition, my Inner Academic had high hopes that many in the audience would send me e-mails and letters marveling at the analytical techniques we used, the breadth of the data, and the many keen insights contained in the narrative and text. How wrong I was. Instead of measured praise from academe, I received several e-mails that went something like this:

> *"Great presentation, but I was hoping to see more 'return on investment' numbers. You see, I really need to convince my boss to help me buy widget _____ (fill in the blank)."*

And then there were the slightly more disturbing comments, like this one:

> *"We have no money for our security program! Oh, woe is me! What I really need is more ROI! Help me!"*

I confess to embroidering the truth a tiny bit here; the second e-mail I received was not nearly so plaintive. But the theme was clear: viewers assumed that because the webcast was about "security metrics," it must be about ROI. Our marvelous metrics were the good deed; their unfulfilled expectations were the punishment.

GOALS OF THIS BOOK

Mercifully, the "security ROI" fad has gone the way of the Macarena. But to be absolutely sure that your expectations are managed (more consultantspeak for you), here is what this book is about, and what it is *not* about.

The primary objective of this book is to quantitatively analyze information security activities. The chapters suggest ways of using numbers to illuminate an organization's security activities:

- **Measuring security:** Putting numbers around activities that have traditionally been considered difficult to measure
- **Analyzing data:** What kinds of sources of security data exist, and how you can put them to work for you

- **Telling a story:** Techniques you can use to marshal empirical evidence into a coherent set of messages

The need for a book like this seems plain to me. Security is one of the few areas of management that does not possess a well-understood canon of techniques for measurement. In logistics, for example, metrics such as "freight cost per mile" and "inventory warehouse turns" help operators understand how efficiently trucking fleets and warehouses run. In finance, "value at risk" techniques calculate the amount of money a firm could lose on a given day based on historical pricing volatilities. By contrast, security has . . . exactly nothing. No consensus on key indicators for security exists.

The lack of consensus on security metrics is, in part, due to the fact that the culture surrounding security is largely one of shame. Firms that get hacked tend not to talk about security incidents in public. Likewise, firms that are doing the right things tend not to talk either, lest giant red bull's-eyes appear on their firewalls' flanks. When they do talk, it is typically under NDA, or at small gatherings of like-minded people. Therefore, this book, as a secondary objective, documents effective practices of firms that take the responsibility of measuring their security activities seriously.

NON-GOALS OF THIS BOOK

This book is first and foremost about *quantifying security activities*. It identifies ways to measure security processes that many enterprises consider important. The metrics and analysis techniques I document here are partly of my own devising but are drawn primarily from examples collected over the course of consulting in the software, aerospace, and financial services industries. I have met and exchanged notes with many people who have started their own metrics programs and are passionate about security metrics. At a minimum, I hope you will regard this book as a useful synthesis of current security measurement practices.

The word "practices" in that last sentence is important. I chose it carefully because of the implicit contrast with an opposing word: theory. In this book you will find plenty of anecdotes, lists of metrics, and ways of measuring security activities. But I have devoted only a small part of the text to *modeling* security risks—that is, figuring out which threats and risks are the right ones to worry about. Risk assessment is a broad field with many schools of thought. Smart people have spent many megawatts of brainpower modeling threats, modeling the effectiveness of security countermeasures, and simulating perimeter defenses.

The first non-goal of this book, therefore, is enterprise risk modeling and assessment. This is an important endeavor that every enterprise must undertake, but specific techniques are beyond the scope of this book. Risk assessment is an organization-specific activity, and I did not want to spend half of my pages disclaiming things because "it depends on what risks your organization feels are the most important." Moreover, I did not wish to add to what is already an exceptionally rich canon of works devoted to the subject of risk modeling and assessment.

To this rather significant and somber-sounding non-goal I would like to add three more. The dearth of generally accepted security metrics often means that unscrupulous vendors manufacture blood-curdling statistics in a vacuum, devoid of context and designed to scare. Middle managers with agendas promptly recycle these metrics for their own purposes. Therefore, this book also is not about the following:

- **Budget justification:** How to convince your boss to spend money on security. If your company has not yet figured out that it needs to spend money on security, it likely has deeper problems than just a lack of statistics.

- **Fear, uncertainty, and doubt (FUD):** How to abuse or misrepresent data for the purpose of manufacturing security scare stories. I derive no pleasure from this, and it makes me feel cheap and dirty.

- **Funny money:** Any and all topics relating to "return on security investment." In addition to its dubious merit as a measure of security effectiveness, ROSI (as it is sometimes called) is a needless distraction from empirical security measurement.

Of course, because no good deed goes unpunished, it is entirely likely that this book will be used for those purposes regardless. But that, as a student of security analysis might say, is a risk worth taking.

AUDIENCE

I wrote this book for two distinct audiences: security practitioners and the bosses they report to. Practitioners need to know how, what, and when to measure. Their bosses need to know what to expect. Not for nothing has the security domain resisted measurement. As the bedraggled security manager of a household-name financial services firm recently told me, "My boss doesn't understand what I do every day. All he understands are numbers." Bridging the yawning gap between practitioners and management is what this book aims to achieve.

OVERVIEW OF CONTENTS

This book is divided into eight chapters:

- **Chapter 1, "Introduction: Escaping the Hamster Wheel of Pain":** The state of security metrics today eerily resembles a hamster wheel that spins continuously around an axis of vulnerability discovery and elimination. Thinking about security as a circular, zero-sum game cripples our ability to think clearly. This introductory chapter advocates replacing the hamster wheel with key indicators—metrics—that measure the efficiency of key security activities.

- **Chapter 2, "Defining Security Metrics":** This chapter describes the philosophy behind metrics, describes business pressures driving their adoption, suggests criteria for evaluating "good metrics," and warns against red herrings and other "bad metrics."

- **Chapter 3, "Diagnosing Problems and Measuring Technical Security":** Leading firms measure security activities differently, depending on need and context. This chapter catalogs the types of measurements that firms use to diagnose security problems. These include practical metrics for such topics as coverage and control, vulnerability management password quality, patch latency, benchmark scoring, and business-adjusted risk.

- **Chapter 4, "Measuring Program Effectiveness":** Beyond purely technical security measures, organizations need methods for measuring strategic security activities, for tracking security acquisition and implementation efforts, and for measuring the ongoing effectiveness of security organizations. This chapter catalogs dozens of program-level metrics, using the COBIT framework as an organizing principle.

- **Chapter 5, "Analysis Techniques":** To create metrics, analysts must transform raw security data into numbers that provide richer insights. This chapter describes essential techniques for arranging, aggregating, and analyzing data to bring out the "headlines." It also describes advanced analytical techniques such as cross-sectional and quartile analyses.

- **Chapter 6, "Visualization":** Even the most compelling data is worthless without an effective way of presenting it. This chapter presents a myriad of visualization techniques, ranging from simple tables to two-by-two grids and intricate "small multiple" charts.

- **Chapter 7, "Automating Metrics Calculations":** Most organizations have plenty of security data available to them, although they are often trapped inside proprietary tools and information islands. This chapter suggests likely sources for finding appropriate data, including firewall logs, antivirus logs, and third-party auditor reports. It also describes techniques for transforming acquired data into formats that lend themselves to aggregation and reporting.

- **Chapter 8, "Designing Security Scorecards":** After an organization collects and analyzes its security metrics, only one step remains: creating a scorecard that pulls everything together. This chapter presents several alternative approaches for designing security "balanced scorecards" that present compact, holistic views of organizational security effectiveness.

In addition to these topics, this book contains a generous sprinkling of anecdotes and war stories from my personal experiences, as well as those of my interview subjects.

Thank you for purchasing this book. I hope you enjoy reading it as much as I have enjoyed writing it.

Acknowledgments

It is a dark and stormy night. Thanksgiving 2006, the occasion on which I write these words, has brought some of the worst rain and wind in my memory. Not that the weather matters one whit. Blissed out on tryptophan, pie, and stuffing, I could care less about the sheets of rain outside my window.

Food seems an appropriate metaphor today—not just because of the occasion, but because it reminds me of a simile for *Security Metrics*. The endeavor of writing this book has been, as the expression goes, like eating an elephant. The only way to do it is one bite at a time.

I first glimpsed the elephant while I was working at @stake, an Internet security consultancy I helped start in 1999. One of my colleagues was a cheerful, pint-sized young woman named Heather Mullane. She worked in Marketing as an event planner, and she was the perfect colleague—prompt, efficient, and scrupulously organized. Her work was always done on time, and her desk was always insufferably spotless and neat. Several prank-loving colleagues and I liked to wind her up by moving around her staplers and tape dispensers after hours. Of course, she always noticed when something was out of place and scolded us for our transgressions.

In one of @stake's lowest moments, Heather's job was made redundant, so she went to work at Addison-Wesley as an editorial assistant. But she still kept in touch, and she would cross the Charles River to see all of us occasionally. Nearly every time she would encourage me to write. "So, when will you write a book on metrics?" she inquired, offering to introduce me to some of the editors. After two years of persisting, I finally gave in and started work on the book you now hold. Heather has since left Addison, married, and moved westward. I have lost touch with her, but I am glad she thought enough of my work to recommend me. Thanks, Heather, for your benevolent pestering.

This book represents the culmination of several years of effort, based on observations and ruminations about how to put numbers around information security. It has progressed in fits and starts—mostly fits. Although my name appears on the cover, I cannot claim sole authorship. I am especially grateful for the contributions of Betsy Nichols, who is the primary author of Chapter 7, "Automating Metrics Calculations." Her company, Clear Point Metrics, does amazing work automating metrics definition, collection, aggregation, and reporting activities, and I highly recommend their products. In addition, the first half of Chapter 2, "Defining Security Metrics," is derived from the IEEE article "The Future Belongs to the Quants," written by Dan Geer, Kevin Soo Hoo, and me.

Many of the metrics discussed in Chapter 3, "Diagnosing Problems and Measuring Technical Security," and Chapter 4, "Measuring Program Effectiveness," draw from the work and stories of fellow diners at the pachyderm picnic that is this book. These practitioners include Jayson Agagnier, Jerry Brady, Rob Clyde, Mark Curphey, Dennis Devlin, Royal Hansen, Mark Kadrich, John Kirkwood, Pete Lindstrom, Rhonda MacLean, Tim Mather, Betsy Nichols, John Nye, Gunnar Peterson, Tom Quinn, Kevin Soo Hoo, Andrew Sudbury, Phil Venables, Phebe Waterfield, Bob Westwater, and many others. All were kind enough to sit for interviews, speak with me informally, or otherwise inspire me by their examples. The 250-plus members of the securitymetrics.org mailing list, many of whom attended the inaugural MetriCon 1.0 conference in Vancouver in August 2006, have also been a tremendous source of collective wisdom.

Eating an elephant often results in indigestion. I have been blessed with a group of manuscript reviewers who, in between the repast of the draft and the *digestif* of the finished manuscript, have helped critique and contain my occasionally sprawling prose. They gently corrected me when I was flat wrong about things and offered valuable suggestions on how to make the material more accessible. These include Olivier Caleff, Alberto Cardona, Anton Chuvakin, Fred Cohen, Mark Curphey, Dennis Devlin, Alex Hutton, John Leach, Dennis Opacki, Jon Passki, Adam Shostack, and Chris Walsh. Gentlemen, thank you.

First-time authors often turn into gibbering, nervous fools during the course of writing and production. For their patience and indulgence, I would like to thank the iron-stomached crew at Addison-Wesley: Jessica Goldstein, Romny French, Karen Gettman, Kristin Weinberger, and Chris Zahn. Others who have bucked me up or given me needed what-fers include Linda McCarthy (Symantec), Steve Mulder (Muldermedia), Becky Tapley, the elusive Catherine Nolan, my dad, and my brother Russ. Despite being not at all connected to security, he offered to read an early draft of one of my chapters and cracked up while reading it. Russ' laughter reassured me that, for all the book's other faults, most readers should find it entertaining at the very least.

Last, I owe thanks to a person I am privileged to call my friend, Dan Geer. In addition to being a ponytailed-and-muttonchopped orator, metrics crony, raconteur, Renaissance man, and beekeeper extraordinaire, Dan is a tremendously humane man. He did for me what the best bosses always find a way to do: put me in a position to be successful. I thank him for igniting and sustaining my interest in security metrics. I hope this book will sustain yours.

Andrew Jaquith
Boston, Massachusetts
November 2006

About the Author

Andrew Jaquith is the program manager for Yankee Group's Enabling Technologies Enterprise group, with expertise in compliance, security, and risk management. Jaquith advises enterprise clients on how to manage security resources in their environments. He also helps security vendors develop strategies for reaching enterprise customers. Jaquith's research focuses on topics such as security management, risk management, and packaged and custom web-based applications.

Jaquith has 15 years of IT experience. Before joining Yankee Group, he cofounded and served as program director at @stake, Inc., a security consulting pioneer, which Symantec Corporation acquired in 2004. Before @stake, Jaquith held project manager and business analyst positions at Cambridge Technology Partners and FedEx Corporation.

His application security and metrics research has been featured in *CIO, CSO, InformationWeek, IEEE Security and Privacy*, and *The Economist*. In addition, Jaquith contributes to several security-related open-source projects.

Jaquith holds a B.A. degree in economics and political science from Yale University.

Introduction: Escaping the Hamster Wheel of Pain

If you're in a security-based startup company, then you'll know that making money requires making excitement, even if the excitement is somebody else's public humiliation.

—Daniel E. Geer, Sc.D., "Risk Management Is Where the Money Is" (1998)

RISK MANAGEMENT IS WHERE THE CONFUSION IS

Call me Analyst.

I am blessed with a lucky job: customers pay my firm money to help them navigate the product-and-services markets for information security. I write original research, speak with enterprise customers, and speak with product vendors on a regular basis. Lately I have been accumulating a lot of slideware from security companies advertising their wares. In just about every deck the purveyor bandies about the term "risk management" and offers its definition of what that is. In most cases, the purveyor's definition does not match mine.

I first encountered the term "risk management" used in the context of security in 1998, when I read Dan Geer's landmark essay "Risk Management Is Where the Money Is."[1] If you've never read it, it describes how forward-thinking vendors, primarily banks,

---

[1] D. Geer, "Risk Management Is Where the Money Is," speech to the Digital Commerce Society of Boston, November 3, 1998, http://www.stanford.edu/~hodges/doc/Geer-RiskManagement.txt.

will be compelled to build security products to underpin electronic commerce transactions. The idea was that the trustworthiness of a commercial entity has an intrinsic value—and that value can be bonded and underwritten. At its core lies a simple premise: the notion that the world ought to be a place where digital security risk becomes reducible to numbers.

At the time, I was gobsmacked by Geer's thoughtfulness and rhetorical force. The essay was like a thunderbolt of lucidity; several days later, I could still smell the ozone. Nearly nine years later, I have found that much of what he wrote stands up well. Unfortunately for Dan's employer at the time, purveyors of bonded trading partner identities did not flourish and monetize electronic commerce security as he had predicted. But he was absolutely correct in identifying digital security risk as a commodity that could be identified, rated, mitigated, traded, and, above all, quantified and valued.

Most of the slide decks I see miss this last point. Nearly everyone shows up with a doughnut-shaped "risk management" chart whose arrows rotate clockwise in a continuous loop. Why clockwise? I have no idea, but they are always this way. The chart almost always contains variations of these four phases:

1. Assessment (or Detection)
2. Reporting
3. Prioritization
4. Mitigation

Of course, the product or service in question is invariably the catalytic agent that facilitates this process. Follow these four process steps using our product, and presto! You've got risk management. From the vendor's point of view, the doughnut chart is great. It provides a rationale for getting customers to keep doing said process, over and over, thereby remitting maintenance monies for each trip around the wheel. I can see why these diagrams are so popular. Unfortunately, from the perspective of the buyer the circular nature of the diagram implies something rather unpleasant: lather, rinse, repeat— but without ever getting clean. (I have been collecting these charts, by the way. Soon, I hope to be able to collect enough to redeem them for a Pokemon game.)

Figure 1-1 shows the cynical version of the "risk management" doughnut, which I call the "Hamster Wheel of Pain":

1. Use product, and discover you're screwed.
2. Panic.
3. Twitch uncomfortably in front of boss.
4. Fix the bare minimum (but in a vigorous, showy way). Hope problems go away.

The Hamster Wheel of Pain

An Alternative View of "Risk Management"

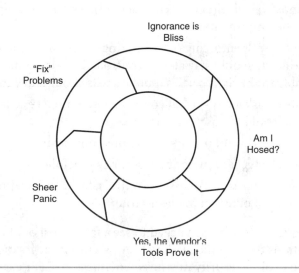

Figure 1-1   The Hamster Wheel of Pain

The fundamental problem with the Hamster Wheel model is simple: it captures the easy part of the risk management message (identification and fixing things) but misses the important parts (quantification and triage based on value). Identifying problems is easy, because that is what highly specialized, domain-specific diagnostic security tools are supposed to do. They find holes in websites, gaps in virus or network management coverage, and shortcomings in user passwords. Quantifying and valuing risk is much harder, because diagnostic tool results are devoid of organizational context and business domain knowledge. To put this simply, for most vendors, "risk management" really means "risk identification," followed by a frenzied process of fixing and re-identification. Serial elimination has replaced triage.

That is not good enough if you believe (as I do) that risk management means quantification and valuation. If we were serious about quantifying risk, we would talk about more than just the "numerator" (identified issues). We would take a hard look at the denominator—that is, the assets the issues apply to. Specifically, we would ask questions like these:

- What is the value of the individual information assets residing on workstations, servers, and mobile devices? What is the value in aggregate?

- How much value is circulating through the firm right now?
- How much value is entering or leaving? What are its velocity and direction?
- Where are my most valuable (and/or confidential) assets? Who supplies (and demands) the most information assets?
- Are my security controls enforcing or promoting the information behaviors we want? (Sensitive assets should stay at rest; controlled assets should circulate as quickly as possible to the right parties; public assets should flow freely.)
- What is the value at risk today—what could we lose if the "1% chance" scenario comes true? What could we lose tomorrow?
- How much does each control in my security portfolio cost?
- How will my risk change if I reweight my security portfolio?
- How do my objective measures of assets, controls, flow, and portfolio allocation compare with those of others in my peer group?

These are not easy questions. I am privileged to see a fair snapshot of the debate around many of these questions daily on the mailing list of securitymetrics.org, an organization I founded in 2004 to explore security measurement questions. For example, a long, raging thread on asset valuation highlighted how difficult achieving consensus on just one of these questions can be. I do not claim to have any of the answers, although some of the folks I have invited to be on securitymetrics.org have taken (and are taking) a shot at it. What I do know is that none of the commercial solutions I have seen (so far) even think about these things in terms of the questions I have posed.

Instead, it is the same old Hamster Wheel. You're screwed; we fix it; 30 days later, you're screwed again. Patch, pray, repeat. The security console sez you've got 34,012 "security violations" (whatever those are). And, uh, sorry to bother you, but you've got 33 potential porn surfers in the Finance department.

We are so far away from real risk management that it is not even funny, and I am wondering if it is even worth the effort in the short term.

Is it time to administer last rites to "risk management"? I think it is. This is not as controversial a statement as it might sound. For example, risk management is often confused with risk modeling—an entirely different but vital part of security analysis. Risk modeling research helps us understand how security works (or doesn't). Research from people like Dan Geer, Kevin Soo Hoo, Mark Kadrich, Adam Shostack, Chris Walsh, Pete Lindstrom, Gerhard Eschelbeck, and others continues to astound and amaze me. Economists we need; what we do not need are traveling salesmen bearing Wheels of Pain.

My point is that "risk management" as an overarching theme for understanding digital security has outlived its usefulness. Commercial entities abuse the definition of the term, and nobody has a handle on the asset valuation part of the equation. It is time to throw out the bathwater; we drowned the baby already in a frothy bath of snake oil.

METRICS SUPPLANT RISK MANAGEMENT

If "risk management" is not the answer, what is?

Even though he was not the first to say it, Bruce Schneier said it best when he stated "security is a process." Surely he is right about this. But if it is a process, exactly what sort of process is it? I submit to you that the hamster wheel is not what he (or Dan) had in mind. Here is the dirty little secret about "process": process is boring, routine, and institutional. Process does not always get headlines in the trade rags. In short, process is operational. How are processes measured? Through metrics and key indicators—in other words, numbers about numbers.

In mature, process-driven industries, just about everyone with more than a few years of tenure makes it their business to know what the firm's key barometers are. Take supply chain, for example. If you are running a warehouse, you are renting real estate that costs money. To make money you need to minimize the percentage of costs spent on that real estate. The best way to do that is to increase the flow of goods through the warehouse; this spreads the fixed cost of the warehouse over the higher numbers of commodities. Unsurprisingly, the folks running warehouses have a metric they use to measure warehouse efficiency. It is called "inventory turns"—that is, the average number of times the complete inventory rotates (turns) through the warehouse on a yearly basis.

When I was at FedEx in the mid-'90s, the national average for inventory turns was about 10 to 12 per year for manufacturers. But averages are just that; all bell curves have tails. The pathetic end of the curve included companies like WebVan, which forgot that it was really in the real estate business and left one of the largest dot-com craters as a result. No density == low flow-through == low turns == death. Dell occupies the high end: back in 1996, its warehouses did 40 turns a year. 40! Dell's profitability flows directly from its inventory management and supply chain excellence; Michael Dell surely eyes this number like a hawk.

I use this (simple) example only because it illustrates how a relatively simple key indicator speaks volumes about company operations. It is not the only number warehouse operators watch, but it is one of the most important. Supply chain operators also tend to look at freight cost per mile, percentage of "empty" (non-revenue-generating) truck miles, putaway and pick times, and distribution of "A" / "B"/ "C" velocity SKUs, among others.

Several themes emerge from the supply chain key indicators list. All of the indicators in the list:

- **Incorporate measures of time or money.** Because time multiplied by labor costs yields money, it is fair to say that they all ultimately reduce to monetary measures. This is a language that investors, the public, and all C-level executives understand.
- **Are well understood across the company.** Most business units know what their indicators measure and what they signify about the health of the enterprise. Moreover, the numbers are *shared* widely across the firm—not hidden.
- **Are well understood across industries and are consistently measured.** That means they lend themselves to benchmarking, in the sense that a high-priced management consultancy could go to a wide variety of firms, gather comparable statistics, gain useful analytical insights, and make a buck on the analysis.
- **Are calculated mechanically.** Although the numbers themselves may not always be straightforward to calculate, they can nonetheless be gathered in an automated way.

I think this is where we need to go next. What I want to see nowadays from vendors or service providers is not just another hamster wheel. I want a set of key indicators that tells customers how healthy their security operations are, on a stand-alone basis and with respect to peers. Barbering on about "risk management" just misses the point, as does fobbing off measurement as a mere "reporting" concern. If solution providers believed that particular metrics were truly important, they would benchmark them across their client bases. But they do not; nearly every vendor I have posed this idea to looks at me like I have two heads.

My short list of (mildly belligerent) vendor questions, therefore, includes these:

- What metrics does your product or service provide?
- Which would be considered "key indicators"?
- How do you use these indicators to demonstrate improvement to customers? And to each customer's investors, regulators, and employees?
- Could you, or a management consultant, go to different companies and gather comparable statistics?
- Do you benchmark your customer base using these key indicators?

I want to see somebody smack these out of the ballyard, but somehow I think I will be waiting a while.

Time to get off the Hamster Wheel of Pain. Next up are metrics and key indicators.

SUMMARY

Security may well be a process, but it should not be seen as one solely governed by the continuous detect-fix-patch-pray cycle that is the Hamster Wheel of Pain. Although the Wheel helps justify the existence of security vendor products, it does nothing to help enterprises understand the effectiveness of their security programs.

Moving beyond the Hamster Wheel requires practitioners to think about security in the same ways that other disciplines do—as activities that can be named, and whose efficiencies can be measured with key indicators. These key indicators should incorporate time and money measures, should be measured consistently, and should be comparable across companies to facilitate benchmarking.

This chapter's primal scream sets us up for Chapter 2, "Defining Security Metrics." It describes why measurement matters, what makes for good and bad metrics, and what measurement models security practitioners can look to for inspiration.

Defining Security Metrics

2

The revolutionary idea that defines the boundary between modern times and the past is the mastery of risk: the notion that the future is more than a whim of the gods and that men and women are not passive before nature. Until human beings discovered a way across that boundary, the future was the mirror of the past or the murky domain of oracles and soothsayers who held a monopoly over knowledge of anticipated events.

—Peter Bernstein, *Against the Gods: The Remarkable Story of Risk*

Information security is in the first stages of the journey Bernstein describes as distinguishing the modern era.[1] Since the dawn of modern computing, security has been left to computer security experts—chiefly technologists whose technical understanding qualified them to shoulder the responsibility of keeping computers and their valuable information safe. The rapid growth of society's dependence on information systems, particularly the Internet, has drawn attention to the glaring vulnerability of this fragile infrastructure.

Most organizations call security a "top management priority," and chief executive officers rank security as 7.5 out of 10 in importance.[2] In recent years, Sarbanes-Oxley (SOX)

---

[1] P.L. Bernstein, *Against the Gods: The Remarkable Story of Risk*, John Wiley & Sons, 1996, p. 1.

[2] M. Gerencser and D. Aguirre, "Security Concerns Prominent on CEO Agenda," *strategy + business*, 12 Feb., 2002, http://www.strategy-business.com/press/enews/article/?ptag-ps=&art=254087&pg=0. The 10-point scale represents relative priorities, where 10 represents the highest ones.

and the Windows security pandemic have caused funding levels to rise significantly. In 2002, the average firm's security budget (excluding staff) was about US$1.1 million, which translated into a grand total of US$196 spent on security per employee per year.[3] Budgets have increased annually at a nearly 20 percent clip since then—but most of the spending has gone to product, not process, which, as Bruce Schneier points out, is backward: security is not a product, it's a process.[4] Why the disconnect? Information security experts meet simple questions, readily answered in any other business context, with embarrassed silence. These questions include the following:

- Is my security better this year?
- What am I getting for my security dollars?
- How do I compare with my peers?

Although measurement has detractors, leading companies and entire industry sectors view it as the only viable means for dealing with information security risks. The alternative is a return to the murky domain of oracles and soothsayers who dispense security advice that companies follow, hoping it will keep them safe. In this old-world model, fear of the catastrophic consequences of an information attack, uncertainty about their vulnerability, and doubts about the sufficiency of current safeguards drive organizations' security decisions.

This chapter formally defines security metrics. I discuss the drivers and impediments to security measurement and present my own definition of what makes for effective metrics:

- "Security Measurement Business Drivers" discusses the importance of security metrics and the business pressures that are driving organizations to adopt them.
- "Modeling Security Metrics" defines "security modelers," how they differ from "security measurers," and why we should leverage the experiences of other fields to develop effective metrics.
- "What Makes a Good Metric?" defines five essential qualities that every security metric should have.
- "What Makes a Bad Metric?" describes the converse.
- "What Are Not Metrics?" discusses shortcomings, popular misconceptions, and red herrings to avoid when creating metrics.

---

[3] A. Carey, "Worldwide Information Security Services Forecast, 2001–2006," IDC report no. 26899, Apr. 2002.

[4] B. Schneier, *Secrets & Lies*, John Wiley & Sons, 2000.

SECURITY MEASUREMENT BUSINESS DRIVERS

Formal security measurement seeks to move beyond fear, uncertainty, and doubt (FUD) to a framework in which organizations can quantify the likelihood of danger, estimate the extent of possible damage, understand the performance of their security organizations, and weigh the costs of security safeguards against their expected effectiveness. Four important realizations are pushing companies away from FUD and toward risk management:

- **Information asset fragility:** Companies in most industries realize that efficient operation of their complex enterprises depends on information. Every known instance of critical information corruption, damage, or destruction intensifies their concern over this dependence. Both awareness of information security and the will to address it are spreading.

- **Provable security:** Because no good, consistent security metrics are available, companies find themselves unable to accurately gauge the suitability or effectiveness of different security options. Consequently, the amount a company can spend on "improving" security has no natural bounds beyond the company's ability to pay.

- **Cost pressures:** Economic pressures and the rising cost of security solutions mean security vendors must compete with other infrastructure projects for information technology dollars. Cost-benefit analyses and return-on-investment calculations are becoming standard prerequisites for any information security sale.

- **Accountability:** Various industry-specific regulatory bodies, recognizing the growing exposure of their industries to information security risks, are mandating mechanisms for managing those risks. For example, the Basel II Capital Accords will soon require banks to set aside capital reserves explicitly to cover operational risks, including information security risks. Both the Gramm-Leach-Bliley Act and the Health Insurance Portability and Accountability Act compel companies in the U.S. to be accountable for information security, and the Sarbanes-Oxley Act includes mandatory reporting of material business changes, including serious information security incidents. Finally, when considering the tender ministrations of New York Attorney General Eliot Spitzer, whose apparent goal is to craft an investor-protection regime centered on the avoidance of information sharing, there's no doubt that some form of accountability is here to stay.

Early adopters are already applying risk-management tools to information security. Security measurement and quantification is a stumbling block, however. In spite of nascent efforts to perform security return-on-investment and cost-benefit analyses, reliable, statistically representative information security metrics do not exist.

ROADBLOCKS TO DATA SHARING

If information security were a public health problem, individual companies might have some rudimentary understanding of their own information security health, but we have no aggregate basis for public policy because organizations do not share their data.

Anonymized data sharing among companies is an important tool for obtaining aggregate security metrics. In the same way that a doctor might share anonymous patient information with the U.S. Centers for Disease Control (CDC), companies could share details of their information security experiences to help each other see the overall security picture. Several practical challenges, legal concerns, and incentive failures have stalled and continue to stall this type of data sharing.

Practical challenges range from the lack of common definitions for terms and metrics to determining how to share information meaningfully. The vocabulary of information security is fraught with imprecision and overlapping meanings. Fundamental concepts and words, such as incident, attack, threat, risk, and vulnerability, mean different things to different people. Basic metrics for counting events are difficult to collect because the terms are unclear. More complicated metrics, such as consequences of security breaches, present even greater challenges because of the time, effort, and uncertainty involved in assessing them and the inherent influence of subjective judgment. Few companies will divert scarce security resources from security system implementations in favor of collecting and sharing security metrics. Finally, even if companies try to pool data regularly, no underlying infrastructure for compiling data for analysis exists to support the collection efforts.

Policy makers in Washington, D.C. studied private industry's reservations about sharing information security data in an attempt to discover whether government could facilitate information sharing. From a legal perspective, sharing information among industry competitors could constitute collusion and therefore violate U.S. antitrust laws. In addition, as information about security practices and incidents becomes well known, sharing data might increase the risk of liability lawsuits. If a government agency participates in the sharing, it might be compelled to disclose data to the public under the Freedom of Information Act (FOIA), even if the data are proprietary and confidential.

Fortunately, policy makers have addressed many of these legal concerns, including antitrust concerns and obligations under the FOIA (though, as we write this, the situation is fluid and the preconditions for sharing are still vulnerable to election-year demagoguery).

The unwillingness of many companies to share security information points to a general failure in the marketplace to provide appropriate incentives. Concerns over reputation and losing customers to competitors tend to suppress many companies' inclination to report incidents, much less share information about them. Furthermore, the desire to protect confidential and proprietary information that might have been compromised reinforces the silence.

Ultimately, the problem is lack of trust. Many companies believe that disclosing sensitive security information, even anonymously, will hurt future business. Without a structure to contradict this, their fears are as rational as the fundamental necessity of sharing.

MODELING SECURITY METRICS

As you might conclude from the preceding discussion, security measurers find themselves in a bit of a quandary. Business pressures are clearly driving enterprises to adopt better methods for measuring the effectiveness of their security programs. But at the same time, the lack of a tradition of data sharing prevents the sort of free-flowing discussion that forges consensus on methods. In short, with regard to security metrics, lots of people are asking, but nobody is telling.

MODELERS VERSUS MEASURERS

In security, we are hardly inventing anything revolutionary when we support decision-making under uncertainty. Whenever data are scarce, the standard approach is to build models from other fields and insert expert opinion to supplement the data. Thus, some well-informed modeling can help us figure out what good security metrics ought to look like.

Modeling relates quite naturally to measuring. In the information security world, most observers who speak about "security metrics" generally think about them from the point of view of *modeling* threats, risk (or perceived risk), and losses. A vocal minority cares less about the modeling aspects per se and would rather just *measure* things. At the risk of being simplistic, modelers think about risk equations, loss expectancy, economic incentives, and why things happen. Measurers think more about empirical data, correlation, data sharing, and causality. (See Table 2-1.) These two viewpoints hark back to the classic division between scientific theorists and experimentalists, as explained by my colleague John Leach:

> "*The scientific research world has always split into those two broad camps. The theorists rely on the experimentalists to gather the data by which competing theories are tested, and the experimentalists rely on the theorists to show how to extract order, structure and knowledge out of the mass of data.*"[5]

---

[5] John Leach, securitymetrics.org mailing list message, "Modelers v measurers (was: Risk metrics)," January 31, 2006.

Table 2-1   Views of the World: Modelers and Measurers

Modelers	Measurers
Risk equations	Empirical data
Loss expectancy	Cross-sectional and time-series analysis
Linear algebra	Correlation
Attack surfaces	Essential practices
Information flow	Information sharing
Economic incentives	Economic spending
Vendors	Enterprises
Why	Before and after

On the securitymetrics.org[6] metrics discussion list I run, the preponderance of comments concern risk modeling rather than risk measurement. Our group has spun many long threads about vulnerability disclosure models but very few about developing a "top 10" list of favorite metrics.

I am in the latter camp. I do not have the math background to come up with a sufficiently sophisticated model to explain how, why, or how much risk a company has or should bear. At the risk of being simplistic, I figure that if I can collect enough data on enough things, perhaps I can put everything in a blender and tease out the relationships via correlation.

That said, I appreciate and understand the importance of modeling in driving forward security measurement. In fact, it is hard to do a good job with measurement without knowledge of modeling. John Leach tells us why:

> "[The Information Security Forum] collects a load of data about the breaches companies suffer from and the things they do to protect themselves, and then does loads of correlation analysis. . . . They have found that there is a correlation, that the companies which suffer the fewest problems (normalized to the size of the company) all tend to do a particular selection of ten controls well. So the recommendation from the ISF has been 'do these ten key controls well and you will significantly reduce your risk.'

---

6 http://www.securitymetrics.org.

However, I asked them once if they had any idea why those ten controls rather than a different set of ten seemed to be the ones which made the difference, what reasoning could they put behind their selection. And, to shorten a long answer, they said No, they had no idea. . . . Correlations are sometimes interesting but if they don't lead to an understanding of the dynamics that give rise to the correlation, then you have barely moved forward. . ."

So, from these I take two lessons. First, you have to measure the threat, not just the incidents and controls people apply, if you want to know why some incidents happen and others don't. Second, you need a model, because correlations on their own are sterile.[7]

Good models supply us with rationales for measurement. Other industries can provide clues about what models we should use for security. We can update and calibrate the models as new data become available, perhaps completely replacing expert opinion with objective measurements in the future. It might be an evolutionary process, but that is certainly no reason for us to start from scratch.

Industries that incorporate formal measurement models include manufacturing, quality assurance, public health, finance and portfolio management, and insurance. As Picasso said, "Good artists copy. Great artists steal." So let's do some rational stealing.

QUALITY ASSURANCE LITERATURE

The quality control literature is vast, is close in spirit to the literature the security world needs to develop, and has been quite successful over the last two decades. The mantra of the 1980s was "Quality is free," and without a doubt, the average product quality has improved since then, as measured in any number of ways. A classic study of software quality convincingly demonstrated that developers should work on quality early in the process.[8] Table 2-2 shows how the cost to fix defects increases in later development stages. We can steal much more from the quality control literature, particularly if we treat security flaws as special cases of quality flaws, assuming they are accidental, and not the fruits of sabotage.

---

[7] John Leach, securitymetrics.org mailing list message, "Modelers v measurers (was: Risk metrics)," January 31, 2006.

[8] IBM Systems Sciences Institute, *Implementing Software Inspections*, monograph, IBM, 1981.

Table 2-2   Relative Cost to Correct Security Defects, by Stage

Stage	Relative Cost
Design	1.0
Implementation	6.5
Testing	15.0
Maintenance	100.0

PUBLIC HEALTH TERMINOLOGY AND REPORTING STRUCTURE

Public health tries to answer questions about disease incidence, prevalence, and spread—that is, to get the "big picture," literally. The choice of the term "virus" to describe the electronic malady was fitting and naturally suggests that we consider public health's terminology and reporting structure as models for security.

Consider the epidemiologic concept of herd immunity, which means what it sounds like: for a population to survive, not every member need be immune to a pathogen. Rather, just enough of the population must be immune to prevent an epidemic. In the natural world, species and individual diversity are protective; in the electronic world, standardization on overwhelmingly dominant vendors creates a near-monoculture of limited, if any, herd immunity.

Consider the Nimda worm. Even had we known the precise susceptibility characteristics of each of Nimda's transmission vectors, we would not have guessed what Nimda could do by merging several vectors into one. In this sense, diseases that mutate quickly or that affect the immune system are like Nimda. Similarly, little difference exists between an asymptomatic disease carrier (a Typhoid Mary) and a distributed-denial-of-service (DDoS) zombie waiting to be triggered. Other parallels are easy to draw.

We already have a model for measuring public health when virulence and mutation of existing disease vectors are the issue: the CDC, which is supported by American taxpayers but plays a worldwide role. Specialists from several allied institutions have called for the creation of a CDC for the Internet, with electronic analogs to the CDC's epidemiologic coverage: mandatory reporting of communicable diseases, statistical identification of excess incidence, and longitudinal trend analysis to calibrate epidemiologic models.[9]

---

[9]   S. Staniford, V. Paxson, and N. Weaver, "How to Own the Internet in Your Spare Time," Proceedings of the USENIX Security Symposium, USENIX Assocation, 2002, pp. 149–167.

PORTFOLIO MANAGEMENT

Generally, portfolio management strategy aims to balance risk and reward and, when necessary, cap risk. Portfolio theory calls for managers to measure unique and systematic risk factors, calculate industry and company betas, and rigorously apply well-understood financial yardsticks.[10] Systems administrators who plan workable modes of diminished operation for computer systems are doing precisely the same thing as portfolio managers who hedge their investment positions. Portfolio management tries to tie reward to risk and to do so as risk and the need for reward change. If the official measure of homeland security risk today moved from yellow to orange, what knobs would you adjust? If you answer, "We don't have knobs to adjust," or "All of our knobs are already turned all the way up to distort," you clearly need a better risk model, one hedged and calibrated enough to respond to external risk indicators. If you have not calibrated the model with measurement, only one thing is certain: You will either overspend or under-protect. Recognizing this fault, analyst firms such as Forrester are explicitly touting portfolio management as an essential IT management skill and strategy.[11]

ACCELERATED FAILURE TESTING

Measurement drives reproducibility in manufactured goods, just as reproducibility drives productivity gains, and productivity gains create wealth. Accelerated failure testing is the calibration of manufacturing quality under the constraint of time compression.

To test a toaster, evaluators move the handle up and down 5,000 times, make toast at −40°, observe the effects of exploding bagels, and so forth. Their purpose is to give the toaster a lifetime of abuse all at once—that is, to compress time. In principle, the difference between testing a toaster and performing a serious penetration test of a web server is very small. Thus, we might learn from the accelerated failure time testing literature.

For the toaster, we ask, "How much abuse before it breaks?" not "Can we break the toaster?" In security, the measure of interest is parallel. The level of effort to subvert—how hard it is for the attacker to penetrate the web server, not whether the attacker can—yields the highest return value to the upstream client. With a trustworthy answer, a rational decision-maker can decide whether a plausible threat to the business exists. Without a trustworthy answer, the decision-maker falls prey to FUD. If FUD represents the dark ages, measurement is the means to enlightenment.

---

[10] A.R. Jaquith, "Learning from Wall Street," *Secure Business Quarterly*, vol. 2, no. 1, 2002, http://www.sbq.com/sbq/app_security/sbq_app_wall_street.pdf.

[11] C. Gliedman, "Managing IT Risk with Portfolio Management Thinking," *CIO* (Analyst Corner), http://www.cio.com/analyst/012502_giga.html.

Having measured the level of effort to subvert, however, does not mean we assume the device, software, or system will never fail. Rather, we can now judge whether natural product rollover intervals are sufficient or if we need to build in such strategies as mandatory upgrade, anti-retention, or even automatic reinstallation. Some well-known products already use these strategies. The Windows Media Player's end-user license agreement, for example, has had mandatory upgrade and anti-retention for several years. Research at the University of Maryland frames the issue as determining the interval between flaw discovery and population-based patch installation.[12]

INSURANCE

Insurance is about estimating risk better than the counterparty to the transaction and deciding whether to underwrite it or lay it off via reinsurance. In most of the world, steadily accumulating actuarial data and learning from them brings success. In the Internet business world, however, such a strategy is almost impossible.

Actuarial data require some basic stability of the underlying entity being measured. When the underlying measurement entity is subject to change, the best alternative is a moving window (left censoring) rather than a full data capture. For example, pricing life insurance based on the average life expectancy over the last thousand years would make no sense, because the change in average human life expectancy has been too great.

In the electronic business world, the technical flux of change is high—so high that actuarial data are practically impossible to obtain. Add configuration complexity and variability to technical flux, and the chance of finding any two sites with substantially the same operating environment is almost zero. For this reason, information risk insurance generally protects against named hazards (if a specific thing happens, the insurance company will pay) rather than an umbrella (no matter what happens, the insurance company will pay).

Insurers must answer the same question that those who worry about the critical infrastructure of any major country must answer: What risk aggregation is inherent in the portfolio? Or, in computerese, how likely is cascade failure (a failure that spreads from one system to another in a domino effect)? Many of the most important security events, such as the Nimda worm or the Ohio Edison power outage,[13] have been cascade failures.

---

[12] W.A. Arbaugh, W.L. Fithen, and J. McHugh, "Windows of Vulnerability," *Computer*, vol. 33, no. 12, 2000, pp. 52–59.

[13] People familiar with the 2003 Ohio Edison SCADA failure that darkened New York City tell me that the root cause was the failure to isolate a Slammer-infested computer inside the production network, which in turn wiped out the grid monitoring systems.

The challenge for insurers is to insure many parties against all sorts of electronic failures without subjecting their portfolios to risk aggregation. They do not want to structure their insurance products thinking they are insuring against house fires (one event equals one claim), only to discover that they are insuring against earthquakes (one event equals many claims).

Until we can measure the risk of cascade failures, measuring species (platform) diversity in the computing environment will have to suffice. The data on diversity in this environment are not good, with a handful of companies dominating every aspect of it.[14] In fact, species diversity is one of the great security tensions today. From the systems administration viewpoint, nothing is so sweet as having all platforms be alike. From the security administration viewpoint, however, nothing is so frightening as having all platforms be alike.

WHAT MAKES A GOOD METRIC?

As I mentioned in the preceding chapter, information security is one of the few management disciplines that has yet to submit itself to serious analytic scrutiny. In settings that require balancing the cost of countermeasures against the cost of risk, decision support is precisely the point of any measurement exercise. Getting the right measurements depends on knowing the right questions. In medicine, a doctor asks what the patient's malady is. In public health, the questions are how many patients have this malady and how they got it. In security, business leaders ask the following:

- How effective are my security processes?
- Am I better off than I was this time last year?
- How do I compare with my peers?
- Am I spending the right amount of money?
- What are my risk transfer options?

Were we talking about some other field, we could look to prior art and industry-specific knowledge—for example, derivatives pricing in vertical industries like finance, health and safety in pharmaceutical manufacture, and reliability in power distribution. Likewise, most enterprises' horizontal functions—human resources, finance, manufacturing, supply chain, call center, e-commerce, and operations—measure their performance by tracking a handful of key performance indicators (see Table 2-3). These indicators

---

[14] J.S. Quarterman, "Monoculture Considered Harmful," *First Monday*, vol. 7, no. 2, http://www.firstmonday.dk/issues/issue7_2/quarterman.

include statistics such as call volumes per associate, inventory turns, customer conversion percentages, manufacturing defect rates, and employee turnover.

Table 2-3 Sample Business Metrics

Discipline or Vertical Market	Key Metrics
Freight	Freight cost per mile (total spent on truck or rail carriage divided by mileage)
	Load factor (percentage utilization of total capacity)
	Empty miles (percentage of trips that carried no inventory)
Warehousing	Cost per square foot (total warehouse operating costs divided by size)
	Inventory turns (total cost of goods sold annually divided by average inventory value for the period)
E-commerce	Website conversion rate (percentage of unique visitors to the website who buy something)
Cable and satellite	Subscription cost to acquire (cost of all marketing, subsidies, and discounts divided by the number of acquired customers)
	Average revenue per user (ARPU)

These indicators share three characteristics. First, they are simple to explain and straightforward to calculate. Their transparency facilitates adoption by management. Second, they are all expressed in terms of time, money, or a measure derived from these. Third, they readily lend themselves to benchmarking.

On occasion, enterprises share them as part of a management consulting survey and attempt to compare their own key indicators against those of other companies they know. In so doing, they gain insights about their own performance relative to peers and other industries. A quick glance at the *Harvard Business Review* or *McKinsey Quarterly* confirms that benchmarking in enterprises continues to be a healthy, vibrant, established pillar of modern management. The ideal benchmarking data are cheap to gather, are expressed as numbers, contain units of measure, are objectively and consistently gathered, and are relevant to a decision-maker.

Information security has no equivalent of the *McKinsey Quarterly*, nor of the time-honored tradition of benchmarking organizational performance. Analytical rigor receives little attention, while nebulous, nonquantitative mantras rule: "defense in depth," "security is a process," and "there is no security by obscurity," to name a few. The numbers that do exist, such as those provided in vulnerability and threat reports from Symantec, Webroot, Qualys, and others, provide macro-level detail about the prevalence of malware or missing patches but little else that enterprises can use to assess their effectiveness comparatively against others. Numbers provided by anti-malware, vulnerability management systems, and SIM/SEM systems certainly add value, but to date, no entity has yet attempted to aggregate and compare these data across enterprises.

So what makes a good metric, and what should we measure? Let's address the first part of that question here. We will address the second part in the next two chapters.

"METRIC" DEFINED

Before writing this book, I was curious to see if I could find a consensus definition of what a "metric" is. According to *Oxford's American Dictionary*, a metric is "a system or standard of measurement." In mathematics and physics, it is "a binary function of a topological space that gives, for any two points of the space, a value equal to the distance between them, or to a value treated as analogous to distance for the purpose of analysis."

Specific to IT metrics, Maizlitsh and Handler further discriminate between metrics used for quantifying value (doing the right things) and those used to measure performance (continually doing those things better):

> "There are two fundamental types of metrics that must be considered before commencing with IT portfolio management: value delivery and process improvement. Value delivery consists of cost reduction, increase in revenue, increase in productivity, reduction of cycle time, and reduction in downside risk. Process improvement refers to improvements in the IT portfolio management process. While the metrics are similar and in many ways interrelated, process metrics focus on . . . effectiveness. Is the process improving? Is the process providing perceived value? Is the process expanding in scope? More and more, leaders are looking into the metrics microscope to eliminate non-value-added activity and focus on value-added activity."[15]

These two definitions certainly help, but, like most definitions, they grant us a rather wide scope for discussion. Just about anything that quantifies a problem space and results in a value could be considered a metric. Perhaps we ought to refocus the discussion on the goals of what a metric should help an organization do. The primary goal of metrics is to quantify data to facilitate insight. Metrics do this by:

- Helping an analyst diagnose a particular subject area or understand its performance
- Quantifying particular characteristics of the chosen subject area

---

[15] B. Maizlitsh and R. Handler, *IT Portfolio Management: Step by Step*, John Wiley & Sons, 2005, p. 53.

- Facilitating "before-and-after," "what-if," and "why/why not" inquiries
- Focusing discussion about the metrics themselves on causes, means, and outcomes rather than on methodologies used to derive them

As an analyst, I am keenly interested in making sure that persons examining a "metric" for the first time should see it for what it is—a standard of measurement—rather than as something confusing that prompts a dissection of the measurer's methods.

Metrics suffer when readers perceive them to be vague. For example, I have seen a widely publicized paper that proposes benchmark security effectiveness, but in its key graphical exhibit, the author's metric is described only as a "benchmark" with a scale from 1 to 5; it does not contain a unit of measure or further explanation.[16] The authors undoubtedly intended to spark discussion about the metric's causes and drivers, but the exhibit instead makes readers scratch their heads about what the metric *is* and how it was defined.[17]

To keep organizations from trapping themselves in tar pits of hand-wavery and vagueness, metrics should be clear and unambiguous. Specifically, good metrics should be consistently measured, cheap to gather, expressed as a number or percentage, and expressed using at least one unit of measure. A "good metric" should also ideally be contextually specific. Table 2-4 summarizes the qualities of good metrics; the next sections describe them further.

Table 2-4   The Definition of a Good Metric

A metric is a consistent standard for measurement.
A good metric should be
• **Consistently measured,** without subjective criteria
• **Cheap to gather,** preferably in an automated way
• **Expressed as a cardinal number or percentage,** not with qualitative labels like "high," "medium," and "low"
• **Expressed using at least one unit of measure,** such as "defects," "hours," or "dollars"
A good metric should also ideally be
• **Contextually specific**—relevant enough to decision-makers so that they can take action

---

[16] Heimerl and Voigt, "Measurement: The Foundation of Security Program Design and Management," *Computer Security Journal*, 2005.

[17] Heimerl and Voigt define their benchmark metric formally elsewhere in the paper. I do not mean to suggest that the metric itself suffers from vagueness—although the exhibit *does*. I revisualize this exhibit in Chapter 6, "Visualization."

CONSISTENTLY MEASURED

Metrics confer credibility when they can be measured in a consistent way. Different people should be able to apply the method to the same data set and come up with equivalent answers. "Metrics" that depend on the subjective judgments of those ever-so-reliable creatures—humans—are not metrics at all. They are ratings. The litmus test is simple: if you asked two different persons the same measurement question, would they produce the same answer?

Metrics are computed either by hand or by machine. In the former case, you can ensure consistency by documenting the measurement process in a transparent and clear way. When people understand how and why to do something, they tend to do it in a more consistent fashion. Keeping measurement questions short and factual (yes/no-oriented) helps, too.

Even better than manual data sources, however, are automated ones. After they are programmed, machines faithfully execute the instructions provided by their programmers. They execute their tasks the same way each time, without mistakes.

Consistently measured metrics need not always come from primary data sources. They can also be calculated or derived. For example, a derived metric that calculates the rate of change of employee entitlements might need to combine records from the HR information system with data from the corporate LDAP server and from application systems. Derived metrics should be as transparent as possible, however. If the derivation formula takes a PhD in math to understand, it is probably too complicated. Complicated formulas just give doubters reasons to pile on.

CHEAP TO GATHER

Every metric takes time to compute. All metrics start their lives as raw source data and then—through the magic of computation—become something more insightful. That means that somebody or something needs to obtain the data from a source, massage and transform the data as needed, and compute and format the results. For some metrics, these steps collapse into a single, fast process; a simple SQL statement or API method call delivers the goods. But other metrics require screen scraping, phone calls, and spreadsheet hackery. Inefficient methods of gathering data cost organizations valuable time that they could have put to better use on analysis.

I firmly believe that metrics ought to be computed at a frequency commensurate with the process's rate of change. For most security processes, such as those for operations and crisis management, "often" is better than "sometimes." Metrics with short sampling intervals help companies analyze their security effectiveness on a day-to-day and week-to-week basis rather than through a yearly rearview mirror (see Figure 2-1). It stands to reason that if a metric needs to be computed frequently, the metric's source data should be cheap to gather in terms of time or money.

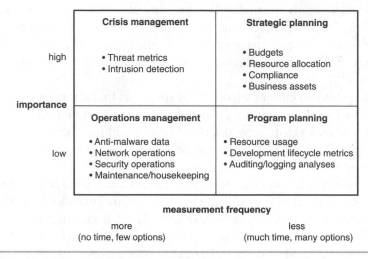

Figure 2-1   Frequently Computed Metrics Should Be Cheap to Gather

Before-and-after comparisons are not something organizations should be forced to do once a year because of inefficient data gathering. For a given metric, ask yourself if you could compute it once a week if you needed to. How about every day? If not, you might want to reconsider the metric—or consider methods of speeding up the measurement process. As with the point about consistency, the criterion that good metrics ought to be cheap to gather favors automation.

Expressed as a Number or Percentage

Good metrics should be expressed as a number or percentage. By "expressed as a number," I mean a *cardinal* number—something that counts how many of something there are—rather than an *ordinal* number that denotes which position that something is in.

For example, "number of application security defects" evaluates to a cardinal number that can be counted. By contrast, subjective high-medium-low ratings that evaluate to 1, 2, and 3 are ordinal numbers that grade relative performance scores but do not count anything.

Metrics that are not expressed as numbers do not qualify as good metrics. "Traffic light" inputs (red-yellow-green) are not metrics at all. They contain neither a unit of measure nor a numerical scale.

Traffic lights *colors* can be used, sparingly, as a presentation strategy to supplement numerical data or draw attention to outliers. But these should overlay or accent cardinal numbers, not replace them. If your data contain more precision than three simple gradations, why dilute their value by obscuring them with a traffic light?

EXPRESSED USING AT LEAST ONE UNIT OF MEASURE

Good metrics should evaluate to a number. They should also contain at least one associated unit of measure that characterizes the things being counted. For example, the metric "number of application security defects" expresses one unit of measure—namely, defects. By using a unit of measure, the analyst knows how to consistently express results of a measurement process that looks for defects.

It is often better to use more than a single unit of measure. The single unit of measure for the "number of application security defects" metric makes it hard to compare dissimilar applications on an apples-to-apples basis. But if one unit of measure is good, two are better. For example, a better metric might be "number of application security defects per 1,000 lines of code," which provides two units of measure. By incorporating a second dimension (dividing by 1,000 lines of code), we have constructed a metric that can be used for benchmarking.

CONTEXTUALLY SPECIFIC

Good metrics mean something to the persons looking at them. They shed light on an underperforming part of the infrastructure under their control, chronicle continuous improvement, or demonstrate the value their people and processes bring to the organization. Although specificity is not required for all good metrics, it helps to keep each of them scoped in such a way that a reader could receive enough insight to make decisions based on the results.

"Contextually specific" is a shorthand way of saying that a good metric ought to pass the "smell test." You do not want managers wrinkling their noses and asking belligerent questions like "And this helps me *how*?"

For example, defining an "average number of attacks" metric for an entire organization doesn't help anybody do their jobs better—unless the indirect goal is an increased security budget. But scoping the same metric down to the level of a particular business unit's e-commerce servers can help much more, because they can make specific decisions about security provisioning and staffing for these servers based on the data.

WHAT MAKES A BAD METRIC?

Now that I have explained what makes a good metric, we should spend some time discussing what makes a *bad* one. The obvious (and short) explanation is that a bad metric fails to exhibit any of the qualities mentioned previously. In other words, it is inconsistently measured, cannot be gathered cheaply, or does not express results with numbers or units of measure. Overly exuberant uses of security frameworks like ISO 27002/17799 also make bad metrics, as do the annualized loss expectancy (ALE) scores. Let's step through each in turn.

INCONSISTENTLY MEASURED

Any metric that relies too much on the judgment of humans cannot be relied on, because the results cannot be guaranteed to be the same from person to person. They are necessarily subjective. Ratings-oriented "metrics" suffer from this deficiency in particular.

An example from my career stands out. Several years ago, a large services firm in Boston built a security "program maturity" questionnaire that attempted to measure competency levels for a dozen different areas of security. As questionnaires go, it was mercifully simple: about 50 questions. For each question, respondents were asked to rate their teams' competency using a scale of 1 to 5, where 5 represented the pinnacle of organization, achievement, and enlightenment. The company got good response rates and pronounced itself extremely satisfied with its metrics efforts.

Questionnaires like these are not bad things; they are extremely useful in "taking an organization's temperature." They can reveal hot spots and gaps in coverage. But the results of these efforts, regardless of the elegance of their expression, do not make good metrics.

Many years ago, at a White House press conference, a reporter lobbed Ronald Reagan a softball question: "Mr. President," he asked, "how would you rate your presidency so far?" Reagan chuckled and replied genially, "Well, I'd have to give myself an A-plus." Self-assessed security control questions are like that too. Rating guidelines must be exceptionally detailed and clear for respondents to answer correctly; usually they are not.

Beyond the pitfall of limited clarity, there is also the question of bias and honesty. Have some respondents inflated their scores (to hide something) or downplayed them (to try to get bigger budgets)? Or did respondents simply shade their answers a bit, in the way that citizens and presidents do when they are asked to evaluate themselves? Few people are outright dishonest, but everyone has biases.

Metrics that require human discernment to compute should be avoided unless they possess controls to guarantee consistency. Organizations need to provide respondents with guidelines on exactly how to answer questions. They also need the internal audit equivalent of the Fourth Estate's Helen Thomas to keep everyone honest.

CANNOT BE GATHERED CHEAPLY

Certain management tools that security managers rely on, such as broad questionnaires and self-evaluations, can be extremely helpful but are labor-intensive to administer. They also must be "spaced out" so as not to annoy their subjects. Critically, the persons answering the questionnaire actually need to do the work. As a result, measurement tools like this are typically fielded infrequently, typically on a quarterly or yearly basis.

Another factor that can produce an "expensive" metric is the sheer drudgery of production. Most people work with all sorts of IT systems on a daily basis, and invariably the numbers and data that these systems possess do not talk to each other. Sometimes the data we want are not exposed to an automated interface. As a result, the act of computing the metrics we would like is reduced to a manual counting and computation exercise, often aided and abetted by spreadsheets.

Because of the expense of production, many security professionals simply punt by defaulting to long sampling intervals. This may not be a bad thing for certain types of broad, program-level metrics such as security budget and cost figures. For processes with long planning cycles, infrequent sampling is fine. But for metrics that are more operational or diagnostic in nature, long sampling intervals will not cut it.

DOES NOT EXPRESS RESULTS WITH CARDINAL NUMBERS AND UNITS OF MEASURE

As I mentioned previously, good metrics should express results using numbers rather than high-low-medium ratings, grades, traffic lights, or other nonnumeric methods. Ordinal numbers—created by assigning a series of subjective scores numeric equivalents—are functionally equivalent to ratings.

There is nothing fatally wrong with any of these methods, of course, and in many cases they can be used in combination with other empirical data to create some rather compelling exhibits. But none of these techniques counts things, so they do not make good metrics.

What Are Not Metrics?

Good metrics facilitate discussion, insight, and analysis; bad metrics prompt furious bouts of head scratching. Reasonable people can agree or disagree on exactly which camp a particular metric belongs in. That said, two hallowed traditions in information security seem to keep creeping into nearly every discussion about security metrics:

- Security framework "measurements," particularly those related to ISO 17799
- Annualized loss expectancy (ALE)

These traditions are fine things, but they have no place in any serious discussion about metrics, regardless of the elegance of their expression or slickness of presentation. They are the ants at every metrics discussion's picnic and the pushy and uninvited friends at every cocktail party. I reserve special vitriol for these two topics largely because they detract attention from more important subjects, such as process measurement and key performance indicators.

Misuse of Security Taxonomies

A common theme I have encountered in my review of security metrics methodologies is an unnatural fixation on using established security taxonomies as the basis of measurement programs. Many large-scale compliance "metrics" projects focus on subjective assessments against an established taxonomy. Most of these methodologies use the ISO 17799 security framework, which defines a structured approach to framing and addressing the problem space of information security.[18]

For example, security software firm Espiria offers a security assessment program and benchmarking service based on self-assessment against the ISO 17799 standard. In 2004, Symantec developed a sales-oriented self-assessment tool designed to quantify risk based on the ISO standard and the ALE method. And Villarrubia et al. proposed a series of security metrics based on the ISO 17799:2000 edition of the standard.[19]

Make no mistake—the ISO 17799 provides an excellent lens for viewing the subject of information security. It carves the security problem space into a taxonomy of 10 subject domains ranging from security policy to physical security, access control, and systems development.[20] These subject domains break down further into about 150 control areas,

---

[18] ISO/IEC: ISO/IEC 17799, Code of Practice for Information Security Management, 2000.

[19] C. Villarrubia, E. Fernandez-Medina, and M. Piattini, "Analysis of ISO/IEC 17799:2000 to be used in Security Metrics," *Security and Management*, pp.109–117, 2004.

[20] The ISO 17799:2005 edition of the standard adds an eleventh category.

as shown in Figure 2-2. As taxonomies go, it is relatively well thought out and does exactly what a mutually exclusive, conceptually exhaustive (MECE) framework should do: it covers the waterfront, and nothing overlaps.[21] In addition, it benefits from the blessings of the International Organization for Standardization (ISO), which declared it a standard in 2000. Most organizations have either heard of, are implementing, or are intimately familiar with ISO 17799 or its successor, ISO 27002. And finally, the ISO standards also serve an important function for auditors—they are often used as guidelines for assessing compliance with good industry practices.

Figure 2-2   ISO 17799 Framework

The use of ISO 17799 as a basis for a metrics program derives from its status as an auditing standard. It is a safe horse to bet on—I refer to it as the "sloucher's choice" for this reason. That said, for all its strengths as a taxonomy and audit standard, ISO 17799 suffers from serious deficiencies as a metrics framework.

---

[21] Actually, a few things *do* overlap, but not in a meaningful way.

My reservations about using the ISO as a metrics framework derives from three objections, which are rooted in deficiencies in the standard itself. Critics of ISO 17799 will tell you that the standard suffers from the following:

- **Excessive focus on audit:** The authors of the ISO 17799 standard intended it to help organizations identify IT security control *requirements*; they did not intend it to be a guidebook for security *management*. It is fair to say that the standard was written with security auditors in mind, not managers. As such, ISO 17799 portrays information security controls as things to be assessed, selected, and implemented. But it makes almost no practical recommendations about how to manage, monitor, and measure the effectiveness of these controls. The unintended consequence of this bias is that it makes complying with the audit's requirements the highest form of achievement. Actually, decreasing risk or increasing computing security are merely side effects caused by having the right policies and passing the audit. I view ISO 17799 as a fully self-powered perpetual-inertia machine: it forces organizations to engage in continuous assessment, not continuous improvement. Indeed, most organizations would say the same thing about Sarbanes-Oxley. My colleague Alex Hutton calls ISO "a hamster wheel the size of the London Eye."[22]

- **Subjective success criteria:** ISO 17799 contains a great deal of excellent guidance in its hundred-plus pages. If you're curious about recommended practices for creating good passwords or deploying "duress alarms," the ISO standard can suggest some good ones. But the flip side of ISO 17799's guidance is that the recommendations are never firm; interpretation is an exercise left to the reader (or auditor, as the case may be). In short, the standard is highly descriptive, but rarely prescriptive. As a result, no consensus for objective success criteria exists for ISO 17799, making it impossible to create repeatable measurement processes.

- **Insufficient attention to measurement:** As mentioned, the ISO 17799 standard focuses primarily on requirements enumeration and auditing. The word "audit" appears dozens of times in the text. By contrast, "measurement" appears in the document just once, and the word "metric" not at all. For measurement, the ISO 17799 document acknowledges that "a comprehensive and balanced system of measurement which is used to evaluate performance in information security management"[23] is a critical success factor for information security. But the standard provides no further guidance on the subject. This is not surprising, considering the standard's lack of objective success criteria.

---

[22] From private correspondence with me.

[23] ISO/IEC: ISO/IEC 17799, "Code of Practice for Information Security Management," 2000, p. ix.

Recent revisions to the ISO 17799 framework, notably the 2005 version and its successor, ISO 27002, attempt to address some of these shortcomings. According to what I've read about the new versions, control guidelines are firmer and contain less room for interpretation. Another standard, ISO 27003, will contain specific implementation guidelines. Likewise, the authors appear to agree that the lack of metrics is a serious deficiency. As a result, ISO plans a standard called 27004 that addresses metrics and measurement. The revisions to the ISO standards are good news for security metrics practitioners. In the meantime, though, the current 17799 standard is all we have.

With the current ISO 17799 framework, security professionals possess a well-constructed security taxonomy. This provides a shared vocabulary for framing and discussing the problem domain of information security. Security taxonomies can serve as useful classification schemes for grouping metrics. Indeed, I discuss appropriate uses of security frameworks in Chapter 4, "Measuring Program Effectiveness," and again in Chapter 8, "Designing Security Scorecards."

But just because the standard exists does not automatically mean companies should base measurement programs on it. In its current form, ISO encourages prospective measurers to think more about compliance with the standard and less about effectiveness.

The ISO framework, and similar frameworks like NIST, COBIT, and other security standards, wraps metrics in a straitjacket. If we intend—as a profession—to connect with the corner office, we should think about metrics in more creative ways. Free your mind—forget about ISO-based "metrics" for now.

ANNUALIZED LOSS EXPECTANCY

A popular paradigm in the information security world is the concept of annualized loss expectancy, which models the impact that security events have on assets. ALE is a relatively easy idea to grasp, because at its core is a simple algebraic formula that multiplies the value of a discrete loss event (the single loss expectancy) by its expected annual occurrence. The following sidebar gives a representative definition of ALE.

ALE occupies hallowed ground in the world of information security. Nearly every security training course for practitioners provides space on their agendas for it. A quick review of curricula shows that the SANS Institute,[24] the CISSP certification tests, and CERIA all teach or require knowledge of ALE. Even Bruce Schneier, as grand an ambassador as information security possesses, gives ALE space in his bestselling book *Secrets and Lies*.[25]

---

[24] SANS Institute, Management 414 course curriculum. See http://www.sans.org/ondemand/description.php?cid=764.

[25] B. Schneier, *Secrets and Lies*, John Wiley & Sons, 2000, pp.301–302.

THE DEFINITION OF ANNUALIZED LOSS EXPECTANCY

The ALE is the monetary loss that can be expected for an asset due to a risk over a one-year period. It is defined as

ALE = SLE * ARO

where SLE is the single loss expectancy and ARO is the annualized rate of occurrence.

   An important feature of the ALE is that it can be used directly in a cost-benefit analysis. If a threat or risk has an ALE of $5,000, it may not be worth spending $10,000 per year on a security measure that will eliminate it.

   One thing to remember when using the ALE value is that, when the ARO is on the order of one loss per year, there can be considerable variance in the actual loss. For example, suppose the ARO is 0.5 and the SLE is $10,000. The ALE is then $5,000, a figure we may be comfortable with. Using the Poisson Distribution we can calculate the probability of a specific number of losses occurring in a given year:

Number of Losses in Year	Probability	Annual Loss
0	0.3679	$0
1	0.3679	$10,000
2	0.1839	$20,000
3	0.0613	$30,000
4	0.0153	$40,000
>4	0.0727	≥$50,000

We can see from this table that the probability of a loss of $20,000 is 0.1839 and that the probability of losses being $50,000 or more is approximately 0.0727. Depending on our tolerance to risk and our organization's ability to withstand greater losses, we may believe that a security measure that costs $10,000 per year to implement is still worthwhile, even though it is less than the expected losses due to the threat.

Source: Risky Thinking (http://www.riskythinking.com/glossary/annualized_loss_expectancy.php). Reprinted per site guidelines, and lightly edited.

There is just one problem with ALE: the old dog will not hunt. As my friend Dan Geer wryly puts it, "the numbers are too poor even to lie with."[26] There are three reasons for this:

---

[26] Interview with Dan Geer, December 29, 2004.

- The inherent difficulty in modeling outliers
- The lack of data for estimating probabilities of occurrence or loss expectancies
- Sensitivity of the ALE model to small changes in assumptions

First, ALE is not nearly as simple a problem as the math might indicate. Outliers dominate loss events—one cannot characterize what a "typical" loss event looks like. My former @stake confederate Andrew Sudbury observes, "Security events are low frequency and high severity. That makes them hard to model."[27] This forces practitioners to compromise and make unreasonable assumptions such as those made in the following physics joke:

A dairy farmer . . . in a fit of desperation over the fact that his cows won't give enough milk consults a theoretical physicist about the problem. The physicist listens to him, asks a few questions, and then says he'll take the assignment. A few weeks later, he calls up the farmer and says, "I've got the answer." They arrange for him to give a presentation of his solution to the milk shortage. When the day of the presentation arrives, he begins his talk by saying, "First, we assume a spherical cow. . ."[28]

ALE is security's spherical cow. It encourages practitioners to think about dollar impact on an aggregate, averaged basis, in spite of the fact that losses do not gravitate to the middle; they cluster on the far edges.

Second, practitioners of ALE suffer from a near-complete inability to reliably estimate probabilities or losses. My colleague Andrew Stewart observes that it is "difficult to predict the probability that a loss event will occur, and there is a similar challenge in predicting the effect of a loss event on intangible assets."[29] Schneier refers to ALE as "a lot of guesswork."[30] Even one of the security professionals who's keenest on ALE (Cybertrust's Peter Tippet) advises attendees of his ALE lectures to use plug figures for occurrence rates because "we don't really know what the probability is."[31]

---

[27] Andrew Sudbury, response to "'Risk' metrics" topic, securitymetrics.org mailing list, February 1, 2006.

[28] Recounting of a famous physics joke, as told by Chad Orzel. http://scienceblogs.com/principles/2006/06/assume_a_spherical_cow.php, June 21, 2006.

[29] Andrew Stewart, response to "ALE & NPV" topic, securitymetrics.org mailing list, May 23, 2005.

[30] B. Schneier, *Secrets and Lies*, John Wiley & Sons, 2000, p.302.

[31] P. Tippett, "Management That Measures Up: Metrics for Information Risk Reduction and Decision Analysis" (paraphrase of oral commentary), February 17, 2005.

The same is true for loss estimation, although that has not kept otherwise well-intentioned people from swinging wildly at the piñata that is the CSI/FBI's annual computer crime survey. Security professionals who have few other sources of industry loss data tend to use the study's "average loss" figures as sources for their ALE models. This is absurd, crazy, foolish, and misguided. Saying organizations should model security programs using "average" losses reported by the CSI is like trying to pick specific stocks using the Russell 2000 index. Both the CSI numbers and the Russell 2000 index have their place, but they should be used as bellwethers, not proper benchmarks.

The third strike against ALE relates to the lack of probability-and-loss data. When models contain only a few variables, they become extraordinarily sensitive to small changes in assumptions. Figure 2-3 shows a detailed exhibit from a loss-expectancy model I built in 1995 to analyze the likelihood and cost of failure for a customer. This customer, a large computer manufacturer, wanted us to recommend options for its business continuity strategy. My firm provided outsourced technology services, and it was our responsibility to model the options and make recommendations.

Exhibit C — Component-Level Analysis

Component (Implementation Option)	Based on	Cost Equipment	Cost WAN	Cost EDI	MTBF	Availability	Average Downtime
C-S1 **SMS UNIX Cluster (AT&T+Lifekeeper)**		$ 300,000			3,376	99.970%	5.89
UNIX Hardware Cluster	UXHW	$ 300,000			40,512	99.998%	23.50
Disk array		incl.			n/a	n/a	n/a
Motherboard/system bus		incl.			n/a	n/a	n/a
NIC		incl.			n/a	n/a	n/a
UNIX OS	UNIX	incl.			13,504	99.993%	5.67
Sybase DB	SDB	n/a			10,128	99.990%	4.31
Sybase App	SAPP	n/a			10,128	99.990%	3.25
C-E1 **EDI Translator (ES-9000)**		n/a		$ 779,025	626	99.840%	1.00
ES-9000 host hardware		n/a			333	99.850%	1.00
Gentran Application/DB		n/a		$ 779,025	10,128	99.990%	1.00
C-E2 **EDI Translator (UNIX -- assumes hardware)**		$ 65,460			10,128	99.990%	1.00
Excel Application/DB		$ 65,460			10,128	99.990%	1.00
C-F1 **UNIX Firewall**		$ 70,000			10,128	99.990%	0.25
C-N1 **NetWare Server (Standard)**		$ 13,200			5,936	99.983%	3.00
NetWare Hardware		incl.			20,000	99.995%	3.00
Motherboard/system bus/NIC		incl.			n/a	n/a	2.00
Disk array		incl.			n/a	n/a	4.00
NetWare OS	NWOS	incl.			8,440	99.988%	2.42
C-N2 **NetWare Server (Mirrored Servers)**		$ 45,000			7,221	99.986%	0.25
NetWare Hardware		incl.			50,000	99.998%	0.25
Motherboard/system bus/NIC		incl.			n/a	n/a	0.25
Disk array		incl.			n/a	n/a	0.25
NetWare OS	NWOS	incl.			8,440	99.988%	0.25
C-PC **PC Workstation**		$ 3,000			15,000	99.993%	2.00
Motherboard/system bus/NIC/disk		incl.			15,000	99.993%	2.00
C-RD **Router/DSU**		$ 12,000			10,128	99.990%	4.00
Router	ROUT	$ 10,000			10,128	99.990%	4.00
DSU		$ 2,000			n/a	n/a	n/a
C-WL **WAN/Local Loop (LEC only, 2 56K lines)**			$ 14,400		515	99.806%	0.50
C-WS **WAN/Long Haul (Single IEC, 2 56K lines)**			$ 19,500		602	99.834%	0.50
C-WR **WAN/Long Haul (Redundant IECs, 2 56K lines)**			$ 26,400		1,203	99.917%	0.50
C-H1 **Hub**		$ 1,800			40,000	99.998%	1.00
C-PR **Label/Impact Printer**	PSRV	$ 3,000			9,495	99.989%	0.50
C-SC **Bar code scanner**	PSRV	$ 2,000			9,495	99.989%	0.50
C-P1 **Power/Momentary Loss (Protected site)**					-	100.000%	-
C-P2 **Power/Momentary Loss (Unprotected site)**					100	99.000%	1.00
C-P3 **Power/Utility Outage (Protected Site)**					-	100.000%	-
C-P4 **Power/Utility Outage (Unprotected Site)**					15,000	99.993%	15.00

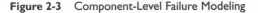

Figure 2-3   Component-Level Failure Modeling

As part of my analysis, I built a huge, glorious Excel model that estimated the likelihood of losses and the cost of each single occurrence. As it happened, the customer's downtime cost exceeded $10,000 per minute. After building the assumptions for each component, I began combining components into 16 business continuity scenarios. Figure 2-4 shows a graphical depiction of each scenario's forecast annual cost (including expected losses). As you can see, the various scenarios caused the total costs to vary by nearly $700,000—and this was before flexing any of the inputs for downtime cost or expected loss frequency. The latter inputs, by the way, were a shot in the dark despite the fact that I dedicated weeks to the task of obtaining the very best and reliable mean time between failures (MTBF) numbers I could find.

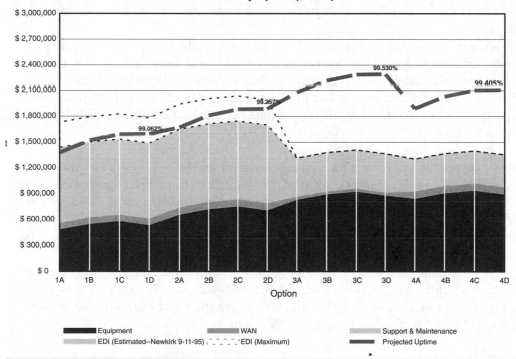

Figure 2-4 Scenario Analysis of Loss-Expectancy Model

I mention this example partly because it illustrates how far you can take ALE-style models if you are so inclined. You can develop complex spreadsheets that have all the elegance of the Grand Unified Theory, the breadth and depth of the Grand Canyon, and formulas so dense that you would need a PhD math student to decipher them.

But ultimately, the model you build still depends on data that, to put it charitably, are not based on actuarially sound principles.

This brings me to the second reason I recount this story about my marvelous model from 1995. Despite the extraordinary care with which I had constructed the model, and the absolute certainty I possessed in the correctness of its results, my boss would have none of it. As it happened, my recommendations—supported by the model—would have caused her organization to lose over $1 million a year in direct electronic data interchange (EDI) revenues from the customer. As justification, she slyly intimated that I had cooked the books: "Andy," she said, "you can make those numbers say anything you want."

As much as I hated to admit it at the time, she was right—a little fiddling with the assumptions could have gotten her a more favorable answer. That is the real tragedy of ALE: it's really just a funny little model that anyone can game for his or her own purposes.

I am not against ALE *as a concept*. If we had good incidence rate numbers and a decent formula for valuing individual items, I would be all for it. But we do not have a decent formula, and we will never get good data. Because of the model's sensitivity to changes in assumptions and the fact that neither the probability of occurrence nor the expected loss can be estimated with any confidence, I think that we can safely say that ALE is no good.

Even though most security practitioners realize that ALE has serious—I would argue fatal—shortcomings, we keep trotting it out as if it meant something. Thus, the real reason I dislike ALE is because its continued use distracts us from discussing practical alternatives. We should be talking about things that people actually measure, not about the same hokey pseudoscience that security experts have been espousing for years. As a model and as a putative measurement technique, ALE needs to be thrown out the window, spit on, run through a tree chipper, and generally discredited.

When I was an undergrad, a physics professor was my academic advisor. The mere mention of "soft sciences" like political science and economics caused him to giggle uncontrollably because of his rather dim view of the analytical methods used in those fields. ALE, frankly, gives *me* the giggles. We can do better.

SUMMARY

Metrics are an emerging field of study for information security professionals. Drawing from examples in fields like manufacturing, logistics, and finance, security metrics attempt to put numbers around activities that safeguard information resources.

Good metrics facilitate discussion, insight, and analysis; bad metrics prompt furious arguments about methodology. Metrics should never require a rocket scientist, witch doctor, or polymath to explain; they should be transparent enough that their calculations are easy to understand.

Good metrics should be

- **Consistently measured,** without subjective criteria.
- **Cheap to gather,** preferably in an automated way.
- **Expressed as a cardinal number or percentage,** not with qualitative labels like "high," "medium," and "low."
- **Expressed using at least one unit of measure,** such as "defects," "hours," or "dollars."
- **Contextually specific** and relevant enough to decision-makers that they can take action. If the response to a metric is a shrug of the shoulders and "So what?", it is not worth gathering.

Bad metrics

- **Are inconsistently measured,** usually because they rely on subjective judgments that vary from person to person.
- **Cannot be gathered cheaply,** as is typical of labor-intensive surveys and one-off spreadsheets.
- **Do not express results with cardinal numbers and units of measure.** Instead, they rely on qualitative high/medium/low ratings, traffic lights, and letter grades.

Taxonomies like the ISO 17799 framework help explain and organize the security problem space but make terrible foundations for metrics programs. Organizations looking to start a security metrics program should think less about taxonomies and more about key indicators that quantify particular security activities. They should also rid themselves of the boat anchor called ALE, a spherical cow whose theories of average losses are belied by the realities of dominant outliers.

The next two chapters set aside nice theories about criteria for good metrics and jump right into the metrics definitions themselves. Chapter 3, "Diagnosing Problems and Measuring Technical Security," discusses metrics used to diagnose problems and measure technical security activities. Chapter 4 identifies ways to measure overall program effectiveness.

Diagnosing Problems and Measuring Technical Security

McKinsey has developed a strong, fact-based culture . . . many alumni are surprised at the lack of concrete data analysis in their new organizations.

—Ethan Raisel and Paul Friga, The McKinsey Mind

The discipline of measurement underpins many of society's most revered professions. Young physicists, chemists, and engineers are indoctrinated into science at an early age through the "scientific method"—a controlled and well-defined process for exploring and proving theories about the natural world. When the scientist is investigating a phenomenon, the method requires the scientist to:

- Formulate a hypothesis about the phenomenon
- Design tests to support or disprove the hypothesis
- Rigorously conduct and measure the results of each test
- Draw a conclusion based on the evidence

Nearly everyone who has taken high school biology or chemistry has experienced the scientific method firsthand. All science lab experiments—such as dissecting a frog, generating "steam" using dry ice, or building a chemical "volcano"—have the same basic steps. In short: write a hypothesis, conduct the experiment, analyze the results, and write up the conclusion. Measurement is core to the scientific method. Without it, experiments cannot be reproduced; without reproduction, a scientist's analysis and conclusions cannot be trusted.

Beyond the domain of the laboratory, hypothesis testing and rigorous measurement underpin certain disciplines in the commercial world, too. Modern management consulting, for example, focuses on marshalling empirical evidence to diagnose organizational problems and to confirm hypothetical strategies for fixing underperforming operations. It is no accident that the entrée engagement for McKinsey & Company, for example, is a short data-gathering and needs-assessment exercise called a *diagnostic*. The resemblance to the laboratory procedure of the same name is—I am quite sure—strictly intentional.

Usually, anyone using "scientific method" and "security" in the same sentence sends his or her listener into fits of giggles. This is largely because little consensus exists on what questions to ask, or how to measure. As my colleague Fred Cohen notes:

> *"The vast majority of information security-related measurement measures what is trivial to measure and not what will help the enterprise make sensible risk management decisions. Very few people seem to know what they want to measure."*[1]

To my eyes, the historical lack of consensus about security measures only means that we have not applied enough thought to the endeavor. Thus, taking our cue from scientists and management consultants, the next two chapters describe how to use empirical measures to diagnose issues with an organization's security controls. In security, metrics help organizations:

- Understand security risks
- Spot emerging problems
- Understand weaknesses in their security infrastructures
- Measure performance of countermeasure processes
- Recommend technology and process improvements

The need for metrics is great, because all companies suffer from security-related aches and pains. Sometimes the pain is sharp and incapacitating, such as when an intruder defaces a public-facing website. Perhaps, as with the now-defunct Egghead Software, an intruder successfully obtains sensitive customer data, and the resulting embarrassment causes business losses. Sharp pains are the kind that put companies "on the front page of the *Wall Street Journal*," as the expression goes. Far more common are the dull aches: an unsettling feeling in the CIO's stomach that something just isn't right. Regardless of the source of the pain, security metrics can help with the diagnosis.

---

[1]   Fred Cohen, e-mail to securitymetrics.org mailing list, January 1, 2006.

To that end, this chapter formally defines a collection of common security metrics for diagnosing problems and measuring technical security activities. I have grouped them into four categories: perimeter defenses, coverage and control, availability/reliability, and applications. Chapter 4, "Measuring Program Effectiveness," discusses metrics for measuring ongoing effectiveness: risk management, policies compliance, employee training, identity management, and security program management. Chapter 8, "Designing Security Scorecards," uses both sets of metrics to build a "balanced security scorecard."

But first, a short case study will describe in more detail exactly what I mean by "diagnostic" metrics.

USING METRICS TO DIAGNOSE PROBLEMS: A CASE STUDY

A few years ago my former employer was called in by the CTO of a large, well-known maker of high-end consumer electronics. This company, which prides itself on its progressive approach to IT management, operates a large, reasonably up-to-date network and a full suite of enterprise applications. The CTO, Barry Eiger,[2] an extremely smart man, is fully conversant in the prevailing technology trends of the day. In manner and in practice, he tends to be a conservative technology deployer. Unimpressed with fads and trends, he prefers to hydrofoil above the choppy technological seas with a slightly bemused sense of detachment. Facts, rather than the ebbs and flows of technology, weigh heavily in his decision-making. In our initial conversations, he displayed an acute awareness of industry IT spending benchmarks. We discovered later that he had spent significant sums of money over the years on advisory services from Gartner Group, Meta Group, and others.

If he is so well informed, why did he call us in I wondered? Barry's problem was simple. His firm had historically been an engineering-driven company with limited need for Internet applications. More recently, his senior management team had asked him to deploy a series of transactional financial systems that would offer customers order management, loan financing, and customer support services. These public-facing systems, in turn, connected back to several internal manufacturing applications as well as to the usual suspects—PeopleSoft, SAP, Siebel, and Oracle. A prudent man, Barry wanted to make sure his perimeter and application defenses were sufficient before beginning significant deployments. He wanted to know how difficult it might be for an outsider to penetrate his security perimeter and access sensitive customer data, product development plans, or financial systems.

---

[2] Pseudonym.

Barry asserted that his team had done a good job with security in the past. "What if you can't get in?" he asked rhetorically. Despite his confidence, his dull ache persisted. His nagging feeling compelled him to find out how good his defenses really were. He also wanted to get some benchmarks to see how well his company compared to other companies like his.

Barry wanted a McKinsey-style "diagnostic." This kind of diagnostic first states an overall hypothesis related to the business problem at hand and then marshals evidence (metrics) that supports or undermines the theory. The essence of the McKinsey diagnostic method is quite simple:

- **The analysis team identifies an overall hypothesis to be supported.** Example: "The firm is secure from wireless threats by outsiders."

- **The team brainstorms additional subhypotheses that must hold for the overall hypothesis to be true.** For example, to support the wireless hypothesis we just identified, we might pose these subhypotheses: "Open wireless access points are not accessible from outside the building" and "Wireless access points on the corporate LAN require session encryption and reliable user authentication."

- **The team examines each subhypothesis to determine if it can be supported or disproved by measuring something.** If it cannot, the hypothesis is either discarded or decomposed into lower-level hypotheses.

- **For each lowest-level hypothesis, the team identifies specific diagnostic questions.** The answers to the questions provide evidence for or against the hypothesis. Diagnostic questions generally take the form of "The number of X is greater (or less) than Y" or "The percentage of X is greater (or less) than Y." For example, "There are no open wireless access points that can be accessed from the building's parking lot or surrounding areas" or "100% of the wireless access points on the corporate LAN require 128-bit WPA security." The diagnostic questions dictate our metrics.

The primary benefit of the diagnostic method is that hypotheses are proven or disproven based on empirical evidence rather than intuition. Because each hypothesis supports the other, the cumulative weight of cold, hard facts builds a supporting case that cannot be disputed. A secondary benefit of the diagnostic method is that it forces the analysis team to focus only on measurements that directly support or disprove the overall hypothesis. Extraneous "fishing expeditions" about theoretical issues that cannot be measured automatically filter themselves out.

So far, the sample hypotheses and diagnostic questions I have given are rather simplistic. Why don't we return to our friend Barry's company for a real-world example?

Recall that Barry's original question was "Is my company's customer data secure from outside attack?" Our overall hypothesis held that, indeed, the company was highly vulnerable to attack from outsiders. To show that this statement was true (or untrue), we constructed subhypotheses that could be supported or disproven by asking specific questions whose answers could be measured precisely and empirically. Table 3-1 shows a subset of the diagnostics we employed to test the hypothesis. Note that these diagnostics do not exhaust the potential problem space. Time and budget impose natural limits on the number and kind of diagnostics that can be employed.

Table 3-1 Diagnostic Metrics in Action

Subhypotheses	Diagnostic Questions
The network perimeter is porous, permitting easy access to any outsider.	How many sites are connected directly to the core network without intermediate firewalls?
	How many of these sites have deployed unsecured wireless networks?
	Starting with zero knowledge, how many minutes are required to gain full access to network domain controllers?
An outsider can readily obtain access to internal systems because password policies are weak.	What percentage of user accounts could be compromised in 15 minutes or less?
Once on the network, attackers can easily obtain administrator credentials.	How many administrative-level passwords could be compromised in the same time frame?
An intruder finding a hole somewhere in the network could easily jump straight to the core transactional systems.	How many internal "zones" exist to compartmentalize users, workgroup servers, transactional systems, partner systems, retail stores, and Internet-facing servers?
Workstations are at risk for virus or worm attacks.	How many missing operating system patches are on each system?
Viruses and worms can spread to large numbers of computers quickly.	How many network ports are open on each workstation computer?
	How many of these are "risky" ports?
Application security is weak and relies too heavily on the "out of the box" defaults.	How many security defects exist in each business application?
	What is the relative "risk score" of each application compared to the others?

continues

Table 3-1 Diagnostic Metrics in Action (Continued)

Subhypotheses	Diagnostic Questions
The firm's deployments of applications are much riskier than those made by leaders in the field (for example, investment banking).	Where does each application rank relative to other enterprise applications @stake has examined for other clients?

To answer the diagnostic questions we posed, we devised a four-month program for Barry's company. We assessed their network perimeter defenses, internal networks, top ten most significant application systems, and related infrastructure. When we finished the engagement and prepared our final presentation for Barry, his team, and the company's management, the metrics we calculated played a key role in proving our hypothesis. The evidence was so compelling, in fact, that the initial engagement was extended into a much longer corrective program with a contract value of several million dollars.

The preceding story illustrates the role that metrics can play in diagnosing problems. The remainder of this chapter describes, in a more systematic way, the types of metrics that can be useful for diagnostics.

DEFINING DIAGNOSTIC METRICS

This chapter defines about seventy-five different metrics that organizations use to assess their security posture, diagnose issues, and measure security activities associated with their infrastructure. Because the list of potential metrics is long indeed, I have split the discussion into two chapters. This chapter focuses on technical metrics that quantify each of the following:

- **Perimeter defenses:** To help understand the risk of security incidents coming from the outside, organizations measure the effectiveness of their antivirus software, antispam systems, firewalls, and intrusion detection systems (IDSs).

- **Coverage and control:** Companies that run "tight ships" know how important it is to extend the reach of their control systems as widely as possible. Metrics can help us understand the extent and effectiveness of configuration, patching, and vulnerability management systems.

- **Availability and reliability:** Systems that companies rely on to generate revenue must stay up, without being taken out of service due to unexpected security incidents. Metrics like mean time to recover (MTTR) and uptime percentages show the dependencies between security and profits.

- **Application risks:** Custom and packaged line-of-business applications that enterprises depend on need to be developed in a safe manner that does not result in unnecessary security exposures. Application security metrics such as defect counts, cyclomatic complexity, and application risk indices help quantify the risks inherent in homegrown code and third-party software.

Each of the four metrics sections is largely self-contained and follows the same formula. First the metrics subject area is defined, explaining exactly what I mean by, say, "perimeter security and threats." That is followed by a table containing a list of representative metrics for the subject area. Each metric has a *purpose* and a representative list of typical *sources*. Note that for the sources, generally I have listed the system originating the metric, not necessarily the one that calculates the metric. In many cases, the originator passes its data to a downstream system for further processing—for example, to a SIM/SEM system.

Many of the metrics may not always seem intuitively obvious; thus, after the table I explain selected metrics in more detail: the value they bring, who uses them, why, and whether they possess special characteristics you should be aware of. But most of the metrics should be fairly self-explanatory.

If you are reading this as a member of a company or organization looking to implement a metrics program, I hope that you will find the metrics presented in this chapter (and in the next one) helpful in your endeavors. But before getting into the details, please be aware of three caveats.

First, the metrics I discuss here should not be considered the last word. A large number of organizations and industry initiatives have begun creating metrics lists, notably the Corporate Information Security Working Group (CISWG), NIST, ISSEA, US CERT, and my own initiative, securitymetrics.org.

Second, these metrics are mostly observed rather than modeled. I have derived the metrics herein from multiple sources: interviews with enterprise subject matter experts, publicly available documents, and personal experience. They are, in most cases, things that people count, rather than things a risk model says they *should* count. I do not offer a risk model that justifies the selection of particular metrics. In other words, you can use the metrics in this chapter to support or disprove your own hypotheses in targeted areas, but the collective set does not itself imply a grand hypothesis for the overall information security problem space.

Third, not all of these metrics are appropriate for all organizations—the list is not meant to be canonical. When you select metrics for your own use, each must pass the "So what?" test. This means that a particular metric needs to provide insights that you don't already possess, arm you with information you can use to spend your organization's dollars more wisely, or help you diagnose problems better. More important, the metrics you select should mean something to the people responsible for producing them or to their bosses. If the metric fails the test, do not use it, or pick another one that works better.

PERIMETER SECURITY AND THREATS

The classical conception of information security begins with the firewall, starting with the DEC SEAL product and the TIS Firewall Toolkit. In 1993, when it was considered cutting-edge to have an Internet connection—before companies like McAfee, PatchLink, and ArcSight persuaded corporate information security officers to write them into their budgets—most organizations instinctively knew that it was a good idea to buy an ANS InterLock or Raptor firewall. Desktop viruses were rare and spread slowly because floppy disk sharing—not e-mail or the web browser—was the primary propagation vector.

Many companies' conceptions of what it meant to be secure focused on managing access to the Internet via the firewall. In the early days, the telecom group typically managed the firewall in conjunction with the centralized wide-area networking (WAN) group—*never* to be confused with (shudder) the "desktop" networking group. It made sense to have centralized, specialized perimeter security organizations manage centralized, specialized perimeter security products.

A few years later, companies began granting wide access to Internet resources. By 1997, nearly every employee had on his or her desktop a web browser, an e-mail client, and a monumentally insecure Windows operating system. The bad guys figured out this latter feature soon enough, and by 2000, Internet- and e-mail–borne viruses and worms had become the bane of IT departments everywhere.

As a result, antivirus software became a standard corporate budget item. Research from the company I work for, for example, shows that in 2005, 99% of enterprises had deployed antivirus software company-wide.[3] Continuing worries about Internet-based malware threats dominate the pages of most of the IT and trade publications, and a whole cottage industry has sprung up around them: antispyware software, vulnerability scanning tools, patch management software, and related threat and perimeter-oriented security products.

Because of their history of centralization within organizations, long tenure on corporate budgets, and relative maturity of tools, metrics for perimeter security are arguably the best understood of all security measures. To put it more simply, IT groups have been buying firewalls and antivirus software for a long time. It is not surprising that companies think of these products first when thinking about security metrics.

---

[3]   A. Jaquith, C. Liebert, et al., Yankee Group Security Leaders and Laggards survey, 2005.

Table 3-2 shows a representative list of perimeter defense metrics. Most of these metrics should be familiar to most security professionals.

Table 3-2   Perimeter Defense Metrics

Metric (Unit of Measure)	Purpose	Sources
E-mail		
Messages per day (number [#]) • Per organizational unit	Velocity of legitimate e-mail traffic; establishes baselines	E-mail system
Spam detected/filtered (#, percent [%])	Indicator of e-mail "pollution"	Gateway e-mail content filtering software
Spam not detected/missed (#, %)	Effectiveness of content filtering software	Gateway e-mail content filtering software
Spam false positives (#, %)	Effectiveness of content filtering software	Gateway e-mail content filtering software
Spam detection failure rate (%)—not-detected plus false positives, divided by spam detected	Effectiveness of content filtering software	Gateway e-mail content filtering software
Viruses and spyware detected in e-mail messages (#, %)	Indicator of e-mail "pollution"	Gateway e-mail content filtering software Workgroup e-mail content filtering software
Antivirus and Antispyware		
Viruses and spyware detected on websites (#, %)	Propensity of users to surf to sites containing web-based threats	Perimeter web filtering appliance or software
Spyware detected in user files (#) • On servers • On desktops • On laptops	Indicator of infection rate on desktops and servers	Desktop antispyware
Viruses detected in user files (#) • On servers • On desktops • On laptops	Infection rate of endpoints as determined by automated software scans	Desktop antivirus

continues

Table 3-2   Perimeter Defense Metrics (Continued)

Metric (Unit of Measure)	Purpose	Sources
Virus and incidents requiring manual cleanup (#, % of overall virus incidents)	Shows relative level of manual effort required to clean up	Antivirus software Trouble-ticketing system Manual data sources
Spyware incidents cleanup cost • By business unit	Shows labor costs associated with cleanup	Antivirus software Trouble-ticketing system Manual data sources
Virus incidents cleanup cost • By business unit	Shows labor costs associated with cleanup	Antivirus software Trouble-ticketing system Manual data sources
Outgoing viruses and spyware caught at gateway (#)	Indicator of internal infections	Gateway e-mail content filtering software
Firewall and Network Perimeter		
Firewall rule changes (#) • By business unit • By group's server type	Suggests level of security complexity required by each	Firewall management system Time-tracking and charge-back systems
Firewall labor (# full-time equivalents)	Labor required to support business unit firewall needs	HR management system Manual data source
Inbound connections/sessions to Internet-facing servers (#) • By TCP/UDP port • By server type or group	Absolute level of inbound Internet activity	Firewall management system
Sites with open wireless access points (#)	Suggests potential exposure to infiltration by outsiders	Wireless scanning tools (NetStumbler, AirSnort, and so on)
Remote locations connected directly to core transaction and financial systems without intermediate firewalls (#)	Indicates level of compartmentalization of sensitive business assets, and potential exposure to attack	Network mapping software Network diagrams

Metric (Unit of Measure)	Purpose	Sources
Attacks		
Ratio of Internet web sessions to attackers (%) at three levels of event severity: <ul><li>Prospects (initial IDS events)</li><li>Suspects (machine-filtered/ escalated alerts)</li><li>Attackers (manual investigation by staff)</li></ul>	Shows the attack "funnel" by which low-level security events are triaged and escalated, as compared to the overall level of business	IDS Firewall Trouble-ticketing system Manual data sources
Number of attacks (#)	Absolute number of detected attacks, both thwarted and successful	IDS Manual data sources
Number of successful attacks (#, %) <ul><li>By affected business unit</li><li>By geography</li></ul>	Indicates the relative effectiveness of perimeter defenses	IDS Manual data sources

E-MAIL

As you read through the "E-mail" section of Table 3-2, you will recognize some familiar metrics. A chestnut of e-mail security vendors is the classic set of spam and gateway antivirus metrics: percentage of spam detected/filtered, and the number of viruses and spyware detected in e-mail messages. Research by the Robert Frances Group shows that 77% of organizations track the first metric, and 92% track the second.[4]

But it is dangerous to read too much into these. For example, the percentage of e-mails that are spam is often paraded around as evidence that the spam-control software is doing its job. But that metric really does not tell us much about the software's accuracy—only about the overall level of "pollution" in the e-mail stream. In other words, it is an environmental indicator but not necessarily a measure of effectiveness. A better measure of effectiveness is either the percentage of missed spam (as reported by end users) or the percentage of false positives (that is, the messages marked as spam that were not actually spam). A minority of companies watches these metrics—39% and 31%, respectively.[5] Both of these measures can be used together, and the two together comprise what is called the "spam detection miss rate" metric.

---

[4] C. Robinson, "Collecting Effective Security Metrics" *CSO Online*, (2004) http://www.csoonline.com/ analyst/report2412.html.

[5] Ibid

ANTIVIRUS AND ANTISPAM

Under the category of antivirus and antispyware metrics are the usual "fun facts": the number of distinct pieces of malware detected by antimalware software scans. These data are easily gathered from desktop and server antimalware systems. But with a little "enrichment" from manual data sources and trouble-ticketing systems, we can add more context. For example, the "virus incidents requiring manual cleanup" metric tells us which virus outbreaks were bad enough that automated quarantine-and-removal processes could not contain them. Dividing the number of incidents that required human intervention into the total number of incidents gives us a much more honest assessment of the effectiveness of the antivirus system. Labor costs associated with manual cleanup efforts also can give an organization a sense of where its break/fix dollars are going.

Another twist I have added to the traditional antivirus statistics is a simple metric documenting the number of *outbound* viruses or spyware samples caught by the perimeter mail gateway's content filtering software. Why it matters is simple—it is an excellent indicator of how "clean" the internal network is. Organizations that practice good hygiene don't infect their neighbors and business partners. My friend Dan Geer relates this quote from the CSO of a Wall Street investment bank:

> *Last year we stopped 70,000 inbound viruses, but I am prouder of having stopped 500 outbound.*

In other words, the bank's internal network is cleaner than the outside environment by a factor of 140 to 1.

FIREWALL AND NETWORK PERIMETER

Let us move on to firewall and network perimeter metrics for a moment. Recall that firewalls are rarely, in and of themselves, deterrents to attacks at the business or application layer. That said, they do serve an essential function by keeping unwanted Internet traffic away from protected network assets such as application servers. The converse is also true: firewalls also let traffic *in*. In many corporations, the firewall rules can be extremely complex as a result of continuous, "organic" growth in the number of access requests from business units. One aerospace company I am familiar with, for example, has over 50,000 active firewall rules—and a less-than-clear understanding of exactly which business units all those rules are for.

Rhonda McLean, CEO of MacLean Risk Partners and former CSO of Bank of America, turned firewall rule management into a creative set of metrics, which I have partially reprinted in Table 3-2 as the "firewall rule changes" and "firewall labor" metrics. Rhonda's team counted the number and cost of changes in absolute terms to provide a view of the level of effort required to respond to new business requirements. They also broke down these numbers by business unit to encourage accountability and to justify charge-backs for services rendered.

In the "Firewall and Network Perimeter" section of the table, you will note two other metrics. The first one counts the number of open wireless access points for an organization's remote office. By "open" we mean not requiring a WEP, WPA, or RADIUS password, and without restricting access by means such as MAC address filtering. This isn't necessarily the most critical metric for every organization. That said, open access points can present a security risk for firms with many far-flung offices in urban environments—especially when considered in combination with the other metric—namely, the number of remote offices connected directly to core transaction networks. One electronics manufacturer I know, for example, found multiple open wireless access points in several overseas locations. In several cases, these locations were in dense urban neighborhoods—anybody with a laptop could obtain an IP address and sniff around the internal network. Even worse, the company had no concept of network zoning; it did not place any firewalls between the remote locations and its core enterprise resource planning (ERP), financial, customer relationship management (CRM), and order management systems.

ATTACKS

Quantifying security "attacks" is a difficult task, but it is getting easier thanks to continuing improvements to the accuracy of intrusion detection software and, in particular, SEIM[6] software. Security vendors like ArcSight, IBM (Micromuse), and NetForensics attempt to identify attacks by filtering security information into three levels of criticality. The lowest level, security *events*, feed into the SEIM from source systems. These events are processed by the SEIM and are not necessarily intended to be viewed by humans. If certain types of events correlate strongly, the system generates an *alert* and forwards it to a security dashboard, along with supporting data. If the incident response team feels that the alert represents an actual attack, they create an *incident*.

Naturally, we can and should count all of these items, and many do. About 85% of organizations count incidents, and over half (54%) also count successful attacks.[7] These

---

[6] SIM/SEM.

[7] C. Robinson, "Collecting Effective Security Metrics" *CSO Online*, (2004) http://www.csoonline.com/analyst/report2412.html.

statistics are certainly interesting in and of themselves, but they are also interesting in relation to each other. When the corpus of event and incident data can be scoped down to a well-understood and well-defined group of assets—such as public web servers—we can use these numbers to create a "funnel" that shows the ratio of Internet web sessions to prospective attackers, suspected attackers, and actual (manually investigated) attackers.[8] A bank I visited in 2001, for example, charted these ratios regularly; during my visit, I noted that the ratio of valid web sessions to attackers was 500,000 to 1.

You'll note that the "Attacks" section of Table 3-2 leaves out such common statistics as the most commonly attacked ports and the most "dangerous" external URLs. I have omitted them deliberately, because they don't pass the "So what?" test. Reed Harrison, CTO of E-Security (now part of Novell), explains:

> "The typical 'Top 10 Ports,' 'Top 10 Attacking IP Addresses,' and 'Top 10 URLs' are really just watch lists. Our customers don't consider them compelling metrics; they prefer to measure operational efficiency and the effectiveness of their control environment."[9]

These are not even "so-what" metrics; they are just plain useless.

COVERAGE AND CONTROL

Coverage and control metrics characterize how successful an organization is at extending the reach of its security régime. Most security programs are full of good intentions, usually expressed formally through some sort of policy. But the reality of suboptimal implementation and poor end-user compliance often puts the shaft to all those good intentions. Coverage and control metrics, then, are essential to helping managers understand the size of the gap between intentions and facts on the ground.

Let's define the terms a bit more precisely. By *coverage* we mean the degree to which a particular security control has been applied to the target population of all resources that could benefit from that control. Coverage metrics measure the security organization's ability to execute on its mandates. Are its eyes, as the saying goes, bigger than its proverbial stomach, or can the organization meet its coverage goals?

Mark Kadrich, a manager formerly with Sygate, explains why achieving good coverage is essential to running an effective security program:

---

[8]   In Table 3-2, I use the terms prospects, suspects, and attackers instead of events, alerts, and incidents.

[9]   Interview with author, April 2006.

"We found that the dark matter on our network had a higher percentage of vulnerabilities when they were finally identified. Remotely managed systems could be systems that are controlled by patch management systems or centrally managed AV systems. You can track that metric over time and create trends that you can correlate to other events."[10]

That said, perfect coverage is impossible. The eligible population may not represent the full set of resources that could be covered. Often, security organizations must grant dispensations or exceptions to embedded, turnkey, or managed systems. Olivier Caleff, who spent several years working for a major defense contractor, explains why: "With turnkey dedicated servers supplied by a vendor, the security group cannot do anything to the system because the vendor will no longer support you otherwise. You have to live with these vulnerable systems and put compensating controls in place to prevent problems from spreading." Fragile legacy systems might also be excluded: "I have a customer who still runs PCs with OS/2 with his own applications. We allow them to connect to IT and production networks, but only with very strict security and very specific network filters." In short, systems with dispensations cannot be included in coverage metrics.

Control means the degree to which a control is being applied in a manner consistent with the security organization's service standards, across the scope of covered resources. In other words, for the things we've got covered, are we getting the results we want?

Table 3-3 shows a sample set of recommended coverage and control metrics. For the purposes of this chapter, I have limited the list of metrics to those that an organization might reasonably measure with its technical infrastructure. Thus, Table 3-3 includes topics such as antivirus, patch management, host configuration, and vulnerability management.

Table 3-3 Coverage and Control Metrics

Metric	Purpose	Sources
Antivirus and Antispyware		
Workstations, laptops covered by antivirus software (number [#], percent [%])	Extent of antivirus controls, for eligible hosts	Antivirus software Network management system
Workstations, laptops covered by antispyware software (#, %)	Extent of antispyware controls, for eligible hosts	Antispyware software Network management system

continues

---

[10] Mark Kadrich, e-mail to securitymetrics.org mailing list, March 20, 2006.

Table 3-3   Coverage and Control Metrics (Continued)

Metric	Purpose	Sources
Servers covered by antivirus software (#, %)	Extent of antivirus controls, for eligible hosts	Antivirus software Network management system
Workstations, laptops, servers with current antivirus signatures (#, %)	Service level agreement (SLA) attainment of antivirus	Antivirus software
Workstations, laptops, servers with current antispyware signatures (#, %)	SLA attainment of antispyware	Antispyware software
Patch Management		
Hosts not to policy patch level (%) • For workstations • For servers • For laptops • For critical systems • By OS: Windows, Linux, UNIX, Mac • By business unit • By geography	Identification of gaps in patch management process	Patch management software Vulnerability management system Systems management software
Number of patches applied per period (#, # per node)	Identifies cumulative workload for previous reporting periods	Patch management software
Unapplied patches (mean and median per node) • For critical patches • By business unit • By geography	Identifies current workload of patches that need to be applied	Patch management software
Unapplied patch ratio (patches per host)[11]	Identifies relative patch workload per host	Patch management software

---

[11] P. Mell, T. Bergeron, and D. Henning, "Creating a Patch and Vulnerability Management Program," NIST Special Publication 800-40, November 2005, http://csrc.nist.gov/publications/nistpubs/800-40-Ver2/SP800-40v2.pdf.

Metric	Purpose	Sources
Unapplied patch latency (age of missing patch, per node)[12] • For critical patches • For noncritical patches • By business unit • By geography	Shows potential size of window of vulnerability for missing patches	Patch management software
Patch testing cycle time (time) • For critical patches • For servers versus workstations • For noncritical patches	Measures time of exposure due to elapsed time between release of official patch and time of completion of patch testing	Patch management software
Patch distribution cycle (time) • For critical patches	Measures time of apply patches	Patch management software
Patches applied outside of maintenance windows (#, %) • For critical systems	Indicates whether control processes are "panicked" or predictable	Change control software Manual controls
Patch SLA attainment (%) • For all systems • For critical systems • Trend versus previous month	SLA attainment for patch management process	Patch management software Vulnerability management system Systems management software
Cost of patch vulnerability group (cost [$])[13]	Total cost of applying a set of patches, including management software, hardware, and labor	Patch management software Time-tracking software
Host Configuration		
Workstation and laptop benchmark score	Standardized configuration benchmark characterizing the degree of lockdown measures applied to the operating system	Desktop benchmarking tools (such as CIS)
Workstations, laptops using standard build image (%)	Conformance of workstations to an organization's standardized operating system build image	Desktop management software

[12] NIST refers to this metric as "patch response time."

[13] NIST ibid.

continues

Table 3-3 Coverage and Control Metrics (Continued)

Metric	Purpose	Sources
% systems in compliance with approved configurations	Shows conformance against configuration standards, regardless of how the system was built	Change control software Desktop management software
Network services ratio (services per host)[14] • All ports • Unnecessary ports • By system type	Identification of potential network ingress points on nodes; suggests divergences from standard builds	Port scanning tools
Remote endpoint manageability (%)	Systems that can be remotely administered by security personnel and that are subject to antimalware and patch management controls	Systems management software Patch management software Antivirus/antispyware software
Business-critical systems under active monitoring (%)	Identifies the extent of uptime and security monitoring controls	Security event management system
Logging coverage (# of nodes, %)	Determines how many hosts forward system and security events to a centralized log server	Systems management software Syslog server logs SNMP traps
NTP server coverage (# of nodes, %)	Determines how many hosts synchronize clocks via a standardized time server	Systems management software Time server logs
Emergency configuration response time (time)[15] • By business unit • By geography • By operating system	Time to reconfigure a given set of nodes in the event of zero-day outbreaks or security incidents	Time-tracking software
Vulnerability Management		
Vulnerability scanner coverage (#, %, frequency) • By business unit • By geography • By network or subnet	Shows the extent of vulnerability scanning operations as compared to the total number of IP addresses Frequency measures how often scans are performed	Vulnerability management software

[14] NIST ibid.

[15] NIST ibid.

Metric	Purpose	Sources
Vulnerabilities per host (#)[16] • Critical vulnerabilities • By system type • By asset class	Indicates the relative level of potential insecurity based on the number of vulnerabilities per host	Vulnerability management software
Monthly vulnerability counts (#) • By criticality • By business unit • By geography • By system type	Raw numbers that, over time, paint a picture of the overall vulnerability workload	Vulnerability management software
Monthly net change (+/−) in vulnerability incidence • By criticality • Critical assets • Other assets	Shows that change in workload from month to month	Vulnerability management software
Vulnerability identification latency (time)	Shows the degree of responsiveness of the vulnerability triage process	Vulnerability management software Time-tracking software
Time to close open vulnerabilities • For critical assets	Characterizes the level of responsiveness in fixing important vulnerabilities that affect critical assets	Vulnerability management software Trouble-ticketing software
Time to fix 50% of vulnerable hosts (# days), aka "half-life" • For critical vulnerabilities	Identifies the "half-life" of the window of vulnerability for an organization's assets. Measures the effectiveness of remediation activities.	Vulnerability management software
Systems requiring reimaging (# per period, % per period)	Trailing indicator of potential downstream workload impact due to (in)security	Spreadsheets Manual tracking

continues

---

[16] NIST refers to this as the "vulnerability ratio."

Table 3-3   Coverage and Control Metrics (Continued)

Metric	Purpose	Sources
Workstation, laptop, server survival (time)	System integrity/survivability; systems with few vulnerabilities should survive much longer	Honeypot software Manual tracking
Time to re-create fully backed-up server from scratch (time as % of SLA)	Efficiency in restoring services to a resource within business requirements	Manual tracking

ANTIVIRUS AND ANTISPYWARE

In the preceding section, I mentioned that the most common antivirus and antimalware statistics are best viewed as "fun facts." My colleague Betsy Nichols has a different label for them: she calls them "happy metrics." Regardless of the label, we both agree that trivial statistics about numbers of blocked viruses don't say anything about the effectiveness of antivirus software in stopping unknown threats, and they don't say anything about the program's overall effectiveness. I do not discount their value in helping educate management about the sheer size of the malware problem, or their usefulness in justifying continued purchase of antivirus software. But to understand the consistency of implementation of desired antivirus controls—in other words, whether there is a gap between policy and practice—we need broader coverage and control metrics.

Coverage metrics identify implementation gaps: of the eligible workstations and servers, how many have antivirus and antispyware software? And of the machines covered by the software, how many have updated signature and policy files? Metrics such as "workstations covered by antivirus software" and "workstations/servers with current antispyware signatures" help administrators understand the extent of their control régime.

For most of the antivirus and antispyware metrics, I have suggested using two units of measure: absolute numbers (#) and percentages (%) of the overall installed base. For the most part, absolute numbers matter less than percentages. In most large companies, knowing (for example) that 688 workstations run the approved antivirus software is less interesting than the fact that this number represents only 54% of the eligible hosts according to what the security policy dictates.

I have not included nearly as many metrics in the "Antivirus and Antispyware" section of Table 3-3, in part because these controls are relatively easy to assess—a workstation or server either has the software on it, or it does not. In addition, I have left out many of the metrics having to do with maintenance activities. As it happens, the most salient mainte-nance process—signature updating—is largely a solved problem. Although antivirus DAT file updates do occasionally cause issues,[17] for the most part update processes are automated. Most administrators can simply slam down the latest signatures without effort or adverse consequences.

PATCH MANAGEMENT

Patch management metrics will strike some readers as controversial. Not everyone believes that patching systems in a timely fashion increases security in a meaningful way. CyberTrust's Peter Tippet, for example, asserts that timely patching is woefully ineffective at stopping the spread of worms and network-borne viruses. He points out that tight router configurations (putting them in "default-deny mode") are much better at throt-tling viral epidemics.[18]

That said, patching is an essential part of keeping systems up-to-date and in a known state. In other words, it is part of an overall portfolio of security controls. The degree to which an organization keeps its infrastructure up to patch indicates the effectiveness of its overall security program. It is likely that organizations that do not patch their systems have highly variable system configurations that render other security controls ineffective. Putting it another way, it may not be true that consistent patching is associated with high levels of security, but it is probable that inconsistent patching correlates highly with *in*security.

Patching can be a labor-intensive exercise, especially for large organizations with weak technical controls and large desktop populations. Identifying what systems require particular patches, and determining which ones get them first, can be extremely costly in terms of time and soft labor dollars. The chief security architect of a large, decentral-ized commercial bank I know of, for example, estimated that coping with the Microsoft Windows ASN.1 encoding vulnerability and the subsequent patch cost $1 million—and that was just for the time spent in *meetings*, never mind all the visits to individual desktops.

Thus, the metrics in the "Patch Management" section of Table 3-2 attempt to characterize the effectiveness of an organization's patching program. The first metric,

---

[17] In March 2006, a McAfee antivirus update accidentally identified Microsoft Office products as malware. Although that may have caused Richard M. Stallman to rub his hands with glee, most IT managers were not amused.

[18] Lawrence Walsh, "Stop: Deny Everything," *Information Security*, March 2003, http://infosecuritymag.techtarget.com/2003/mar/news.shtml.

"Hosts not to policy patch level," quantifies how many hosts have not been patched to current levels. By "policy patch level" we mean the appropriate number and kind of patches for a particular operating system and type of host. Workstations, for example, might require all vendor patches, regardless of criticality, whereas mission-critical servers might need only the most critical ones. Because different types of hosts need different numbers and kinds of patches, most organizations typically aggregate patch level metrics by type of host (laptops and workstations versus servers), critical systems, and operating system. For organizations with federated IT operations, aggregation by business unit can help identify which parts of the business are doing better (or worse) than others.

Related to patch policy levels is workload. How many patches did the organization apply during the most recent reporting period, and how many remain to be applied? Proxies for workload measures ("number of patches applied," "unapplied patches") show what the organization has done and must do. Simple aggregates of patch figures are not always helpful for workload metrics; cross-sectional analyses by business unit or criticality are better.

"Unapplied patch latency" is a key indicator; it measures the average (or median) number of days between the initial patch announcement and verified installation on target systems. When aggregated and grouped by business unit or type of host, the numbers can be extremely revealing. For example, several years ago I was asked to perform a due-diligence security assessment on a small, private firm that was in negotiations with a potential acquirer many times its size. As part of our assessment, we did a quick scan of all their workstations (fewer than 100) and servers (about a dozen) using Microsoft's Baseline Security Analyzer tool. Using some clever scripting and a dash of XSLT, we crunched MBSA's cheerfully verbose output files and calculated patch latency numbers. Once we did so, we discovered something as dangerous as it was blindingly logical: the Internet-facing production servers were in much worse shape (11 missing critical patches per server, averaging 400 days old) than the internal workstations (two missing, average 25 days old). The latency numbers, when presented, had the desired effect: they helped bring beneficial changes to the way the company patched its servers.

Related to latency are overall cycle times. Patching can be thought of as having at least three distinct steps: identification of target systems that need particular patches, patch testing, and patch distribution and installation. For purposes of simplicity, I have omitted the metric for patch identification in Table 3-3—although one might argue that our banking friends mentioned several paragraphs ago could benefit from it. For most companies, the real bottlenecks are testing and mass distribution. Cycle times for testing require manual effort to measure because automated patch "test harnesses" don't exist. But most patch management software can easily calculate the distribution cycle times.

As it happens, in many companies patch testing for workstations is becoming less common, due to the ever-decreasing window between the release of a patch and its evil twin, the follow-on malicious exploit. It is becoming too risky to wait. Some companies have made it official policy to slam down patches to workstations as soon as they become available, without *any* testing.[19] These companies are not necessarily convinced that patching software has become miraculously more effective; rather, they believe it is less labor-intensive to deal with infrequent patch-related instability issues than to go through the effort of testing.

The last metrics in Table 3-3 are programmatic in nature. "Patches applied outside of maintenance windows" denotes how many patches were deemed so exceptional or critical that they demanded an out-of-cycle installation. Interestingly, this metric comes to us from Microsoft's internal IT operations group. Brian Keogh, the Group Manager for Server Patch Management, explains this metric as follows:

> *"Part of the way that we manage unexpected reboots or patching servers when they shouldn't be patched, that kind of thing, is by working with the server owners to define maintenance windows. These are windows basically when the server owners have said, Hey, yes. You can apply this patch, a patch, and reboot a server at this time during the week. Each server has a predefined maintenance window associated with it. . . . One of the key business metrics that we use to measure our success is the number of servers that are patched outside of their maintenance windows. For example, if we apply a patch outside of a server's predefined maintenance window, that's going to be a ding against our success. Another metric is going to be the number of servers patched by deadline."[20]*

Related to maintenance windows are service level agreements (SLAs). Although each organization defines SLA differently, I like defining patch management SLA to mean that a given set of target machines has had the appropriate set of patches applied within a desired latency window. Thus, a typical SLA might say that 100% of all critical servers must have patches applied within five calendar days of release (that is, patch latency of less than five days), and all patches must be applied within scheduled maintenance windows.

---

[19] A particular investment bank that I am familiar with has an official policy to forcibly update both workstations and servers immediately.

[20] Brian Keogh, Paul Thomsen, and TechNet Radio, "Patch Management at Microsoft," published June 23, 2004, http://www.microsoft.com/technet/community/tnradio/rdotrns01.mspx (defunct).

The final metric, "cost of patch vulnerability group," reflects the all-in cost of managing the patching process. It should generally include the pro rata cost of patch management software, staff, storage resources, and bandwidth needed to identify, test, and distribute patches to servers and workstations. The cost figures can either be in aggregate or on a per-node basis.

HOST CONFIGURATION

Host configuration metrics provide ways to measure the span and extent of control over networked assets, primarily desktops and servers. One could also argue that routers and mobile phones qualify as "hosts" and that we ought to measure their controls also. This is a fair point, but at present these devices rarely present problems for administrators. Router and phone security metrics don't (yet) pass the "So what?" test.

The most important point about host configuration metrics is that they measure whether workstations and servers are configured in a manner that allows the organization's security objectives to be achieved. What this means in practice is that machine configurations are at least partially locked down and that the attack surface they present is within the bounds of acceptable risk.

What represents "acceptable risk"? Most security experts agree that the default out-of-the-box configuration of the dominant corporate operating system, Microsoft Windows, represents an *unacceptable* risk. Although I do not wish to come across as a Microsoft-basher, some of the security choices the company has made with respect to the default security posture are maddening:

- By default, Windows 2000 opens eight listening TCP/IP network sockets; Windows XP opens ten. Some of these, like the NetBIOS listeners and the Universal Plug and Play feature, have been shown to be susceptible to buffer overflow attacks. It is no accident that year in, year out nearly every IP address on the Internet is scanned by anonymous attackers at least once a minute, looking for open Windows NetBIOS listeners that they can compromise.

- Prior to the release of Windows XP Service Pack 2, Microsoft Windows did not ship with a built-in host firewall, or, if it did, it was not turned on by default.

- Every Windows version since 3.1, by default, grants new users root-like (administrator) privileges by default. A successful virus infection that compromises these users will necessarily have the run of the entire system.

- The most popular file systems for Windows (FAT and FAT32) do not possess the concept of file ownership or access control privileges. Any user or process can read, write, or replace any file in the file system, with few limitations.

- The default Windows web browser Internet Explorer, in addition to having a sorry history of bugs and buffer overflow flaws, features a type of "plugin" called ActiveX that extends the browser's functionality. Web pages trigger execution of ActiveX controls, which run as native code using the privileges of the current user. When this aspect of ActiveX is considered in combination with the preceding two issues, you can see why spyware has become an epidemic.

Again, I do not mean to bash Windows—not too much, anyhow. The key point is that the default security posture is terrible. Microsoft knows this, and has worked hard to decrease the attack surface of its new operating system, Windows Vista. Although Vista will someday be widely deployed, in the meantime most organizations need to spend significant amounts of time reconfiguring their Windows workstations and servers to reduce the number of ways they could be compromised by attackers. Thus, it would be handy to have a way to measure the relative security configuration of an organization's Windows PCs—particularly laptops and desktops, whose security states vary from moment to moment due to the activities of the people who operate them.

To that end, an important tool in the security administrator's arsenal is the Windows benchmarking standard from the Center for Internet Security (CIS). The CIS itself produces a free stand-alone benchmarking tool that is suitable for individual use but not for larger enterprises. Other products, like Elemental Security's ESP product, produce a much more robust, enterprise-grade solution. Regardless of which tool you use, all the benchmarking tools do more or less the same thing: they scan each host, looking for security risks. For example, the benchmarking tool looks for unnecessary Windows network services (for example, Server, Universal Plug and Play, and Windows Messenger), checks whether users possess administrative privileges, and examines certain access control settings in the file system. At the end of the scan, the tool scores the host's relative posture against a supplied "benchmark," such as the "High Security Workstation" or "NSA" benchmark. The numerical scores range from 0 (the worst score) to 10 (the best). For the record, when I ran the CIS tool on my current employer's standard workstation build, it scored a 0.

In Table 3-3, the "workstation benchmark score" means the CIS High Security benchmark. It is a very good standard. It reflects the consensus view from the NSA, NIST, and other experts of what a securely configured Windows system should look like. However, many organizations have other tools they prefer to use, such as network-based vulnerability management tools such as Qualys and Foundstone. These are fine, although their scanning and scoring methodologies are geared more toward finding vulnerabilities than benchmarking the compliance of the system's configuration. (We will discuss vulnerability management in the next section.)

A second host configuration metric is "workstations using standard build." By this we mean workstations that were built using an organization's standard build image. The "image" is a customized version of the operating system with a standard complement of productivity software and hardened security settings. Most organizations with mature desktop operations groups typically have at least one "standard image" or "gold master" that they maintain. With a few tweaks, desktop management software such as Microsoft SMS can often reliably detect whether a workstation was built using the standard build. But "reimaging" is not usually that common an activity; simple tracking spreadsheets work, too. Regardless of the method used, understanding the number and percentage of desktops built in a standard way is an essential security metric for understanding the scope of an IT organization's controls.

As I mentioned earlier, Microsoft operating systems by default open an excessive number of network listeners. Other operating systems open ports too, even if they don't have them open in the out-of-the-box configuration. For example, Mac OS X's default configuration opens no network ports. But users with sufficient privileges can enable file sharing, iTunes music sharing, and other services that open listening network ports. These listeners can be key ingress points for network worms or malicious attackers. Thus, the number of open network ports per host helps security administrators understand whether systems are in default states and the extent of divergence from the corporate standard configuration. The "network services ratio" shows the number of listening network services for each host. Organizations may find it helpful to adjust the numbers to take into account only unnecessary services, and ignore required listeners such as network backup software or client agents for system administration tools. Good sources of network services metrics are port-scanning tools such as Nmap and Nessus and vulnerability management software. Both types of tools can generally "fingerprint" each endpoint's operating system, which makes it straightforward to slice and dice the results by operating system.

The next three metrics—"business-critical systems under active monitoring," "logging coverage," and "NTP server coverage"—refer to the relative coverage of remote network management tools, event-logging controls, and synchronization of system clocks. The latter two metrics are important for security incident handing; when problems occur, investigators need access to event information from individual workstations and servers. One way to make this happen is to forward security events to centralized servers. It is straightforward to do this with UNIX and Linux-based hosts; Windows hosts require additional software.[21] Related to logging controls is clock synchronization—essential for ensuring that event information from multiple hosts can be reconstructed faithfully in the correct order. By default, modern Windows and OS X machines synchronize their

---

[21] Representative software includes WinSyslog and Kiwi Syslog Daemon (freeware).

clocks with Microsoft- and Apple-managed external network time protocol (NTP) servers automatically, and UNIX and Linux machines typically require only minimal configuration to do the same. Many organizations prefer to synchronize with an internally managed NTP server or a trusted external one, such as tick.mit.edu.

The last metric, "emergency configuration response time," quantifies the extent of an organization's control over assets. Most security administrators would like to have a Big Red Button that they can press when disaster strikes. When something goes wrong, how long does it take to implement emergency countermeasures? A typical countermeasure might be remotely shutting down a system, reconfiguring the host firewall to block all traffic other than administrative commands, pushing a virus update, or forcing the installation of a software package. The exact test and measurement method varies from company to company. The important point is to be consistent.

VULNERABILITY MANAGEMENT

Like it or not, vulnerabilities are the mother's milk of today's IT security climate. *Proof-of-concept exploit code*, *Patch Tuesday*, *Zero Days*, and *buffer overflow* are relatively new terms for most IT professionals; they have all been introduced to the lexicon in the last five years. And yet, these and other phrases dominate the IT trade rags. The phenomenon of "vulnerabilities" has done more than any other to fuel the recent, spectacular rise in security spending. Patch management, vulnerability management, antispyware, and intrusion prevention vendors owe their livelihoods in large part to the continued presence of vulnerabilities.

Vulnerabilities—unforeseen flaws in the design or implementation of a software program that enable attackers to evade security controls—are not just an annoyance. Vulnerabilities per se are not harmful until exploited; many are benign. But the most critical ones are downright dangerous. Unlike the occasionally academic vulnerabilities of the past, today's serious vulnerabilities are being immediately turned into mass exploits by a criminal underground that seeks to surreptitiously install spyware, keyloggers, and Trojan horses.

Thus, every organization's security program should include metrics that give a clear-eyed view of the vulnerabilities present in its network and, in particular, on its hosts. Vulnerability metrics tell you how sound your hosts are.

Vulnerability metrics are similar in composition to those for patch management presented earlier. Instead of patches per host, a typical metric is "vulnerabilities per host" grouped by criticality, system type, or asset class. This statistic identifies the number of open or current vulnerabilities in a group of hosts. Commercial vulnerability management systems from Qualys, Foundstone, nCircle, and other vendors calculate these figures as part of their normal scanning processes.

Per-host vulnerability metrics show the relative number of vulnerabilities per host or asset. The absolute number of open vulnerabilities on a per-business-unit basis, quantified over a monthly reporting period ("monthly vulnerability counts"), shows the remediation workload for IT operations staff. A variation on this metric, "monthly net change," shows only the net increase or decrease in vulnerability counts. Both of these metrics can help prioritize day-to-day IT activities; a particularly bad month might require staff to drop nonessential projects and focus on plugging holes. Coverage metrics like "vulnerability scanner coverage" help managers understand what percentage of their IP address space is regularly scanned.

Two cycle-time metrics, "vulnerability identification latency" and "time to close open vulnerabilities," measure how long it takes security operations staff to identify vulnerable hosts and close vulnerabilities discovered by periodic scans. Identification latency is the difference between a vulnerability announcement and the identification of hosts to which it applies. For companies without an automated vulnerability scanning system, this process can be time-consuming and error-prone. Time-to-close metrics are usually derived from the ticket open/close timestamps in trouble-ticketing systems. Modern vulnerability management systems, such as Foundstone, can automatically create trouble tickets when they find vulnerabilities on hosts and then auto-close the tickets later if subsequent scans show that the issue has been fixed.

Some of the best measurement work that has been done to date on vulnerability cycle times has been done by vulnerability management vendor Qualys, which provides managed remote scanning services for its customers. Among other things, Qualys' scanning service attempts to detect the presence (or absence) of security vulnerabilities on target workstations and servers. The results of each scan are stored in a central database managed by Qualys, with all the customer-specific information stripped out.

In 2002 Gerhard Eschelbeck, the then-CTO of Qualys, initiated an empirical study of vulnerability management practices across Qualys' entire customer base.[22] The analysis examined how quickly companies patched 1,500 critical Windows vulnerabilities, such as those that were the root cause of the Blaster and Witty worms. In total, Qualys analyzed over 32 million vulnerability scans. Gerhard found that most companies patch large numbers of machines at first and then progressively fix the remainder in smaller and smaller batches. When displayed on a graph, the overall effect is asymptotic. Although

---

[22] G. Eschelbeck, "The Laws of Vulnerabilities," 2005 Edition, November 2005.

the time frames differed from issue to issue, the overall *pattern* of patching behaviors was so consistent that Qualys could generalize its results as follows:

- For critical vulnerabilities on Internet-facing networks, 50% of vulnerable systems are fixed every 19 days.
- For critical vulnerabilities on internal networks, 50% of vulnerable systems are fixed every 48 days.

Eschelbeck calls the amount of time required to fix 50% of vulnerable systems the "vulnerability half-life"—an apt title, because the decrease in vulnerability seems to resemble a process much like radiation emission. I have added this metric to the list of vulnerability metrics shown in Table 3-3.

A revealing workload-related indicator that few companies track today is the rate at which workstations and servers need to be rebuilt due to security issues ("systems requiring reimaging"). In 2005, Yankee Group's Security Leaders and Laggards survey showed that, on average, a company with 10,000 desktops and laptops rebuilt 175 PCs per week.[23] Assuming a 50-week working year, that means that about 85% of all PCs are rebuilt at least once a year. Not all of these rebuilds were directly related to security issues; the leading reason was system instability of various kinds. However, spyware and viruses were cited as the primary reason by 39% and 50% of respondents, respectively.

The final vulnerability metric in the table is one that measures the overall integrity of a host based purely on its capability to resist attacks. Popularized by the SANS Institute, the "survival time" metric measures how long a new, unpatched machine exposed to the Internet stays uncompromised, based on reports from probes on participating systems. In November 2004, the survival time for a Windows workstation was 18 minutes; by December 2006 it had risen, to about 25 minutes. In contrast, survival times for unpatched UNIX hosts have continually exceeded 600 minutes.[24]

Survival-time metrics from SANS are not just "fun facts"; they can also be used as benchmarks to prioritize security program investments. Rhonda MacLean has used the SANS survival time benchmark to drive investments in patch and vulnerability management software. By standardizing on a hardened workstation image, automating patch management, and regularly scanning for vulnerabilities, MacLean was able to increase the survival time of her company's hosts to over 69 hours.

---

[23] 2005 Yankee Group Security Leaders and Laggards survey, November 2005.

[24] "SANS Survival Time History" at http://isc.sans.org/survivalhistory.php.

AVAILABILITY AND RELIABILITY

Security, availability, and reliability cleave together because severe security incidents often lead to downtime. Putting it another way, maximizing uptime requires *minimization* of security issues that could cause downtime. In my own experience, I have detected a durable security management trend from the past few years: the merging of security and reliability. Dan Geer, for example, has long argued that security is a subset of reliability, particularly for the enterprises with the largest and most mature security operations teams. And at Goldman Sachs, the Managing Director in charge of IT reliability and disaster recovery is also the same person who manages security operations, and he encourages his team to view both as part of the same problem space.

This book is not intended to serve as a reference for IT operations metrics. However, because of the relationship between availability and reliability, it is worth examining some basic IT operations metrics on subjects such as uptime, system recovery, and change control. Table 3-4 shows a representative set of availability and reliability metrics.

Table 3-4 Availability and Reliability Metrics

Metric	Purpose	Sources
Uptime		
Host uptime (percent [%], hours) • For critical hosts • For all hosts	Availability measure for critical hosts and other systems	Host/application monitoring software Spreadsheets Manual tracking
Unplanned downtime (%)	Shows the amount of change control process variance. Larger numbers indicate a less "controlled" environment.	Spreadsheets Manual tracking
Unplanned downtime due to security incidents (%, hours)	Shows the amount of change control process variance that can be pinned on security issues	Spreadsheets Manual tracking
Mean/median unplanned outage (time) • Due to security incidents	Characterizes the seriousness of a "typical" unplanned outage	Spreadsheets Manual tracking
System revenue generation (cost [$] per hour) • For critical hosts	Shows business value associated with systems. Can be co-graphed with downtime incidents to show the explicit relationship between incidents and revenue.	Spreadsheets

Metric	Purpose	Sources
Unplanned downtime impact ($)[25]	Quantifies foregone revenue due to the impact of incidents	Spreadsheets
Mean time between failures (time)	Characterizes how long systems are "typically" up between failures	SpreadsheetsManual tracking
System Recovery		
Support response time (average time)	Average time from outage to response	Spreadsheets
Mean time to recovery (time)	Characterizes how long it takes to recover from incidents	Spreadsheets
Elapsed time since last disaster recovery walk-through (days) • For nominated business-critical systems	Shows relative readiness of disaster recovery programs	Spreadsheets Manual tracking
Change Control		
Number of changes per period (#)	Measures the amount of periodic change made to the production environment	Change control software
Change control exemptions per period (#, %) • By business unit	Shows how often "special exceptions" are made for rushing through changes	Change control software Spreadsheets
Change control violations per period (#, %) • By business unit	Shows how often change control rules are willfully violated or ignored	Change control software Spreadsheets

UPTIME

The classic metrics used to measure operations include "uptime" and "downtime." For the purposes of discussion, *downtime* refers to periods of time when a computing resource such as a server, application, service, or device is not running or operational. Typically, downtime can be thought of as being either *planned* or *unplanned*. By "planned downtime," we mean those periods when operations personnel have taken the resource out of service for normal maintenance activities like scheduled backups,

---

[25] NIST refers to this metric as "cost of program failures."

application upgrades, or periodic housekeeping jobs. For example, most UNIX systems, by default, perform nightly scheduled jobs at 1 a.m. (albeit without taking the machine out of service). More generally, most companies with mature operational environments have regularly scheduled "windows" for performing nightly maintenance activities—this is planned downtime.

Most companies do not count planned downtime when calculating downtime statistics. For the most part, they care only about unplanned downtime—that is, unexpected outages caused by software faults, natural disasters, or other unforeseen problems. Thus, we have the following metrics:

- **Planned downtime** is the total amount of time that resources were out of service due to regular maintenance.

- **Unplanned downtime** is the total elapsed time related to unexpected service outages.

- **Uptime** is the total time for a given period minus any unplanned downtime.

- **Mean unplanned outage length** is the total number of unplanned outages divided by the number of outages.

- **Median unplanned outage length** is the length of the outage halfway between the shortest and longest outages.

- **Mean time between failures** calculates the average amount of uptime between unplanned outages; it is the total uptime divided by the number of outages.

Host uptime for critical hosts helps characterize the overall availability of these resources (see Table 3-4). Unplanned downtime measures the amount of volatility in the operational environment. For the purposes of security, measuring the amount of downtime related to security incidents can be quite revealing.

Many firms operate critical resources that generate revenue, such as order-processing software or electronic commerce web servers. Understanding these revenues can help affix a dollar value to outages. For example, Symantec's electronic commerce website generates in excess of $900 million a year in revenue.[26] On an hourly basis, the e-commerce system's revenue-generating capacity is north of $102,000 per hour. Thus, a 20-minute unplanned downtime incident costs Symantec at least $34,000 in foregone revenue.

---

[26] This is a conservative estimate based on publicly disclosed information. According to Symantec's 10-K statement, 2005 consumer revenues totaled $1.4 billion. About 65% of these revenues ($902 million) were processed electronically through Symantec's electronic channels. Symantec also processes a significant number of enterprise orders electronically; I have not included these revenues in my estimate. Source: EDGAR Online. http://yahoo.brand.edgar-online.com/fetchFilingFrameset.aspx?dcn=0000891618-06-000254&Type=HTML.

All of this sounds terrific, but calculating uptime, downtime, and revenue generation costs is more of an art than a science. For starters, few of these metrics lend themselves to simple calculations, because the overall scope of resources that they cover isn't simple. Uptime statistics for critical resources are easy to calculate when the resource is a single system but are harder to calculate for complex environments. Moreover, nobody has yet invented telemetry equipment that, in addition to magically calculating the overall weighted uptime for an IT environment, automatically divines which incidents should be allocated to security issues.

In the environments that I have worked in (or near), uptime calculations remained the exclusive province of the IT operations staff. The favorite high-tech tool for automatically calculating uptime and downtime metrics was the trusty spreadsheet. And the rules for classifying downtime incidents were tacit rather than automated.

Regardless of the degree of automation applied to uptime and downtime calculations, these metrics can—and should—take security into account.

SYSTEM RECOVERY

System recovery metrics add more texture and depth to availability metrics. They flesh out not the question of how often systems go down, but the level of resilience in an enterprise's response to outages. Although many standard recovery metrics exist, I have highlighted two of the most important ones.

The "support response time" measures how long it takes an organization to recognize a security outage and initiate support activities. "Mean time to recover" (MTTR) identifies the amount of time required to restore operations to inoperable resources once these activities start. Organizations that do not need to distinguish between these two metrics often collapse both into a single consolidated MTTR metric. Both metrics are straightforward to calculate but require the operations staff to keep disciplined start/stop logs or timesheets.

Related to the actual recovery efforts are disaster recovery planning activities. Most businesses with critical assets by necessity implement disaster recovery plans to ensure business continuity in the event of severe system outages. These plans, of course, encompass much more than security-related outages; more commonly they seek to mitigate worst-case scenarios such as natural disasters. It is rare that one sees "hackers steal credit card data" listed in a disaster recovery plan (DRP) manual.

That said, the degree to which an organization regularly performs "dry runs" of its disaster recovery plans serves as an important indicator of disaster readiness. Businesses that actively walk through their plans will probably be better equipped to deal with a security incident. This is in part because most DRPs include detailed crisis communications plans, storage media restoration procedures, and media outreach activities. These are just the sort of things that an organization subjected to a vicious hacker attack needs to be good at, too. Thus, an important system recovery metric is the amount of elapsed time since the most recent DRP walk-through. It is not necessary to track statistics for all systems—just for nominated critical systems.

CHANGE CONTROL

A critical component of any effective security program is the process used to manage changes to the configuration of the environment. Security standards and configuration change management share a natural affinity. In fact, it is hard to see how you could have one without the other; if it is easy to affect an information system's production environment, it is often easy to change its security state as well.

Companies with poor track records in either discipline tend to conflate one with the other. For example, several years ago I was working with a diversified financial institution that operated an interactive website for its customers, who were nearly all consumers. This company had strong security policies but poor change controls and a complete lack of separation of duties.

One day during the spring of 2000, a developer working to improve the company's website uploaded and installed a new version of a particular part of the company's transaction system. He did this because he had a login account on the production machines, and that was what he'd been accustomed to doing. He wasn't forced to write a test plan or a back-out plan, and there was no "production control" group to implement his fixes in a controlled way. He just simply popped the code onto the box and hoped for the best. At some point later, the new module he'd uploaded crashed. It took the rest of the system down with it, including all of the high-availability replicas. The system took eleven feverish, nerve-racking days to troubleshoot, diagnose, and bring back online. *Eleven days!* That's forever in Internet time—and it knocked three full percentage points off the year's uptime figures.

In telling this story, I mean to make a point other than the most obvious one— namely, that change controls and configuration management are essential. I expect you knew that already. No, the real point of the story was the unintended political consequence that stemmed from the lack of change controls. Because of the lack of visibility to the developer's changes, this company did not know what the cause of the problem was—but it was perfectly prepared to blame security anyway. That's right: management circulated the conventional wisdom that "security problems" had caused the outage— when in reality nothing could have been further from the truth. The security monitoring systems worked fine; they had not detected an intrusion, unauthorized security violation, or privacy breach. When the true root cause emerged, my besieged counterpart (the company's CSO) received quite a few apologies. Immediately afterwards, he began lobbying for stronger change controls and clearer separations of duties.

Three key metrics can help organizations understand the degree of change control an organization possesses. All of these assume the organization keeps track of changes to production systems:

- The number of production changes
- The number of exemptions
- The number of unauthorized changes (violations)

These metrics are typically tracked on a per-period basis, and for additional insights they can be sliced by business unit or technology area. The latter two, exemptions and violations, are related. An "exemption" represents a change that was granted for exceptional reasons and required implementation outside of normal maintenance hours. Emergency fixes and other out-of-cycle changes require exemptions.

An interesting variation on the exemption metric is one that divides the number of exemptions into the number of changes. This results in a percentage that shows how many changes are made out-of-cycle. When grouped by business unit, this metric provides evidence that helps IT organizations finger the twitchiest and most cowboy-like business units.

Unauthorized changes, also known as violations, measure the number of changes that were applied without approval. This number, obviously, should be as close to zero as possible.

APPLICATION SECURITY

Applications are the electronic engines that drive most businesses. Microsoft Office, web servers, order-management software, supply chain management, and ERP systems are all applications that businesses rely on every day. Applications automate firms' workforce activities, pay their bills, and serve customers. Applications come in many shapes and sizes: in-house developed, packaged, outsourced, and served on demand.

As important as applications are to the fortunes of most organizations, they also represent points of potential weakness. Application threat vectors, although they are less well understood than network-based threats, are just as important. As long ago as 2002, Garter Group stated that 75 percent of attacks tunneled through or used application-related threat vectors.[27]

---

[27] D. Verton, "Airline Web Sites Seen as Riddled with Security Holes," *Computerworld*, 4 Feb. 2002.

For companies with custom-developed applications, the manner in which the software was developed matters. Software written without sufficient attention to security issues carries much more risk than software that adheres to generally accepted principles for coding secure software—as much as five times more risk, based on my previous research.[28]

Measuring the relative security of application code is hard. The security industry has not arrived at a consensus about exactly what it means to build a "secure application." Although definitions vary, there are at least three potential ways to measure application security (see Table 3-5): by counting remotely and locally exploitable flaws without knowledge of the code (black-box metrics), by counting design and implementation flaws in the code (code security metrics), and by creating qualitative risk indices using a weighted scoring system (qualitative process metrics and indices).

Table 3-5 Application Security Metrics

Metric	Purpose	Sources
Black-Box Defect Metrics		
Defect counting	Shows externally identified defects due to implementation or design flaws	Black-box testing tools
Vulnerabilities per application (number [#]) • By business unit • By criticality • By proximity	Measures the number of vulnerabilities that a potential attacker without prior knowledge might find	Black-box assessments by security consultants
Qualitative Process Metrics and Indices		
Business-adjusted risk	Simple formula for scoring the business impact and criticality of vulnerabilities identified in security assessments	Security assessments Spreadsheets
Application conformance indices	Creates a score for ranking the overall security posture for an application or group of applications	Questionnaires Spreadsheets

---

[28] A. Jaquith, "The Security of Applications: Not All Are Created Equal," @stake, Inc., 2002.

Metric	Purpose	Sources
Code Security Metrics		
Assessment frequency for developed applications • % with design reviews • % with application assessments • % with code reviews (optional) of sensitive functions • % with go-live penetration tests	Measures how often security quality assurance "gates" are applied to the software development life cycle for custom-developed applications.	Manual tracking Lines of code (LOC)
Thousand lines of code (KLOC)	Shows the aggregate size of a developed application	Code analysis software
Defects per KLOC	Characterizes the incidence rate of security defects in developed code	Code analysis software
Vulnerability density (vulnerabilities per unit of code)	Characterizes the incidence rate of security defects in developed code	Code analysis software
Known vulnerability density (weighted sum of all known vulnerabilities per unit of code)	Characterizes the incidence rate of security defects in developed code, taking into account the seriousness of flaws	Code analysis software
Tool soundness	Estimates the degree of error intrinsic to code analysis tools	Code analysis software Spreadsheets
Cyclomatic complexity	Shows the relative complexity of developed code. Indicates potential maintainability issues and security trouble spots.	Code analysis software

BLACK-BOX DEFECT METRICS

Perhaps the most dramatic and headline-grabbing type of application security metric is of the black-box variety—that is, how many holes we can drill in one application compared to another. Black-box testing involves assessing an application, typically remotely via the web. The method of assessment varies. For high-volume testing, automated black-box testing tools from SPI Dynamics, Cenzic, and Watchfire allow companies (or consultants) to quickly scan a large number of deployed applications for potential vulnerabilities.

Automated tools are best suited to testing web applications. A typical black-box web security testing tool "spiders" an application by starting at a known URL (http://www.foo.com/myapp) and following every related hyperlink until it has discovered all the website's pages. After the spider enumerates the application's pages, an automated "fuzzer" or "fault injector" examines the web forms on each page, looking for weaknesses. For example, the fuzzer might see an account registration form that contains a field into which a new user is meant to type her first name. The goal of the fault injector is to see what happens when it sets the field value to something the server-side logic won't expect—like 10,000 letter A's, SQL statements, or shell code.

In the nonautomated camp are security consultants who conduct tests as part of a formally scoped engagement. Consultants tend to be much more expensive than an automated black-box tool but can find issues that the tools cannot. They can also exercise their creativity to dig deeper and find root causes. On the other hand, the level of analytical rigor and degree of methodological consistency vary from consultant to consultant.

Regardless of the method used, the objective of testing is the same: to find vulnerabilities (defects) that can be exploited to compromise the application's integrity, confidentiality, or availability. The categories of flaws that black-box tools and consultants tend to find include:

- **SQL injection:** Manipulating submitted web form fields to trick databases into disgorging sensitive information
- **Command injection:** Executing native operating system commands on the web server
- **Parameter tampering:** Changing submitted web form fields to change the application state
- **Cross-site scripting:** Submitting malformed input that will cause subsequent users to execute malicious JavaScript commands that hijack their sessions or capture data
- **Buffer overflows:** Overfilling a server-side buffer in an effort to make the server crash, or to take it over remotely

At the end of the assessment, the tool or consultant adds up and summarizes any defects found for prioritization. Results of black-box tests are typically simple counts of what defects were found, the category to which they belong, and where. Security consultants generally, as part of the engagement, prioritize the vulnerabilities they find and assign them a criticality rating (high, medium, low).

Enterprises that rely on black-box testing techniques to provide application security metrics, in my experience, do not care too much about defects that aren't marked as critical. They *do* fix severe issues that could lead to a remote compromise or disclose sensitive data. Thus, in Table 3-5 we recommend that organizations group vulnerabilities by criticality. Other cross sections that companies find useful include by business unit and by proximity. Was the defect remotely exploitable, or could the exploit succeed only when the attacker was logged in locally to the server?

QUALITATIVE PROCESS METRICS AND INDICES

Qualitative assessments earlier on in the application life cycle uncover issues before they become bona fide vulnerabilities in the field. Assessments go by many names. During my tenure at @stake, we performed all manner of application assessments at different stages in the application development life cycle (see Table 3-6):

- **Design reviews** at the midpoint of the design stage
- **Architecture assessments** at the midpoint of development
- **Code reviews** (optional) at the end of development for sensitive functions
- **Penetration tests** prior to deployment

Table 3-6 Qualitative Assessments by Phase of Software Development

	Design Review	Architecture Assessment	Code Review	Penetration Test
Test Type				
Goals	Validation of security engineering principles	Verification of implemented security standards	Focused examination of sensitive functions	Identification of deployment flaws
	Identifies gaps compared to security standards	Finds potential architectural weaknesses	Finds development flaws	Finds "real-world" vulnerabilities
Recommended Testing				
External public-facing	Yes	Yes	Yes	Yes
External partner-facing	Yes	Yes	Yes	Yes
Internal enterprise	Yes	Yes	Optional	Optional
Internal departmental	Optional	Yes	Optional	Optional

Enterprises that want to quantify the spread of secure development processes can measure the frequency with which they conduct these activities. Of these activities, penetration tests (also known as "ethical hacking" or "black-box testing") are the best known. Black-box testing uncovers issues in software that an organization has already deployed or has in the field. But not all applications that need testing are always in the field; indeed, one might argue that post-deployment black-box testing comes far too late to uncover important issues. It is always best to detect potential design flaws as early as possible, either through qualitative assessments or via automated code security tools (which I describe later in this chapter).

The first two activities, design reviews and architecture assessments and code, provide qualitative measures of application security. When an organization embarks on a substantive effort to assess applications qualitatively, it must possess a defensible methodology for evaluating and scoring defects. If it does not, the results of different assessments will vary wildly, giving management an excuse not to trust the numbers they see.

Frankly, there is no easy solution for guaranteeing that all team members involved in assessing applications will use the same methodology each time. Every person offers different experiences, creative urges, biases, and interpretations. However, organizations can and should implement standard definitions for terms like "risk" and "impact" that are as unambiguous as possible. In addition, managers should ask team members to agree to use a standard formula for "scoring" application assessments. If an organization can standardize on definitions and scoring formulas, it can partially mitigate the risk of inconsistency.

Business-Adjusted Risk

A common scoring technique is to define an index formula that assigns an overall risk number to defects. Here, I will discuss two that I am familiar with: the @stake business-adjusted risk (BAR) formula for scoring vulnerabilities, and a broader, more general application security index suitable for scoring applications as a whole.

BAR is a technique I invented along with colleagues at @stake, an Internet security consultancy. During its life span from 1999 to 2004, @stake conducted hundreds of application assessments using the exact same formula. BAR classifies security defects by their vulnerability type, degree of risk, and potential business impact. When assessing an application, for each security defect we calculated a BAR score as follows:

BAR (1 to 25) = business impact (1 to 5) × risk of exploit
(1 to 5, depending on business context)

Risk of exploit indicates how easily an attacker can exploit a given defect. A score of 5 denotes high-risk, well-known defects an attacker can exploit with off-the-shelf tools or canned attack scripts. A score of 3 indicates that exploiting the defect requires inter-mediate skills and knowledge, such as the ability to write simple scripts. Finally, only a professional-caliber malicious attacker can exploit certain classes of defects; we give these defects a score of 1.

Business impact indicates the damage that would be sustained if the defect were exploited. An impact score of 5 represents a flaw that could cause significant financial impact, negative media exposure, and damage to a firm's reputation. A score of 3 indi-cates that a successful exploit could cause limited or quantifiable financial impact, and possible negative media exposure. Defects that would have no significant impact (mone-tary or otherwise) receive a score of 1.

BAR is a simple tool for scoring applications: the higher the score, the higher the risk. Because BAR includes relative ratings for both likelihood of occurrence and business impact, it moves in the same direction as insurers' annual loss expectancy calculations.

BAR suffers from several defects. First, its estimation method is fast and light rather than precise, and it does not quantify risk in terms of time or money. Second, scores are heavily biased by the availability (or lack thereof) of attack scripts and exploit code. BAR scores, therefore, are necessarily temporal—when a hacker or researcher releases exploit code, it changes the score. We believed that this quality was (and is) true to the way the world works, but in practice it causes BAR scores to understate risks over time as new exploits become available. Newer metrics like the Common Vulnerability Scoring System (CVSS) explicitly support temporal adjustments and as such represent an improvement over BAR.

That said, at @stake we were able to successfully and consistently replicate the BAR method over hundreds of engagements. To give you an idea of how BAR works in prac-tice, in 2002 I released a paper called "The Security of Applications: Not All Are Created Equal," which analyzed 45 e-business applications (commercial packages, middleware platforms, and end-user e-commerce applications). We used outlier analysis on 23 of the assessments in our survey. For each engagement, we calculated an overall business risk index, based on the sum of the individual BAR scores. We ranked engagements by their index scores (highest to lowest) and divided them into quartiles. Engagements with the lowest business risk index formed the first quartile; those with the highest formed the fourth. The most-secure applications in our analysis contained, on average, one-quarter of the defects found in the least-secure. The top performers' reduced defect rates also translated into much lower risk scores. The least-secure applications had a BAR score six times that of the most-secure: the fourth quartile had an average BAR score of 332, and the first had an average score of 60. (You can see a graphical depiction of the BAR scores in Figure 6-8 in Chapter 6, "Visualization.")

Application Scoring Indices

Variations on indices for counting and rating specific application defects, such as the BAR technique I described, are common ways to "score" application security. As I mentioned, however, any risk index technique that relies on humans to discern between qualitative levels of risk is prone to inconsistencies.

An alternative technique to the various vulnerability-rating methods is a scoring technique that eliminates considerations for things that *might* happen (such as a vulnerability that "could result in financial damage to multiple business units") and replaces them with simple, declarative statements about things that *do* happen ("the server encrypts sensitive data"). Although some subjectivity remains, it is easier to debate about facts instead of hypothetical outcomes. Scoring systems do not necessarily linearly relate to risk; they sacrifice a certain amount of precision for speed and repeatability.

A sample scoring technique that focuses on factual questions is something I have loosely called the Application Insecurity Index (AII).[29] The idea is to create a fast and lightweight application scoring method that assigns points based on whether particular applications meet (or do not meet) specific guidelines and practices. Fact-based questions that result in binary yes/no answers serve as the basis of the score. Figure 3-1 shows the Application Insecurity Index components. The potential score ranges from 8 to 48; lower scores are better.

The AII contains three primary areas: business importance, technology alignment (or lack thereof), and assessment oversight activities:

- **Business importance** scores consider the application's importance to the organization: whether the application faces the Internet, contains sensitive data, costs the organization money when down, or processes business transactions.

- **Technology outlier** scores put a number on the degree to which the application follows prescribed organizational guidelines for eight security topics, including authentication, data classification, validation of user input and output, role-based access control, and identity management.

- **Assessed risk** scores highlight the application's relative riskiness based on whether the application might be considered subject to regulatory inspection or review, such as Sarbanes-Oxley or the European Union Privacy Directive. It also scores whether the application carries any risks associated with third-party code development or data storage, and whether the application has received a technical security assessment.

---

[29] Feel free to scream.

Business Importance Score

Business function (1-4 points) ☐
  4 Customer account processing
  3 Transactional/core business
     processing
  2 Personnel, public-facing
  1 Departmental/back office

Access scope (1-4 points) ☐
  4 External public-facing
  3 External partner-facing
  2 Internal enterprise
  1 Internal departmental

Data sensitivity (1-4 points) ☐
  4 Customer data/subject to
     regulator fines
  3 Company proprietary & confidential
  2 Company non-public
  1 Public

Availability impact (1-4 points) ☐
  4 > $10m loss, serious damage to
     reputation
  3 > $2m loss, minor damage to reputation
  2 < $2m loss, mimimal damage to reputation
  1 Limited or no losses

Total (4-16 points) ☐

Technology Outlier Score

Authentication (0-2 points) ☐
  2 Does not meet requirements
     or unknown
  1 Partially meets baseline
  0 Fully meets baseline requirement

Data classification (0-2 points) ☐
  ...

Input/output validation (0-2 points) ☐
  ...

Role-based access control (0-2 pts) ☐
  ...

**Security requirements
documentation (0-2 points)** ☐
  ...

Sensitive data handling (0-2 points) ☐
  ...

User identity management (0-2 pts) ☐
  ...

**Network/firewall architecture
(0-2 pounts)** ☐

Total (0-16 points) ☐

Assessment Risk Score

Technical assessment ☐
  8 Not assessed
  6 High-risk vulnerabilities found
  4 Medium-risk vulnerabilities found
  2 Low-risk vulnerabilities found

Regulatory exposure ☐
  4 Unknown/no regulatory review
  3 Subject to Sarbanes-Oxley, EU
     Privacy Directive, California Online Privacy
     Protection Act (SB 68)
  2 Subject to other regulations
  1 Not subject to regulation

Third-party risks ☐
  4 Code and data offshore
  3 Code offshore
  2 Outsourced development (US)
  1 In-house development

Total (4-16 points) ☐

Figure 3-1   Application Insecurity Index

By design, AII gives the highest scores to applications that serve the most critical business functions, deviate the most from appropriate technical security standards, and have the highest exposures to regulations and identified security vulnerabilities. Also by design, AII focuses on facts that can be quickly ascertained through a lightweight interview process or questionnaire. An application:

- Processes customer transaction data—or not
- Faces the Internet—or not
- Meets requirements for role-based access control to govern authorization—or not
- Handles sensitive data properly—or not
- Has been assessed for application vulnerabilities—or not
- Contains code developed offshore—or not

Criteria for judging standards compliance are likewise straightforward (see Table 3-7). For example, an organization's identity management standard might specify that applications must authenticate users against a centralized LDAP directory, and that external applications used by contractors and partners must be authenticated against a separate directory replica. Scoring compliance for these criteria is easy—the application architects and system administrators will know the answers, and they will not be subject to ambiguity or interpretation.

Lightweight scoring systems like AII should be just that: lightweight. They should take only a few minutes to complete and need not exhaustively score every possible technical or business criterion. When designing such a system, be careful not to rate everything—just high-priority items. It is also important to keep baseline criteria concise and objective. Speed trumps precision.

Table 3-7 Technology Outlier Criteria

Criterion	Standard
Authentication	Sensitive applications require multifactor authentication (username, password, token). Web-based applications require form-based authentication over SSL.
Data classification	The application provides controls for managing different classes of information sensitivity, as appropriate.
Input/output validation	User-supplied input is sanitized before use by the application. Data sent to users are cleansed of malformed or malicious output.
Network/firewall environment	Externally facing Internet applications use a DMZ for web servers, with a separate zone for application servers and databases. Internal core business application servers reside in protected internal subnetworks.
Role-based access control	The application provides separate roles for general users, administrators, and line-of-business roles. Access control rules are expressed as appropriate for roles rather than for named users.
Security requirements documentation	Requirements for authentication, data classification, and so on are explicitly defined in the work order or design documentation.
Sensitive data handling	User credentials are encrypted when in transit. Passwords and sensitive data are encrypted when in storage.
User identity management	For corporate applications, user identities are stored in corporate LDAP or Active Directory. External/partner identities are stored in a dedicated LDAP/AD replica.

AII is not a standard—it is my own interpretation of a method organizations can use to quickly get a handle on potential trouble spots in their application portfolios. More formal methods for assessing application risk exist, of course.

More formal methods for assessing and scoring application risk include the Relative Attack Surface Quotient (RASQ) methodology popularized by Microsoft's Michael Howard and two researchers from Carnegie-Mellon, Jon Pincus and Jeannette Wing. Carnegie-Mellon's OCTAVE method is another.

RASQ attempts to quantify the number and kinds of vectors available to an attacker.[30] At a system level, analysts identify the relative "attackability" of an application by modeling the potential targets, channels facilitating the attack, and access rights. The net result is a single number capturing the relative size of the attack surface. The advantage of RASQ is that it benefits from a formally developed threat model. Howard, Pincus, and Wing's papers contain good discussion and labeling of generic attack vectors, which helps practitioners.

That said, certain aspects of RASQ make it less suitable as an enterprise scoring method for a portfolio of applications. Critically, RASQ works best when it analyzes a single application over time. But its metrics are not comparable across multiple applications (hence the "Relative" part of the name). In short, RASQ has lots of promise, but it is not a useful metric—yet—that can be consistently measured and cheaply gathered. Research continues, however.

CODE SECURITY METRICS

So far I have discussed qualitative metrics for measuring the security of applications. These qualitative metrics are best used to estimate the risk exposure of applications as a whole. They do not assume any particular inside knowledge about the stuff that applications are actually made of: software code.

Code security metrics tackle measurement of software quality directly. A great body of software development metrics, generally speaking, has sprung up over the last twenty years, and many of these are finding their way into security.

First, consider "code volume" metrics. These count the number of lines or code in an application, or the discrete number of features and functions it provides. One of the most common code-volume metrics is "lines of code" (LOC); many people prefer to measure code by thousands of lines as well (KLOC). As an alternative to LOC counting, some methods simply count "statements" instead of lines of code.[31]

---

[30] M. Howard, J. Pincus, and J. Wing, "Measuring Relative Attack Surfaces," 2003, http://www.cs.cmu.edu/ ~wing/publications/Howard-Wing03.pdf. Manadhata and Wing, "Measuring a System's Attack Surface," 2004, http://reports-archive.adm.cs.cmu.edu/anon/2004/CMU-CS-04-102.pdf.

[31] Methodology issues occasionally arise with respect to pure LOC counting. Specifically, what constitutes a "line of code"? Does a single statement, split for readability, count for multiple lines? For this reason, the popular Java tool CheckStyle measures code volume by counting statements rather than lines of code. http://checkstyle.sourceforge.net/.

A more subjective metric is "Use Case Points," which counts the number of "use cases" an application supports by analyzing functions with respect to who uses them and under what scenarios. Use Case Points suffer from methodological inconsistencies and the relatively high amount of effort needed to count them, whereas KLOC can be counted easily by machine.

Code volume metrics are not directly related to security, but they provide texture, depth, and context. They become much more interesting when combined with statistics about security defects. By "defect," we mean a flaw in the code as detected by an automated code-scanning program like RATS, ITS4 (open-source) or Klocwork, Coverity, Ounce Labs, or Fortify Software. Typical flaws detected by these programs include unsafe memory handling, lack of validation of user input, and dead (unreachable) code blocks. Thus, a common code security metric is "defect density," defined as the number of defects per unit of code (such as KLOC). In August 2005, The Software Assurance Metrics and Tool Evaluation (SAMATE) working group, a project of NIST, identified defect density as an important metric.[32]

Defect density is not perfect, because it characterizes only raw ratios of flaws in applications. Density numbers do not prioritize issues or difficulty of exploit, as colleague Adam Shostack explains:

> "I think defect density is hard. I'll trade just about anything for a `gets` on a socket. So if program A has a `strcp` of some data, and program B has a `gets` on that data, I think there's a qualitative difference. Is it quantifiable? Hard to say. You could say either will get you `root`, but maybe one is easier to exploit. Five minutes versus ten is a two-to-one difference."[33]

Other variations on defect density include "known vulnerability density," defined as the number of *known vulnerabilities* per unit of code, and Ounce Labs' "V-density" metric, which is a weighted sum of all known vulnerabilities. V-density corrects for the rawness of pure defect density numbers by giving heavier weights to the most serious security flaws.

Vulnerability density metrics provide rough quantitative scores of software quality. The primary benefit of density metrics is that they can be calculated consistently across an organization's application development portfolio. On the flip side, critics of vulnerability density metrics contend that the state of the art in code scanning is not very good

---

[32] "Metrics for Software and Metrics for Tools," 10 August 2005, SAMATE, Paul Black (PPT), as reported and retyped by Chris Wysopal. A majority of the metrics in the Code Security section are derived from SAMATE's excellent summation.

[33] Adam Shostack, e-mail to securitymetrics.org mailing list, 19 September 2005

and suffers from two problems: accuracy and lack of knowledge of certain classes of flaws. With respect to the first problem, most tools tend to overstate the number of vulnerabilities present in code. Fred Cohen explains why accuracy has long been an issue:

> *"The automated code base checking market is still pretty immature and problematic in several ways, most notably the large number of false positives for most tools. The tools really don't seek to understand the code, they tend to be syntactic-based or based on following paths through execution, but they fail to handle lots of things well. . . . Folks at big software companies have programmers that intentionally avoid the stronger solutions in favor of what they understand or what is easier—seat of the pants, so to speak. But still, [the tools] do successfully find the really obvious ones that cause most of the currently exploited errors."*[34]

Chris Wysopal makes the same point more concisely, and wonders whether automated tools will ever be good enough to detect all the serious types of flaws:

> *"The challenge with vulnerability density scores is this: how do you work in false positive and false negative rates, especially the fact that the tool may not have the capability of detecting many classes of security flaws?"*

Both of these gentlemen, whose opinions I respect greatly, have a point. If you cannot trust the tools, can you trust the metric? Generally, the answer is no.

Thus, to complement (and correct for) vulnerability density metrics, SAMATE recommends a metric called "soundness," which denotes the number of correct defect classifications minus the false positives and false negatives, divided by the total number of defects detected. This metric helps put the defect numbers in perspective by assigning a potential range to the tools' error rate. No tool can calculate soundness metrics automatically. Users must work out these numbers on their own, based on their experiences with the tools.

Sampling methods work well for calculating soundness. Users should select several "typical" code modules and compare the results of a manual code review against an automated scan. To calculate soundness, users count the number of defects the scanner missed and add to this result the number of things the scans flagged incorrectly as defects. Dividing this figure by the number of defects identified by the scan yields the "unsoundness" metric; subtracting this percentage from 100% returns the soundness figure.

---

[34] Fred Cohen, e-mail to securitymetrics.org mailing list, 23 December 2005.

Beyond the direct security issues that scanning products can find and enumerate in code modules, organizations should also consider the broader issue of code complexity. Both Bruce Schneier and Dan Geer are fond of pointing out that "complex systems fail complexly." Modern applications are typically complex code edifices constructed with care, built for extensibility, and possessed of more layers than a Herman Melville novel. This is not necessarily a bad thing, but it makes it harder to find and eliminate the root causes of security problems. Thus, if complexity contributes to insecurity, we ought to devise methods for measuring code complexity as a leading indicator of future security problems. Fortunately, the academy is way ahead of us.

The last twenty years have witnessed quite a bit of prior academic research into the relationship between software complexity, defect rates, and reliability. Researchers have theorized that complexity metrics ought to be a good predictor of reliability and the degree to which a module is prone to faults. For example, in a study of a large telecommunications software project, Koshgoftaar, Allen, Kalaichelvan, and Goel concluded that "design product metrics based on call graphs and control-flow graphs can be useful indicators of fault-prone modules. . . . The study provided empirical evidence that in a software-maintenance context, a large system's quality can be predicted from measurements of early development products and reuse indicators."[35] Other researchers have arrived at similar conclusions.[36]

Although different schools of thought each have their favorites, many researchers feel McCabe's "cyclomatic complexity" metric provides an effective measure of complexity in code. Cyclomatic complexity for a code module is defined as the minimum number of paths that in linear combination generate all possible paths through the module.[37] Modules with a high number of branching instructions, excessive nesting, or if/then statements generate higher scores than simpler modules do. A cyclomatic complexity of 1 to 4 denotes relatively low complexity, 5 to 7 suggests moderate complexity, 8 to 10 denotes high complexity, and anything over 10 is considered highly complex.

Many common development tools can create cyclomatic complexity metrics. An open-source toolkit that works well for Java code, for example, is the Project Mess

---

[35] T. Koshgoftaar, E. Allen, K. Kalaichelvan, and N. Goel, "Early Quality Prediction: A Case Study in Telecommunications," *IEEE Software*, January 1996.

[36] See http://hissa.ncsl.nist.gov/HHRFdata/Artifacts/ITLdoc/235/appendix.htm#418907 for a list of empirical studies investigating the relationship between complexity metrics and reliability. For a contrasting view, see F. Lanubile and G. Visaggio, "Evaluating Predictive Quality Models Derived from Software Measures: Lessons Learned," January 1996, http://www2.umassd.edu/SWPI/ISERN/isern-96-03.pdf.

[37] See NASA's "IV&V Facility Metrics Data Program - Complexity Metrics" web page, at http://mdp.ivv.nasa.gov/complexity_metrics.html.

Detector, aka PMD.[38] The project's slogan, amusingly enough, is "Don't Shoot the Messenger." My own often over-engineered code—in case you were wondering—typically scores between a 4 and 6.

Cyclomatic complexity metrics have the advantage of being relatively easy to calculate. This means that these metrics can be automated and compared across projects. Cyclomatic complexity is the right metric for measuring control flow density on a per-method and per-entity (or per-class) basis. Because security flaws are, at least some of the time, implementation-related, cyclomatic complexity metrics can help predict which classes/methods in an application might experience flaws. That said, the relationship of complexity metrics to security is hypothetical rather than proven. As with any code volume metrics, organizations should consider cyclomatic complexity in the context of additional environmental metrics to produce a true picture of risk.

Code security metrics is one of the most vibrant areas of security metrics. The metrics I suggested in the "Code Security Metrics" section of Table 3-5 represent just a smattering of the ones that groups like SAMATE have been discussing lately. As the software security industry comes closer to consensus on effective code security metrics, more will emerge.

SUMMARY

Security analysts use metrics for many purposes, particularly for diagnosing problems with their organizations' security programs. Diagnostic security metrics borrow from management consulting techniques by asking two questions: what hypothesis can be formed about the efficiency or effectiveness of security controls, and what evidence can be marshaled to support or disprove that hypothesis?

Technical security activities provide a wide variety of metrics that analysts can use as diagnostics. Technical metrics include those that measure:

- **Perimeter defenses:** E-mail, antivirus software, antispam systems, firewalls, and intrusion detection systems

- **Coverage and control:** The extent and reach of controls such as configuration, patching, and vulnerability management systems

- **Availability and reliability:** Systems that ensure continuity and allow recovery from unexpected security incidents

---

[38] "Project Mess Detector" is just one variation on the PMD acronym. See http://pmd.sourceforge.net/rules/codesize.html for the tools—and for more amusing variants on the name.

- **Application risks:** Defects, complexity, and risk indices for custom and packaged line-of-business applications

Technical security metrics should not simply be "fun facts" or "happy metrics" that tell the CSO what a great job the security team is doing, such as the sheer number of spam messages blocked by the firewall. They should reveal more interesting insights, such as gaps in coverage (ratio of inbound to outbound viruses, patch latency), environmental stability (firewall turbulence, net changes in vulnerability incidence, patches within SLA windows), or problems with change controls (number of change control exemptions per period, unauthorized production changes). For all these metrics, historical measurement allows analysts to trace performance over time and detect outliers.

Application security metrics represent an entirely separate measurement domain with its own diagnostics. Black-box metrics count defects detected by scans. Process metrics about the frequency of security reviews and go-live assessments help measure the spread of secure development processes. Application security indices allow organizations to quickly "score" application security risk across an entire portfolio of applications. Code metrics such as vulnerability density and cyclomatic complexity provide raw measures of how secure and reliable code modules are likely to be.

Technical activity metrics are ideally suited to serve as diagnostic metrics because they fulfill many of the qualities that good metrics should have. They are expressed as numbers, incorporate clear units of measure, and can generally be computed on a frequent basis because their data flow from deployed IT and security software packages.

Technical metrics are not the only ones worth considering, of course. Security program metrics incorporate the overall processes that technical systems participate in. We turn to these in the next chapter, "Measuring Program Effectiveness."

Measuring Program Effectiveness

Trust, but verify.

—Ronald Reagan, ca. 1987, quoting Vladimir Ilyich Lenin

My first job out of college was as a self-employed programmer. After a year and a half of steady and profitable work, I realized that I could either continue to burnish my skills as a developer or do something broader and more business-oriented. I interviewed with a gentleman named Ray,[1] an executive with a large transportation services company whose trucks you've probably seen on the highway. Ray was starting a new European subsidiary on behalf of the parent company, and as part of that effort he hired me as a business and technology analyst.

The year was 1993. An ex-consultant with Mercer Management Consulting, Ray was about as organized, analytical, and measurement-oriented a person as I've ever seen. Everything he said or wrote was organized into bullets. I used to joke that even his grocery shopping lists were organized hierarchically. He is a stern, sober fellow—to see him is to be reminded of New York Yankees manager Joe Torre. You know that focused look of Torre's—like a grave digger who's just finished shoveling out a fresh grave. Ray is like that, too: serious.

I worked with Ray initially one-on-one, and then later in a team setting once we'd staffed up the group. From him, I learned firsthand about sensitivity analyses, writing

---

[1] Pseudonym.

business plans, and screening resumes. Ray made a powerful impression on me at a young age. Not just because of his dedication, hard work, and organizational skill, and not because of the formalism with which he analyzed markets and data. Those things go without saying. No, I think the most profound thing he ever told me was also one of the funniest. In the spring of 1993, at the end of a conversation we were having about business management, he tossed off this throwaway line, a favorite saying of his boss, Dan:

Trust is good. Control is better.

Ray wasn't being entirely serious when he said it. He grinned mischievously, and the corners of his mouth stretched up and out, all the way to the sides of his face. For Ray, this was high comedy. (That, plus the time he referred to UPS as "those brown bastards."[2])

Ray's point—summarized as six short words—was that companies can, and should, develop working environments in which managers and employees communicate freely and trust each other. But trust is not the only important ingredient; for an organization to be effective, trust must be backed by systems of accountability. Controls need to be built into the operating environment so that subjectivity is eliminated and so that managers and employees can see for themselves how they will be measured—and will know how to improve. At Ray's company, accountability is hardwired into the corporate medulla.

The relationship of effectiveness to accountability is surely something most information security professionals can identify with. As nearly any serious security publication will tell you, *security is about control.* The prevailing standards and formal literature on security all speak of "security controls." Regardless of the source—be it the ISO 17799 framework, the Control Objectives for IT (COBIT), or the U.S. National Institute of Standards and Technology (NIST)—the notion of control ranks high as one of the key objectives of information security.

Security controls are processes designed to ensure that an organization meets its confidentiality, availability, and integrity objectives. When we speak about security effectiveness, therefore, we are really talking about the effectiveness of the controls in aggregate. Metrics enable us to measure effectiveness—and serve as the underpinnings of a system for ensuring accountability. They are the "verify" part of Reagan's advice.

In this chapter, I describe and catalog metrics that organizations can use to measure the effectiveness of security programs. Among other topics, I discuss metrics for:

---

[2] I am deliberately misquoting Ray. His actual characterization of UPS was slightly more profane, albeit less alliterative.

- Risk management
- Policy development and compliance
- Employee training
- Identity management
- Security program management

and other important security topics. In the same manner as the preceding chapter, I provide tables of pro forma metrics for each major topic area. Color commentary for selected metrics accompanies each table as needed.

USING COBIT, ITIL, AND SECURITY FRAMEWORKS

Metrics promote accountability by quantifying the effectiveness of security processes. They tell us whether our controls are working the way they should by boiling them down into numbers. Nearly every mainstream IT and security framework assumes or requires that practitioners implement reporting and accountability controls of one kind or another.

FRAMEWORKS

As frameworks go, four of the most popular are:

- **Control Objectives for Information Technology (COBIT):** First published by the Information Systems Audit and Control Association (ISACA) in 1996, COBIT provides IT and security objectives for organizations seeking to implement governance programs. COBIT defines thirty-four control objectives, grouped under four domains: planning and organization, acquisition and implementation, delivery and support, and monitoring and evaluation (see Table 4-1). The 4.0 revision of COBIT was released in 2005.
- **ISO 17799:** Often referred to simply as "the ISO standard," the ISO 17799 series grew out of the British Standards Institute 7799 information security standard. ISO divides the universe of security into ten major subject hierarchies containing thirty-six top-level controls, with nearly two hundred recommended policy and standard areas (see Table 4-2). The ISO 27000 series supercedes ISO 17799.
- **Information Technology Infrastructure Library (ITIL):** Focused on the broad technology environment as opposed to security specifically, ITIL defines eight sets of practices for services IT organizations provide to their internal constituents and to

customers (see Table 4-3). In comparison to COBIT and ISO, ITIL concerns itself with service delivery rather than technology (ISO) or control processes (COBIT). It focuses more on practices and metrics than the other two frameworks.

- **U.S. NIST 800 series:** The Unites States National Institute of Standards and Technology Special Publications 800-18 and 800-80[3] specify seventeen high-level security control families (see Table 4-4).

Table 4-1   COBIT Framework Control Objectives

Planning and Organization	Delivery and Support
PO1: Define a strategic IT plan	DS1: Define and manage service levels
PO2: Define the information architecture	DS2: Manage third-party services
PO3: Determine the technological direction	DS3: Manage performance and capacity
PO4: Define the IT processes, organization, and relationships	DS4: Ensure continuous service
	DS5: Ensure systems security
PO5: Manage the IT investment	DS6: Identify and allocate costs
PO6: Communicate management aims and direction	DS7: Educate and train users
	DS8: Manage service desk and incidents
PO7: Manage IT human resources	DS9: Manage the configuration
PO8: Manage quality	DS10: Manage problems
PO9: Assess and manage IT risks	DS11: Manage data
PO10: Manage projects	DS12: Manage the physical environment
	DS13: Manage operations

Acquisition and Implementation	Monitoring and Evaluation
AI1: Identify automated solutions	M1: Monitor and evaluate IT performance
AI2: Acquire and maintain application software	M2: Monitor and evaluate internal control
AI3: Acquire and maintain technology infrastructure	M3: Ensure regulatory compliance
	M4: Provide IT governance
AI4: Enable operation and use	
AI5: Procure IT resources	
AI6: Manage changes	
AI7: Install and accredit solutions and change	

Source: Information Systems Audit and Control Association, COBIT Framework, 4th Edition

---

[3] "Guide for Developing Security Plans for Information Technology," NIST Special Publication 800-18, National Institute of Standards and Technology, U.S. Department of Commerce, Washington, DC, 1998.

Table 4-2   ISO 17799 Security Controls

Security Policy	**Organizational Security**
3.1: Information security policy	4.1: Information security infrastructure
	4.2: Security of third-party access
	4.3: Outsourcing

Asset Classification and Control	**Personnel Security**
5.1: Accountability for assets	6.1: Job definitions and resourcing
5.2: Information classification	6.2: User training
	6.3: Security incident response

Physical and Environmental Security	**Communications and Operations Management**
7.1: Secure areas	8.1: Operational procedures/responsibilities
7.2: Equipment security	8.2: System planning and acceptance
7.3: General controls	8.3: Protection against malicious software
	8.4: Housekeeping
	8.5: Network management
	8.6: Media handling and security
	8.7: Exchanges of information and software

Access Control	**Systems Development and Maintenance**
9.1: Business requirement for access control	10.1: Security requirements of systems
9.2: User access management	10.2: Security in application systems
9.3: User responsibilities	10.3: Cryptographic controls
9.4: Network access control	10.4: Security of system files
9.5: Operating system access control	10.5: Secure development/support processes
9.6: Application access control	
9.7: Monitoring system access and use	
9.8: Mobile computing and teleworking	

Business Continuity Management	**Compliance**
11.1: Business continuity management	12.1: Compliance with legal requirements
	12.2: Reviews of policies and compliance
	12.3: System audit considerations

Source: International Organization for Standardization, ISO 17799:2000 standard

Table 4-3   ITIL Sets and Disciplines

Service Support	Service Delivery
Change Management	IT Financial Management
Release Management	Capacity Management
Problem Management	Availability Management
Incident Management	IT Continuity Management
Configuration Management	Service Level Management
Service Desk	

Planning to Implement Service Management	Security Management

ICT Infrastructure Management	Application Management
ICT Design and Planning	
ICT Operations Management	
ICT Deployment	
ICT Technical Support	

The Business Perspective	Software Asset Management

Source: UK Office of Government Commerce, 2005

Table 4-4   NIST 800-x Security Control Families

Access Control	Audit and Accountability	Awareness and Training
Certification, Accreditation, and Security Assessments	Configuration Management	Contingency Planning
Identification and Authentication	Incident Response	Maintenance
Media Protection Protection	Personnel Security	Physical and Environmental
Planning	Risk Assessment	System and Communications Protection
System and Information Integrity	System and Services Acquisition	

Other common frameworks include the Committee of Sponsoring Organizations (COSO) of the Treadway Commission and vertical, audit-related standards like SAS 70.

This chapter does not compete with any of these standards and should not be seen as a substitute for them. I do not pretend to possess any transcendent insights that will cause you to junk your current controls in favor of some half-baked pseudo-standard proposed in these pages. If you are seeking to translate between portfolios of governance standards, this chapter will not be your Rosetta Stone.[4]

My goal for this chapter is quite modest: to suggest useful metrics that practitioners can use as part of a measurement program, whether or not your organization uses one of the popular frameworks. As you can see from Tables 4-1 through 4-4, the COBIT, ISO, ITIL, and NIST frameworks concern themselves with areas much broader than measurement, although measurement plays a part in each. Your metrics program may take inspiration from one of the frameworks; if so, I think you will find the metrics in this chapter complementary.

As an organizing principle, I have categorized the process effectiveness metrics described in this chapter along the lines of the four high-level COBIT domains:

- **Planning and organization:** Processes for defining strategic security plans, scoping overall program budgets and levels of investment, assessing risk, and managing organizational and human resources
- **Acquisition and implementation:** Processes for identifying, acquiring, developing, and installing security solutions
- **Delivery and support:** Processes for defining service levels; managing internal and third-party access; training end users; handling incidents; and operating programs to secure data, facilities, and operations
- **Monitoring:** Processes for monitoring systems, assessing the effectiveness of security controls, and supporting audit processes

I have patterned these categories after the COBIT domain structure because it is simple. The four domains correspond roughly to typical stages in the system development life cycle: strategy, planning, implementation, maintenance, and support. Moreover, the COBIT domains are technology-agnostic—an important consideration when evaluating processes to determine their effectiveness, efficiency, and potential for improvement.

NOT USEFUL: ASSET VALUATION

Insurers make a point of informing their customers about exactly what their policies cover, and what they do not. Just about every policy I have ever seen contains a list of

---

[4] Readers seeking a Rosetta Stone should read E. Guldentops, T. Betts, G. Hodgkiss, et al., "Aligning COBIT, ITIL and 17799 for Business Benefit: Management Summary," IT Governance Institute and the Office of Government Commerce, 2005. I didn't feel the need to summarize their summary.

specific exclusions that enumerate in glorious detail what areas are not covered. Insurers do this not because they are nice or charitably minded, but because they wish to limit their risk and clarify their position.

In the same spirit, I would like to take a moment to mention two process-oriented subjects that will not be used as inspiration for metrics in this chapter—or in great detail elsewhere in this book, for that matter. I am referring to asset valuation—assigning values to information assets—and its stuttering, one-eyed, web-footed cousin, annualized loss expectancy (ALE).

From Chapter 2, "Defining Security Metrics," you will recall that I do not have much use for the ALE method of risk assessment. At the risk (so to speak) of repeating myself, I think it is a total waste of time. Because neither the expected loss nor frequency can be estimated with precision or consistency, ALE quickly becomes an exercise in pointless spreadsheet engineering. The numbers that come out of any ALE analysis are guaranteed to be subjective and nonreproducible.

The same is true for most methods of asset valuation, except that there appears to be even less consensus on how one ought to estimate the value of information assets. Asset valuation is arguably the "third rail" of information security: you touch it and die. On my securitymetrics.org mailing list, we have had long, raging debates about how to put dollar figures on assets. My esteemed colleague Pete Lindstrom states flatly that the value of an asset must be worth at least what you are willing to pay to protect it. By "what you are willing to pay," he means the all-in cost of hardware, software, personnel, and services:

> *"I actually believe that the amount we put into an asset is the* best *way to characterize at least a minimum value of that asset, particularly when dealing with intangibles. Anything 'wasted' really does get included in that value implicitly. . . . At the very least, as we aggregate this spending from individual assets to broader projects to business functions to organization-wide spending, it gets factored in somewhere as a 'cost of doing business' and therefore was 'worth trying.'"[5]*

On the other hand, Gunnar Peterson suggests that information assets have value only to the extent that they contribute revenues to an organization's business. An asset's value, then, ought to be a pro rata share of the net revenues from customers the asset supports:

> *"Customers and customer relationships, as opposed to a valuation of the amount of gigabytes in the database, have tangible, measurable value to businesses, and their value is much easier to communicate to those who fund the projects. So in an*

---

[5] Pete Lindstrom, securitymetrics.org mailing list, May 5, 2006.

enterprise risk management scenario, their value informs the risk management process. . . . [For example, consider] a farmer deciding which crop to grow. A farmer interested in short-term profits may grow the same high-yield crop every year, but over time this would burn the fields out. The long-term-focused farmer would rotate the crops and invest in things that build the value of the farm and soil over time. Investing in security on behalf of your customers is like this. The investment made in securing your customer's data builds current and future value for them. Measuring the value of the customer and the relationship helps to target where to allocate security resources.[6]

In addition to my securitymetrics.org cronies, other incredibly smart and well-meaning people in the security field, and in other disciplines, have proposed other methods. One common technique states that assets are worth at least what something costs to either acquire or replace—dodging the question of tax treatment and depreciation, of course. Another suggests that cost-of-downtime is the most important driver of information asset values.

I do not have a strong opinion on any of the asset valuation methods. Each has its strengths and weaknesses. That said, I agree that most organizations possess at least one "textbook" example of an asset whose value can easily be calculated because it causes business to screech to a halt when down. Order processing and manufacturing systems clearly have tangible asset values. But once we knock off the low-hanging fruit, every-thing gets muddy. What is the value of the CFO's laptop? How about a customer service representative's PC? Is a perimeter firewall worth more during a period of calm than during a worm outbreak? Could we figure out a formula for valuing these assets consis-tently over time, and in a way that facilitates comparisons between organizations? I have no idea how to answer these questions, and nearly any organization that claims other-wise is either lying or thinking wishfully. And even if they are not lying, nobody else uses the same formula—rendering benchmarking impossible. Frankly, if industry were able to agree on an asset valuation formula, the accountants would have made it canon a long time ago. Moreover, Wall Street traders would have been able to make money buying and selling derivative instruments based on them by now.

Although security professionals find it hard to agree on how to value assets, nearly everyone agrees that "critical assets" are much easier to define. Most people know instinctively how to employ the principle of Occam's Razor to cleave assets into two groups: critical assets and everything else. Critical assets are those for which an organiza-tion possesses zero tolerance for risk. Most companies can easily name their critical

---

[6] Gunnar Peterson, securitymetrics.org mailing list, May 4, 2006 (lightly edited).

assets; typically, they are transaction-processing systems, accounting systems, and machines that contain bulk quantities of customer information. Putting this in the context of risk, assets are like piles of chips that experienced gamblers keep at their tables. The "no-touchies" are those chips (critical assets) that they will not expose or part with. The remaining chips—the "touchies"—are the gambling chips.[7]

I do not mean to totally put down asset valuation formulas. Work in this area continues, but consensus eludes. In the meantime, it is easiest to rely on something other than asset values as the basis of measuring program effectiveness. That is the goal of this chapter.

PLANNING AND ORGANIZATION

COBIT was developed as a formal framework for aligning business requirements, IT processes, and IT resources. It builds on and extends principles for quality, fiduciary requirements, and security requirements:[8]

- **Quality principles:** Cost, quality, and delivery fulfillment
- **Fiduciary principles:** Effectiveness and efficiency of operations, reliability of information, and compliance with laws and regulations
- **Security requirements:** Confidentiality, integrity, and availability

IT resources covered by COBIT include data, application systems, technology, facilities, and people.[9]

COBIT's Planning and Organization domain includes all the processes needed to orchestrate the governance of technology and resources within an organization. COBIT formally defines the Planning and Organization domain as follows:

"[Planning and Organization] covers strategy and tactics, and concerns the identification of the way IT can best contribute to the achievement of the business objectives. Furthermore, the realization of the strategic vision needs to be planned, communicated and managed for different perspectives. Finally, a proper organization as well as technological infrastructure must be put in place."[10]

---

[7]   See R. J. Ringer, "Looking Out for #1" (1977)

[8]   E. Guldentops, J. Lainhart, E. Schuermans, et al., *COBIT Control Objectives*, 4th Edition, IT Governance Institute, 2005, p. 12.

[9]   Ibid, p. 13.

[10]   Ibid, p. 14.

The primary control objectives for the Planning and Organization domain include defining the IT strategic plan and desired architecture; communicating goals and direction; assessing risks; and managing investments in time, money, and capital (see Table 4-5). From the organization's point of view, the Planning and Organization domain sets the tone for the other domains. Without proper planning, the steps the organization takes to manage IT processes cannot be characterized as "controls," because operational activities devolve into reactive, firefighting activities. Thus, Planning and Organization objectives keep an organization's controls, generally speaking, from becoming "out-of-controls."

Table 4-5 shows a sampling of suggested security metrics for processes associated with the Planning and Organization domain. As you might expect, the scope of the Planning and Organization domain is much larger than just security, so focusing the discussion on security requires us to scale back the set of objectives that we consider to be important. From the security point of view, the most important things to measure are how effectively the organization assesses risks, manages security issues associated with personnel, and manages costs. The metrics focus on these areas primarily.

ASSESSING RISK

For assessing risk, the process metrics we care about most measure forward-looking activities. We do not need to know how *well* a particular set of security controls are functioning—at least not as a Planning and Organization metric. Instead, it is more important to capture high-level metrics that quantify what an organization knows (and does not know) about the nature of risk inherent in its infrastructure, people, and information. "Knowing what you do not know" assists with planning tasks because it identifies potential holes in an organization's security posture that affect an organization's most critical assets.

Thus, the metrics for the "assess risk" control objective, shown in Table 4-5, answer the following questions:

- Do critical assets reside on systems that are compliant with an organization's security standards? (Metric: % critical assets/functions residing on compliant systems)
- Has the organization reviewed critical assets and functions for physical and information security risks? (Metric: % critical assets/functions reviewed for physical security risks, % critical assets/functions with documented risk assessment)
- Is the organization prepared to handle compromises of critical assets? (Metric: % critical assets/functions with documented risk mitigation plan, % critical assets/functions with cost of compromise estimated)

Table 4-5 Planning and Organization Metrics

Control Objective	Metric
Assess and manage IT risks	% critical assets/functions residing on compliant systems
	% critical assets/functions reviewed for physical security risks
	% critical assets/functions with cost of compromise estimated
	% critical assets/functions with documented risk assessment
	% critical assets/functions with documented risk mitigation plan
Manage IT human resources	% job performance reviews with evaluation of IS responsibilities and compliance
	% position descriptions defining IS roles, responsibilities, skills, and certifications
	% users who have undergone background checks
	Ratio of business unit (shadow) security teams to security team staff
Manage the IT investment	Budget allocations for security (operational, new programs, discretionary)

Fans of risk management will note that I have not specified any particular metrics to use for quantifying the level of risk per se—in other words, metrics for risk assessment. That is a deliberate omission—in part because risk assessment is a discipline unto itself. Lots of independent bodies have developed a panoply of thoughtfully constructed, well-documented methodologies for assessing risk. In the field of IT security perhaps the best known is Carnegie-Mellon's OCTAVE method. Other worthy methods include Howard, Pincus, and Wing's Relative Attack Surface Quotient (RASQ).

Risk assessments are complicated and take time to perform properly. They require planning, discipline, and a high level of coordination between stakeholders. And when assessing risk, assessors must always leave room for discernment and good judgment. Risk assessments are always, by design, subjective exercises. Note that the relatively high amount of labor required to assess each system—and the subjectivity involved in making the assessments—violate my criteria that good metrics must be cheap to gather and consistently measured. Those risk assessment metrics that *are* cheap to gather and consistently measured are technical metrics of the diagnostic and technical variety (see the section "Vulnerability Management" in Chapter 3, "Diagnosing Problems and Measuring Technical Security").

Because of the difficulties of ensuring a fast, cheap, and consistent risk assessment process, I have shied away from recommending specific assessment metrics for the Planning and Organization domain. Organizations should measure facts about the process of risk assessment itself, rather than worry too much about how to quantify the risk. Scoring a particular critical asset or set of assets as possessing a "high" risk score is almost always a subjective process. For planning purposes, it may be better to simply answer yes or no as to whether the asset has had a risk assessment. Yes/no metrics are cheap to gather, and it is usually fairly easy to guarantee their objectivity. Planning and Organization metrics should avoid complicated risk assessment formulas—however elegantly designed or artfully aggregated—in favor of hard-and-fast facts that can be independently verified.

HUMAN RESOURCES

Human resources security metrics attempt to quantify forward-looking measures of an organization's personnel. As the expression goes, an organization's security is only as strong as the weakest link—and people have been shown time and again to be the weakest link. Aligning the organization's people strategies with security goals, therefore, is a key control objective. Metrics for the "manage human resources" control objective attempt to answer questions such as these:

- Are security responsibilities included in job descriptions and assessed during performance reviews? (Metric: % position descriptions defining IS roles, responsibilities, skills, and certifications, % job performance reviews with evaluation of IS responsibilities and compliance)
- Does the organization face potential downstream issues due to employees without background checks? (Metric: % users who have undergone background checks)
- How well dispersed are security responsibilities throughout the organization? (Metric: ratio of business unit (shadow) security staff to core security team staff)

If you are familiar with COBIT and the ISO 27002/17799 standards, you will recognize most of these metrics. It is well established that job descriptions ought to have security responsibilities documented and that employees should be carefully screened before being hired.

The last metric—the ratio of "shadow" staff to security team staff—is one of my favorites. It reveals much about an organization's success in spreading around security responsibilities. Nearly all organizations, including the one you probably work in, have a centralized security group whose job it is to safeguard all information assets. Sometimes this group reports up through the finance organization; most of the time, it is part of the IT or operations group. Regardless of where it resides in the organizational body politic, it's this group's job to keep everyone safe.

At the same time, most large organizations have discovered that they cannot rely on just a single group of people to do everything. Investment banks, for example, are a perfect case in point. One bank that I'm familiar with has three primary IT groups: one each in London, New York, and Tokyo. The business also manages a wide-ranging portfolio of business units, each one of which has its own technology operations staff. Thus, while it's perfectly accurate to say that the firm has a centralized security group—it does—this group is not the only part of the company charged with formal security responsibilities. Designated persons in the operational groups called "local security coordinators" receive special security training and liaise with the regional and central security staff. Their job is to guide security investments, handle incidents, and coordinate communications within their business units.

The "shadow ratio," then, defines a way of measuring dispersion of responsibilities. All nonsecurity staff whose job contains operational security responsibilities count toward the total. In the case of our investment bank, the ratio of local security coordinators to central security staff is nearly one-to-one.

MANAGING INVESTMENTS

As with just about everything in life, security costs money. And as the last five years have shown, security in particular costs a *lot* of money. As an analyst, I believe that the security spending bubble we have seen—20% annual increases since 2001—cannot last. The Law of Gravity has not been repealed; sooner or later, what goes up must come down.

As information security slides past its frothy crest of irrational exuberance, senior management will increasingly want to know what it is getting for all of its investments. Keeping tabs on costs—knowing what an organization spends, and why it spends it— is key.

Security costs are no different from any other kind of IT cost. Generally, these costs break down into two categories: fixed costs (in-house costs that must be paid, regardless of the size of the business) and variable costs (those that vary with manpower or can be scaled up or down based on activities).

Table 4-6 shows common examples of each type.[11]

---

[11] This table is derived in part from commentary in Maizlish and Handler's excellent chapter, "Building the IT Portfolio." See B. Maizlish and R. Handler, *IT Portfolio Management: Step-By-Step*, p. 184, 2005.

Table 4-6   Fixed and Variable Cost Categories

Fixed Costs	Variable Costs
Hardware	Per-seat software licenses
Depreciation	Training
Real estate	Incremental server capacity
Capitalized development expense	On-demand applications
Maintenance agreements	Managed services
Site licenses for software	Outsourced personnel
Employee salaries	

Beyond consideration of an investment's *type* (fixed or variable), perhaps more important is its *purpose*. One well-known way of thinking about IT investments breaks them down into three categories. IT investments are used to

- Run the business
- Grow the business
- Transform the business

With respect to security, these costs equate to activities that

- Operate the organization's security systems (operational)
- Implement new security controls to meet new requirements (new programs)
- Get out in front of new business requirements (discretionary)

Most security organizations should attempt to categorize their budget items as belonging to one of these three buckets. Furthermore, for the purposes of budgetary metrics, security organizations should track the level of spending for their operational, new/implementation, or discretionary security initiatives.

Most companies will likely spend most of their budgets on operational activities, with a small minority going to new programs. However, forward-thinking businesses will also want to explicitly allocate budget for discretionary activities. These could include proactive consultations with business units, piloting new security technologies ahead of demand, and implementing automation for security measurement activities. Thus, if a normal budget allocates 90% of available funds to operational costs and 10% for new programs, a "stretch goal" might look to shift the balance to 80% operational, 15% new programs, and 5% discretionary.

ACQUISITION AND IMPLEMENTATION

If the Planning and Organization control domain describes what an organization must do, the Acquisition and Implementation domain begins to answer the question of *how*. This domain contains all the activities relating to acquiring, provisioning, and implementing information systems and their associated controls:

> *"To realize the IT strategy, IT solutions need to be identified, developed or acquired, as well as implemented and integrated into the business process. In addition, changes in and maintenance of existing systems are covered by this domain to make sure that the solutions continue to meet business objectives."*[12]

Acquisition and Implementation processes turn the organization's high-level strategy and objectives into reality. As shown in Table 4-7, these processes focus on how an organization defines and documents requirements for the software it uses, acquires or develops solutions to meet those requirements, creates appropriate control processes and procedures, and manages changes to infrastructure and processes. In short, they encompass the broad goal of managing how a company goes about the process of understanding the need for, and managing, beneficial changes to the technology environment.

From the perspective of security, the goal of the Acquisition and Implementation domain is to ensure that appropriate security controls are incorporated into information systems as early as possible. When an organization prepares to buy or build a new information system, it must take steps to ensure that the data it manages are safe from tampering, restricted to those who need them, and kept available for use by the organization. An organization's relative success at doing these things depends largely on its ability to identify appropriate security solutions, install and accredit them properly, develop effective procedures for operating them, and manage changes to their security configurations.

IDENTIFYING SOLUTIONS

Customer-facing systems, or those that store information on their behalf, require particular attention. Thus, the security metrics that measure acquisition and implementation process effectiveness should, among other things, measure how well an organization specifies requirements for safeguarding customer information (see Table 4-7). Security metrics for the "identify solutions" control objective should ask the following questions:

---

[12] Ibid, p. 14.

- How frequently are security teams engaged when business units draw up requirements for new information systems? (Metrics: # security team consultations by business units, % new systems with initial security consultations)
- How much attention do business units pay to customer requirements when planning
  a new information system? (Metrics: # consultations with security teams by externally facing applications teams, # customer consultations with security teams)
- How often are business units requiring controls that ensure that customer information managed by new systems cannot be tampered with by unauthorized parties?
  (Metric: % coverage of integrity controls for data exchanged with customers/
  partners)
- How often are business units requiring controls that ensure the confidentiality of
  customer information managed by systems? (Metric: % coverage of confidentiality controls for data exchanged with customers/partners)

The metrics in the "Identify automated solutions" section of Table 4-7 focus more on
systems that manage customer information than other types of systems. That is because
they are typically the most visible, revenue-generating systems and could cause the most
harm to an enterprise if breached or damaged. These are not the only kind of information systems, of course, and businesses need not ignore other, purely internal types. For
example, human resources information systems have fairly important integrity and confidentiality requirements. Other than the occasional exhibitionist, nobody wants his or
her salary and medical history shared with others. The list of metrics I have provided
should be seen as a starting point, rather than as a canon.

Table 4-7 Acquisition and Implementation Metrics

Control Objective	Metric
Identify automated solutions	% coverage of confidentiality controls for data exchanged with customers/partners
	% coverage of integrity controls for data exchanged with customers/partners
	# consultations with security teams by externally facing applications teams
	# customer consultations with security teams
	# security team consultations by business units
	% new systems with initial security consultations

continues

Table 4-7   Acquisition and Implementation Metrics (Continued)

Control Objective	Metric
Install and accredit solutions and changes	% accredited (signed-off) externally facing and customer-related applications
	% systems with security accreditations (signed-off and risk accepted)
	% systems with security certifications (tested and deemed compliant)
	% information systems with built-in security costs
Enable operation and use	% information systems with operational policies and controls
	% BU heads with implemented operational procedures aligned with controls

Two terms recurring in the metrics merit further explanation. First, the word "coverage" refers to the degree to which organizational requirements are met for a collection of systems. For example, policy might specify that customer data in motion over the Internet must be encrypted using a suitable protocol such as SSL or SSH, and that sensitive data at rest must be "marked" as such and tracked using a database auditing tool. Technical metrics that measure adherence to this policy (as described in Chapter 3) can quantify the relative level of compliance for each system. Aggregation of these metrics over a group of systems enables an organization to state the percentage of systems that are covered by compliant controls.

The second word that recurs is the word "consultation." I believe strongly in formal and informal collaboration between business units and security staff to increase awareness and acceptance of security, especially at the beginning of the system's implementation life cycle. Just about everyone agrees that security requirements should be incorporated into the life cycle as early as possible. Trusting that business units will consider security requirements during the scoping and requirements phases is not enough; verification is better.

Thus, organizations should monitor the number of "consultations," or meetings between security domain experts and their counterparts on the business side, during the acquisition phases of system development and implementation. But just what is a consultation? In my view, it is a face-to-face scheduled meeting with a formal list of attendees and an agenda to review the security requirements of a proposed system, or of an existing system that needs to be upgraded or changed. Requiring face-to-face interaction, and that it be formally scheduled with an agenda, makes it easy to count and prevents "cheating." Shambling down the corridor to a colleague's cube does not count, nor does shoptalk at the watercooler. For the purposes of measurement, the actual proceedings and action items from the consultation meetings matter less than the fact that they happened.

INSTALLING AND ACCREDITING SOLUTIONS

Bringing systems online successfully requires discipline, training, documentation, and effective project planning. Organizations must also ensure that they install information systems correctly, that system owners understand and accept the risks associated with these systems, and that installed systems demonstrably comply with prevailing security standards. We refer to these latter two concepts as processes for *accrediting* and *certifying* information systems.

Accreditation means that the owner of a system has ascertained the security risk associated with a system and has agreed to accept any residual risk that existing controls cannot transfer or mitigate. Fundamentally, accreditation of a system means that the owner is accountable for residual risks. NIST's definition of accreditation is excellent:

"Security accreditation is the official management decision . . . to authorize operation of an information system and to explicitly accept the risk to agency operations, agency assets, or individuals based on the implementation of an agreed-upon set of security controls. . . . Security accreditation provides a form of quality control and challenges managers and technical staffs at all levels to implement the most effective security controls possible in an information system, given mission requirements, technical constraints, operational constraints, and cost/schedule constraints. By accrediting an information system, an agency official accepts responsibility for the security of the system and is fully accountable for any adverse impacts to the agency if a breach of security occurs. Thus, responsibility and accountability are core principles that characterize security accreditation."[13]

Certification, on the other hand, refers to something deeper than the act of accepting risk. Certification of a system means that a trusted party (internal or external) has tested the security controls of an installed system and has judged that it meets organizational security standards. Again, the NIST definition:

---

[13] G. Ross, M. Swanson, G. Stoneburner, S. Katzke, A. Johnson, "Guide for the Security Certification and Accreditation of Federal Information Systems," NIST Special Publication 800-37, National Institute of Standards and Technology, May 2004, p. 1.

"Security certification is a comprehensive assessment of the management, operational, and technical security controls in an information system, made in support of security accreditation, to determine the extent to which the controls are implemented correctly, operating as intended, and producing the desired outcome with respect to meeting the security requirements for the system. The results of a security certification are used to reassess the risks and update the system security plan, thus providing the factual basis for an authorizing official to render a security accreditation decision."[14]

Certification and accreditation go hand-in-hand. System owners cannot make informed decisions about risk acceptance until they understand the effectiveness of an information system's controls. Organizations have different processes for certifying systems. For some, interview-based walkthroughs and assessments suffice; others require control tests such as penetration testing. In addition, the type of testing required varies based on the sensitivity and potential exposure of the system at hand. One firm I know of, for example, requires every new Internet-facing web application to receive a full penetration test from an outside, contracted technical security assessment firm. As a result, every year the firm tests several dozen new applications prior to formal accreditation.

Security measures for the "install and accredit solutions and changes" section of Table 4-7 answer the following questions:

- Do information systems adhere to organizational security standards? (Metric: % systems with security certifications)

- Have the owners of information systems agreed to, and accepted, security risks? (Metrics: % systems with security accreditations, % accredited externally facing and customer-related applications)

- Has the organization included security in the costs of new systems? (Metric: % information systems with built-in security costs)

If you have ever read the annual Federal Information Security Management Act (FISMA) testimonies to Congress, you know they make for interesting reading, but not for the reasons you might think. Let's face it, the writing style and delivery of most testimonies make organic chemistry textbooks seem like Gothic novels by comparison. What I find most interesting are the figures the testifiers choose to cite. Sometimes the figures are "happy metrics"—statistics designed to impress the listeners more than illuminate their

---

[14] G. Ross, M. Swanson, G. Stoneburner, S. Katzke, A. Johnson, "Guide for the Security Certification and Accreditation of Federal Information Systems," NIST Special Publication 800-37, National Institute of Standards and Technology, May 2004, p. 1.

understanding. But invariably, the two numbers that departments cite most often are the percentage of accredited systems and the percentage of certified systems. The annual testimony of U.S. government department heads in front of Congress, as required by the FISMA statute, is a case in point:

> *"The Department's FISMA inventory currently includes approximately 700 systems, and prior to the initiation of the Remediation Project, the number of fully accredited systems was only 26% Department-wide. By the end of February of this year, over 60% of the systems are fully accredited. In just 5 short months the Department has more than doubled the number of accredited systems, and it is on track to make the goal of full remediation by the end of this year. It is clear the Project is positively affecting the security culture of the Department, and recent upward trends in remediation metrics support that view."[15]*

I mention the U.S. federal government not because it is a paragon of security virtue (it is not) but because it is *big* and contains a lot of moving parts. Accreditation and certification processes for large organizations are not easy. Most organizations have hundreds of systems that require accreditation. It takes a great deal of coordinated effort on the part of both system owners and security organizations to rigorously accredit each system. Recent commentary by the U.S. Director of National Intelligence's office shows just how labor-intensive these processes can be:

> *"If we continue on our current path following our existing processes, the cost of re-certifying expiring accreditations for intelligence information systems over the next two years will exceed many millions of dollars and that doesn't include bringing in new capabilities. A significant portion of that cost is due to widely divergent standards and controls, the lack of a robust set of automated tools and reliance upon manual review. . . . Failure to establish uniform certification and accreditation practices throughout government stifles innovation, hinders efforts to automate the process, and sustains cost growth."[16]*

---

[15] Testimony of Scott Charbo, Chief Information Officer, U.S. Department of Homeland Security, before the House Government Reform Committee Hearing on Information Security and Implementation of the Federal Information Security Management Act of 2002, March 16, 2006.

[16] D. Meyrose, "Letter on Certification and Accreditation Revitalization," Office of the Director of National Intelligence, Washington, DC, 5 June 2006.

Clearly, organizations cannot overrely on certification and accreditation metrics. But giving up in despair isn't the answer, either. The key is consistency of effort. Every organization will have its own processes for accreditation and certification. NIST itself provides guidelines for government agencies in the publication I cited for the accreditation definition (Special Publication 800-37). Regardless of how complex the process you use to accredit systems might be, the metric for measuring the relative penetration of accreditation activities is much simpler: do system owners sign off on the security of their information systems, or not? Thus, I recommend using a simple "yes/no" strategy of counting the number of explicit sign-offs an organization receives from its system owners and dividing that figure by the number of systems requiring accreditation.

For certification metrics I recommend a similarly sparse approach. From the total pool of candidate systems that require certification, organizations should identify those systems that have received an appropriate review of their security controls. Each system that has not received a review counts as a "no." You should also give a "no" to each system that has received a review but whose outstanding security issues prevent it from receiving accreditation by its system owner. Those systems that have received both a review of their controls *and* accreditation should each get a "yes" mark.

In addition to certification and accreditation metrics, another key figure that I've seen cited often is deceptively simple: the percentage of systems with built-in security costs. By "built-in" we mean whether the cost of security controls for a system (technical, people, process) were included in either the original acquisitions budget or the operations budget. For example, in 2005 the White House reported that "85% of systems had security costs built into the system life cycle planning costs."[17] What is nice about this metric is that it elegantly packs a lot of meaning into a single statistic. For costs to be built-in, the budget owners must know what they are and must have allocated a portion of their operational budget to them. Depending on how one defines the phrase, "knowing the costs" implies hardware, software, expenses, and (probably) labor allocations. Budget allocations mean just that: the people who own the budgets need to explicitly set aside dollars to support the security functions of the systems they own or use. This implies that budget owners must conscientiously charge back for security services they provide, or allocate funds corresponding to the security-based costs they consume from others. Thus, determining the percentage of systems with built-in security costs enforces a sort of budgetary and planning rigor that most organizations benefit from.

One issue I've skated over is risk classification. In addition to the metrics I have suggested for certification, accreditation, and costing, many companies may also seek to

---

[17] "Federal Information Security Management Act (FISMA), 2004 Report to Congress," U.S. Office of Management and Budget, March 1, 2005, p. ii.

classify new systems as belonging to "high," "medium," or "low-risk" categories. While valuable, risk-based acquisition and implementation metrics are subjective. I have omitted risk metrics in favor of a more factually based determinant: whether a system is customer-facing or Internet-facing. Pugnacious readers are welcome to disagree with me on this point.

DEVELOPING AND MAINTAINING PROCEDURES

Systems do not run themselves; they usually require people. Those people need to know what they are supposed to be doing: how to operate the systems they use in their day-to-day work, how to fix problems they encounter, and what steps to take to keep the system safe.

The tangible forms that instructions take for keeping systems up and running go by many names, such as "procedures," "work instructions," and "operational controls." Regardless of the name used, these instructions typically describe:

- Procedures for starting and stopping the system
- Day-to-day operational responsibilities and tasks
- Availability policy and expected service level
- Monitoring and oversight responsibilities
- Problem management processes
- Business continuity and disaster recovery instructions
- Technical architecture
- Security responsibilities for users and operators
- Data security policy
- System ownership

Some systems will require only a subset of these characteristics. For purposes of security management, the procedures for monitoring, data security, business continuity, and security responsibilities matter most.

Each system that management deems critical needs appropriate operational procedures. Thus, to measure an organization's effectiveness in developing and maintaining procedures, I recommend keeping track of which systems have suitable operational policies and procedures (Metric: % information systems with operational policies and controls).

DELIVERY AND SUPPORT

The previous two domains, Planning and Organization and Acquisition and Implementation, describe how organizations can measure the parts of their security programs devoted to building security strategies and putting in place systems to carry out those strategies. In this section, I suggest metrics for the Delivery and Support domain—the day-to-day control activities that comprise security operations.

The COBIT guidelines define the Delivery and Support domain as follows:

"This domain is concerned with the actual delivery of required services, which includes service delivery, management of security and continuity, service support for users, and management of data and the operational facilities."[18]

Typical activities performed in the Delivery and Support domain include defining service levels for technology operations, training users, helping customers, managing problems and incidents, ensuring continuity of operations, and implementing system access controls.

For the purposes of security metrics, a certain amount of overlap exists between the Delivery and Support approach espoused by COBIT and the metrics discussed in the preceding chapter. Program-level security metrics differ somewhat from largely technical metrics because they cover areas that may span domains beyond just a particular technical area. Of the classic triad of security program elements—technology, people, and process—the latter two can rarely be perfectly described by a simple equation or diagnostic measure. Program metrics try to measure the performance of people and processes, independent of the underlying technologies.

A second difference is that the security program metrics include the "fuzzier" parts of measurement that may not be captured by a particular piece of security widgetry. No antivirus software, intrusion detection system, or vulnerability scanner can possibly tell an organization whether its people possess sufficient security training, for example. These metrics could certainly be calculated in a straightforward and cost-effective fashion, but they won't be obtained through an existing security system.

Table 4-8 shows a concise set of program metrics for measuring the effectiveness of delivery and support processes. COBIT specifies thirteen different control areas, but to keep the discussion simple I've provided metrics for only the most important five controls. These focus on user training and awareness, system security, and data management.

---

[18] Ibid, p. 15

Table 4-8   Delivery and Support Metrics

Control Objective	Metric
Educate and train users	# security skill mastered, average per employee and per security team member
	% new employees completing security awareness training
	% existing employees completing refresher training per policy
	% security staff with professional security certifications
	Fulfillment rate of target external security training workshops and classroom seminars
	By business unit or office, correlation of password strength with training latency
	By business unit or office, correlation of tailgating rate (employees closely following colleagues in the door, to avoid swiping in) with training latency
Ensure systems security	# active user IDs assigned to only one person
	% users with authorized system access
	% users with authorized access to security software
	% highly privileged employees whose privileges reviewed this period
	% highly privileged terminated employees whose privileges reviewed this period
	% information assets with role-based assignments
	% roles, systems, applications implementing segregation of duties in production systems
	% systems implementing account lockout policy
	% systems/applications verifying password policy
	% directory accounts dead or disabled
	Cycle time to remove terminated or inactive users
	Cycle time to deprovision users, by system type
	% inactive user accounts disabled per policy
	% terminated user accounts disabled per policy
Identify and allocate costs	Cost of security for revenue-generating systems
	% security costs charged back to business units
	Estimated damage ($) from all security incidents
	% security incidents that did not cause damage beyond policy thresholds

continues

Table 4-8   Delivery and Support Metrics (Continued)

Control Objective	Metric
Manage data	Data flow (bytes sent to and received by customers, external employees, vendors, partners)
	Toxicity rate of customer data (# of records containing personally identifiable information [PII], and ratio of same to all data records)
	% backup media stored with third parties
	% backup media successfully delivered
	% media sanitized prior to disposal
	# data privacy escalations, and estimated time/cost to fix
Manage third-party services	Cycle time to grant (or revoke) customer/partner access to company systems
	% third-party applicants successfully vetted within service standards
	# authorized (and unauthorized) customer/partner transactions, by application
	% strategic partner/third-party agreements with documented security requirements
	% third-party agreements requiring external validation of procedures
	% third-party users whose privileges reviewed this period

EDUCATING AND TRAINING USERS

End-user education is a cornerstone of modern thinking about information security. It's a well-accepted truth that the more aware people are of their responsibilities as users of computer systems, the more likely they are to exercise due caution and care in their day-to-day activities. Heightened awareness leads to better practices; better practices should result in fewer security incidents, decreased susceptibility to infiltration by outsiders, and (for the engineers) higher-quality systems design. Burton Group's Diana Kelley expresses the sentiment well:

> *"When security becomes everybody's business, the organization gains greater value from its security investments and builds stronger overall business process management and growth."*[19]

---

[19]   Diana Kelley, *ComputerWorld*, "Making Security Everyone's Business," March 21, 2005, http://www.computerworld.com/securitytopics/security/story/0,10801,100375,00.html.

Most security awareness programs target the everyday worker. These programs impart the organization's policies and procedures for such generally applicable security concepts as antivirus protection, "acceptable use" of company resources, software licensing, password policy, social engineering, and recommended steps for reporting security incidents.[20] Some companies extend security awareness and training programs to topics such as application development practices.

Most organizations train users formally in classroom settings. Information security standards like the ISO 27002/17799 framework recommend that companies should, as a condition of employment, periodically require employees to acknowledge their acceptance of the organization's security policies by signing a "user responsibility" document or rider to the employee agreement. My previous two employers did.

Employee training is all well and good, but how does one measure it? For most users, organizations need to determine whether their employees attend "on-boarding" or periodic refresher training classes as their policies dictate. For the security staff, we need different measures. In addition to general training, organizations need to identify whether their security teams are acquiring the specialized security skills they need. And finally, organizations ought to identify methods of determining whether all the effort they are putting into their training and awareness are actually making a tangible difference. Thus, security awareness and training metrics should answer these questions:

- Are employees acknowledging their security responsibilities as users of information systems? (Metric: % new employees completing security awareness training)
- Are employees receiving training at intervals consistent with company policies? (Metric: % existing employees completing refresher training per policy)
- Do security staff members possess sufficient skills and professional certifications? (Metric: % security staff with professional security certifications)
- Are security staff members acquiring new skills at rates consistent with management objectives? (Metrics: # security skill mastered, average per employee and per security team member, fulfillment rate of target external security training workshops and classroom seminars)
- Are security awareness and training efforts leading to measurable results? (Metrics: By business unit or office, correlation of password strength with the elapsed time since training classes; by business unit or office, correlation of tailgating rate with training latency)

---

[20] See NIST special publication 800-50 for an overview of security training and awareness programs. M. Wilson and J. Hash, "Building and Information Technology Security Awareness and Training Program," U.S. Department of Commerce, National Institute of Standards and Technology, October 2003.

The last question—asking whether there is, in essence, a cause-and-effect relationship between training and better security—matters most. But sadly, it is also an unlikely avenue for most companies to explore. In nearly ten years of various and sundry chats with information security managers, I can recall exactly one company that explicitly tried to correlate training and operational security metrics. I do not really know why this is.

Perhaps managers of training programs feel that courses designed to impart a warm glow of security throughout a company's body politic are inherently impossible to measure. Or perhaps some might feel that the numbers might not tell a true story. NIST's guidance on metrics, for example, warns that one of the ironic side effects of increased awareness can be an increase in reported incidents. The measurement goal of showing a "decline in security incidents or violations [might] indicate that the gap between existing awareness programs . . . and identified needs is shrinking," NIST writes. But, paradoxically, "reporting of potential incidents may increase because of enhanced vigilance among users."[21]

I have a funny habit of narrowing my eyes and perking up my ears whenever somebody claims that measurement is impossible. Can't measure the effect of training on security? Ah, but you *can*—you just need to return to first principles: find key indicators that are consistently measured, cheap to gather, and expressed as numbers. What have we got that would work? Here is a hint: most training courses spend a lot of time educating users on how to make "good passwords" and maintain physically secure environments. Surely we can find indicators for success or failure in these areas.

For example, one thing we can measure is passwords—or, more specifically, password *strength*. Most users have passwords for their desktop computer and network; these passwords are usually stored in a Windows server domain controller or Active Directory replica. So, an easy way to measure password strength would be to run a copy of the Windows server's Security Account Manager (SAM) file through a password-breaking tool like LC5 (formerly L0phtCrack), or use an alternate like John the Ripper. These tools will tell you whose passwords are strong or weak, and how long it took to break them. If 90% of a particular office attended security awareness training within the last year, but 75% of all passwords could be broken in less than 15 minutes, that would suggest a problem with the training, the password policy, or both.

A Wall Street security manager related to me a second cause-and-effect metric: correlation of building card read data with training compliance percentages, by site. Specifically, he measures what percentage of employees swipe their building cards an *even* or *odd* number of times. That might sound like a strange thing to measure, until

---

[21] Ibid, p. 39.

you reflect that this company requires its employees to swipe on the way out of buildings, not just on the way in. An odd number of swipes suggests that the employee is a tailgater. This manager hypothesized that sites with poor training class attendance percentages would also have high numbers of tailgaters (as identified by their "oddness"). His data proved him right!

ENSURING SYSTEM SECURITY

One of the key components of the Delivery and Support domain is ensuring system security. If one were to adhere strictly to the COBIT definition of what this means, one might think that any discussion of metrics for this area would lead us down the path of technical security metrics. This seems an obvious conclusion, because many of the things organizations can count come from tactical or operational security products. But then there is the inconvenient fact that this path was well trodden in the last chapter.

Recall that this chapter uses COBIT as a way of organizing our thinking about processes, rather than as a way of creating metrics for COBIT itself. I'm not smart enough about COBIT to even attempt that. I'd rather help readers understand how to take the metrics in this chapter and map them into a framework they already understand. Thus, because we have previously covered many of the metrics that can be garnered from technologies and tools, let us turn the discussion to people and process metrics.

When the words "people" and "security" are uttered in the same breath, many professionals automatically think about things like acceptable-use policies, training, passwords, and responsibilities. From a workforce and organizational standpoint, this makes sense. If one substitutes the word "accountable parties" for "people," the discussion shifts more to the operational aspects of security management—specifically, to concepts like authorization. Put succinctly, we need to know if the right people have access to the right things—and that the wrong people do not.

Put more formally, when you allow somebody to do something, you are *authorizing* him or her to do it. That person, in essence, carries with him or her a *privilege* or *permission*: an action that can be performed on or to a target. Reading a particular file represents a permission; so does the ability to log into a website, correct a patient record, or push a code patch to a production server. Permissions, when granted to a particular person or organizational role, constitute an *entitlement*.

Today's information security battleground is all about entitlements—who's got them, whether they were granted properly, and how to enforce them. Most of the panic-inducing security stories in the media—you know, the ones bemoaning the catastrophic rise in information "leakage,"[22] mobile viruses, piracy, teleworking thieves, and perfidious outsourcers pilfering proprietary secrets—ultimately stem from the same cause: a fear that the reach of an organization's entitlements exceeds its grasp. Understanding the reach of entitlements is what information security is ultimately all about, and it's what any discussion of every complex security issue boils down to.

Thus, when considering process metrics to measure how effectively an organization ensures security, entitlements (who has access to what) figure prominently in the discussion. Pertinent questions to ask, and the metrics that answer these questions, include the following:

- How consistently does the organization implement principles of accountability? (Metrics: % active user IDs assigned to only one person, % systems implementing account lockout policy, % systems/applications verifying password policy)

- How pervasive is the principle of role-based access to systems? (Metric: % information assets with role-based security assignments)

- Does the organization segregate responsibility for production systems to prevent change control problems? (Metric: % roles, systems, and applications implementing segregation of duties in production systems)

- What users possess a significant amount of privileged access to information systems? (Metrics: % users with authorized system access to more than one critical system, % "high-risk" users with application and system access on the same system, % users with authorized access to security software)

- Does the organization review employee entitlements? (Metrics: % of highly privileged employees whose privileges were reviewed this period, % directory accounts dormant or disabled)

- Is the business at risk from terminated employees, especially those with privileged access? (Metrics: cycle time to remove terminated or inactive users, cycle time to deprovision users by system type, % inactive user accounts disabled per policy, % terminated user accounts disabled per policy)

These questions and suggested metrics should be taken as a starting point for a fuller discussion of security entitlements within organizations. The question of role-based access is certainly an important one, because it indicates the degree to which the

---

[22] Whenever I hear the word "leakage," I automatically think of certain pharmaceutical contraindications. Although I prefer plain speaking to gobbledygook, in this particular case I'd welcome a little obfuscation. "Unauthorized information movement" sounds a lot better to me. Even "extrusion" represents an improvement—even though it makes me think of pottery wheels.

organization has thought through its processes for defining and granting entitlements. Systems that define entitlements exclusively through roles tend to have better security architectures than those that rely just on granting privileges to named users. Some kinds of applications, like those written for the J2EE platform,[23] actively discourage defining entitlements for specific users. Broadly speaking, the best practice for granting privileges is to:

- Provision individual user accounts for the system or application
- Define (name) and provision roles for the system or application
- Define application entitlements by assigning the appropriate permissions to each role
- Map users to roles using application-provided tools or a central identity management system

User permissions, therefore, are defined as the union of the permissions they possess explicitly (which should be minimal) combined with those users inherit by virtue of the roles they possess.

On a related note, privileged access is a potentially serious problem for many organizations. The doomsday scenario, the one that CIOs dread, is the "rogue administrator" problem. That is where a disgruntled system administrator uses his privileged access to servers and data to wreak havoc on his way out the door. Just such a nightmare happened in 2002, when a UBS PaineWebber system administrator who had not gotten the bonus he wanted planted a backdoor script that silently deleted server files at random intervals. The code took down over 2,000 servers and crippled access for 8,000 employees, in part because the administrator had broad, root-level access to a large part of the company's infrastructure. To make matters worse, more than forty people shared the root user account, making it difficult to establish lines of accountability or audit trails.[24]

Metrics that measure "highly privileged" system administrators would have helped prevent problems like this one. One revealing metric is the percentage of users who have privileged access to more than one critical system. Another is the percentage of "high-risk" users, defined as those who have access to multiple tiers on the same system, such as database administrator privileges *and* root access. A large East Coast financial services

---

[23] Java 2, Enterprise Edition provides out-of-the box support for centralized role definitions for web applications that conform to the framework. These are defined centrally in a "deployment descriptor" file. There is no built-in support in this file for defining entitlements for individually named users, which has the net effect of discouraging their use—certainly a good thing, in my view.

[24] S. Gaudin, "UBS Trial Puts Insider Security Threats at Center Stage," *Information Week*, June 12, 2006.

company uses this metric to identity users with excessive privileges. Recently, it performed a comprehensive review of user entitlements across all its critical production systems. The company found that out of approximately 2,300 users with access to systems, 290 could be classified as "high-risk." That is about 12% of the user population.

Low-tech metrics can help detect potential insider threats, too. Chris Walsh points out that measuring the percentage of employees who have not taken vacation in a long time might reveal "indispensable" employees at high risk of burnout. "The guy at UBS Paine Webber might have been detected if somebody else had to do his job for two or three weeks per year."

We could certainly imagine more system security metrics than these, especially those related to broad, program-level concerns other than entitlements. For more granular, technically focused metrics, see Chapter 3.

IDENTIFYING AND ALLOCATING COSTS

Pages earlier, in the discussion of Planning and Organization domain metrics, I recommended a key set of metrics for measuring overall program costs: the budgetary allowances for new programs, current programs, and discretionary initiatives. These capture the broad costs of running the security program, but to understand the operational side of security (for the Delivery and Support domain), we need metrics that are a little less coarse. They should capture essential data about security costs incurred during day-to-day operations. Furthermore, they should—to the greatest extent possible—tie directly back to activities that serve the organization's mission. For companies, this means making money.

I won't spend time repeating what I mean by "security costs" (discussed previously in the "Planning and Organization" section), other than to mention that they include operational hardware, software, people, consulting, and outside audit fees. These costs should be totaled up for all security functions across the organization, including for business units that share partial responsibility for operational security. What matters more than composition of costs is how those costs are allocated: to revenue-generating activities, to business units, or to the IT organization.

Another category of cost is security incidents—or, more properly put, hard- and soft-dollar estimates of costs the organization incurs when investigating, reacting to, and reporting on break-ins, data disclosures, and other security problems. During incident post-mortem meetings, organizations should quantify the cost of incidents whenever possible. Hard costs include legal fees, regulatory fines, crisis communications representation, external forensics fees, and extraordinary charges for equipment and software related to the incident. Soft costs include labor for hours spent by internal counsel, IT personnel, and senior management. I tend to take a dim view of most soft-dollar estimates, but most firms should try to capture these as rigorously and consistently as they can.

Summing up the preceding, identification and allocation of security costs means understanding how much money the organization spends on securing its systems. It also means measuring expenses associated with managing security incidents. Metrics that quantify these issues ought to answer these questions:

- What do the security systems managed by the organization cost relative to top-line business activities? (Metric: cost of security for revenue-generating systems)
- How much of the operational security budget ties back to business activities? (Metric: % security costs charged back to business units)
- How significant was the cost impact of security incidents? (Metrics: estimated damage [$] from all security incidents, % security incidents that did not cause damage beyond policy thresholds)

Estimating the cost of security incidents should not present too high a barrier for most companies. Most security groups are accustomed to the notion of after-action reporting, and many even attempt to quantify hard and soft costs as part of the exercise.

Tying back security costs to business units or revenue-generating systems is more difficult. Cost allocation is, for most organizations, a black art. In fact, given the degree of political wrestling that occurs when figuring out charge-back formulas, one might more profitably call it a full-contact sport. Regardless, security organizations should try, to the best of their abilities, to associate specific expenditures with business initiatives.

Certain security costs are easy to allocate, such as outsourced security monitoring services for a demilitarized zone (DMZ), single sign-on (SSO) systems, application monitoring tools, and external audits:

- Outsourced security monitoring services for a demilitarized zone (Strategy: pro rata allocation based on user sessions or bandwidth)
- SSO system (Strategy: pro rata allocation based on deployment of SSO agents on business servers, plus labor allocation)
- Database and web application monitoring tools/firewalls (Strategy: charge-back of per-agent software costs, plus labor allocation)
- Managed intrusion detection
- External audit fees and consulting (Strategy: direct charge-back if audit is for a specific application; otherwise, pro rata allocation based on issues found)

Other costs may be more difficult to allocate, especially those that are incurred by all members of the organization. Security awareness, training, and coordination costs, for example, do not obviously relate to specific business initiatives; neither do directory synchronization and maintenance tools, antivirus software, or other ubiquitously deployed security software. In these cases, it might be best not to allocate them at all (thus relegating them to everyone's favorite nebulous category, "infrastructure." Alternatively, if costs have clear and obvious per-employee expenses (such as antivirus), pro rata allocation to each business unit based on head count represents a fair and transparent method.

MANAGING DATA

Information is the lifeblood of the modern firm. The word "data" denotes all forms of information that can ultimately be distilled into bits and bytes. Data are either at rest (stored in RAM or on disk) or in motion (being transmitted from a sending party to a receiver). Understanding data's direction, magnitude, and sensitivity is an important discipline for information security programs. However, few organizations have any idea of how much information they own, send, or receive.

Not all data are created equal. The departmental project-tracking spreadsheet for the company holiday party is much less sensitive than company financials or product pricing information. Thus, while companies need to understand the broad contours of the data they own or are custodians for, they also need to understand exactly which of these bits are the most sensitive.

Certain classes of data, when mishandled, seem to attract disproportionate press attention and litigation. Inadvertent disclosures of personally identifiable information (PII) about customers have lately become hazardous to the health of public companies. So hazardous, in fact, that one might compare an inadvertent disclosure of customer data to a hazardous-waste spill. But unlike many environmental spills, like with the Exxon *Valdez,* data disclosures affect people rather than the environment. People whose data were mishandled write letters to Congress, start consumer boycotts, sue, demand compensation, and pressure regulatory bodies to levy fines. That is something seagulls and trees cannot do.[25]

Data handling becomes particularly important when sensitive information flows outside the organization, either through a contractual arrangement with a third party, or via

---

[25] According to estimates by Gartner Group, the inappropriate disclosures of 145,000 customer records by ChoicePoint, a data aggregator, cost the company $11 million, equivalent to $75 per account. These charges related to the discovery, handling, cleanup, and reporting of the incident to consumers and regulators. See A. Litan, Testimony to Committee on Veterans' Affairs, May 25, 2006, http://www.house.gov/va/hearings/schedule109/may06/5-25-06/AvivahLitan.html.

a customer-facing medium like a website or portal. In the last few years, high-profile losses of archive tapes by the Bank of America and Fleet highlighted the importance of keeping archives safer through encryption of backup media. Likewise, failure to sanitize hard disks and other storage media properly upon disposal can lead to inadvertent problems later on.[26]

Security metrics for data should measure the amount of data flowing into and out of the organization. They should also identify the amount of potentially "toxic" data that must be monitored, handled properly, and contained. And they should attempt to capture key process indicators for high-risk situations where sensitive information passes from the custodianship of the organization to an outside party. Therefore, here are some questions to ask:

- How much information is flowing into the organization on a daily, monthly, and yearly basis? (Metric: data flow, such as bytes sent to and received by customers, external employees, vendors, partners)

- How much sensitive customer information does the company manage? (Metric: toxicity rate of customer data [# of records containing PII] and ratio of same to all data records)

- How safe are storage media entrusted to third parties? (Metrics: % backup media stored with third parties, % backup media successfully delivered)

- Are media assets decommissioned properly to remove traces of sensitive data? (Metric: % media sanitized prior to disposal)

- How quickly can the organization respond to complaints from employees and customers about potential data privacy or integrity problems? (Metric: # data privacy escalations, and estimated time/cost to fix)

In summary, organizations need to get a handle on the data they create, use, and manage on behalf of their shareholders, partners, and customers.

MANAGING THIRD-PARTY SERVICES

No man, or organization, is an island. Every company and government branch maintains ongoing business relationships with outside parties for services. These third parties back

---

[26] For a dramatic example, see Bob Sullivan, "I Just Bought Your Hard Drive," The Red Tape Chronicles, June 5, 2006. The money quote is at the top: "One year ago, Hank Gerbus had his hard drive replaced at a Best Buy store in Cincinnati. Six months ago, he received one of the most disturbing phone calls of his life. 'Mr. Gerbus,' Gerbus recalls a stranger named Ed telling him, 'I just bought your hard drive in Chicago.'" http://redtape.msnbc.com/2006/06/one_year_ago_ha.html.

up systems, carry tapes back and forth to offsite locations, maintain office buildings, pick up and deliver parcels, write application code, or service office equipment. Customers and citizens, too, often have some access to an organization's information assets. Every one of these parties represents a potential threat to an organization's security—at least in theory.

Thus, every information security management program needs to understand the amount and type of access third parties have to information resources, and the degree of control the organization can exert over this access. Third-party access, like every other type of user access, goes through several distinct phases, starting with requirements, and then moving on to provisioning, and then monitoring, and eventually revocation:

- Understanding requirements for access: scope of access, resources needed, expected duration, and security impact
- Approving access: provisioning user accounts and documenting access grants
- Periodically reviewing access rights
- Removing access: deprovisioning

In addition to the grant/monitor/revoke cycles, consider also the security controls themselves. Privileged third parties often have direct access to an organization's systems via a shared network, extranet, or Internet portal. They may also use, create, or modify upstream or downstream sensitive data. In these cases, it is critical to understand the extent to which third parties implement proper controls. Metrics should attempt to measure whether third parties are implementing the "correct" controls—or, at an even more basic level, whether the organization even knows what the correct controls should be.

To measure the effectiveness of programs for managing third-party access, we need to answer questions that uncover the key performance indicators throughout the life cycle. Thus, metrics ought to answer the following questions:

- How quickly are requests for access by third parties vetted and approved? (Metric: % third-party applicants successfully vetted within service standards)
- Once approval is granted, how quickly can the organization grant access to third-party applicants? (Metric: cycle time to grant, and revoke, customer/partner access to company systems)
- Does the organization understand what security controls are needed for third-party access? (Metric: % strategic partner/third-party agreements with documented security requirements)

- To what extent do third parties implement the correct security controls appropriate to their level of access? (Metrics: % third-party agreements requiring external validation of procedures; % of third parties satisfactorily completing external audits, such as those required by SAS 70)

- How frequently are the access rights of third parties reviewed? (Metric: % third-party users whose privileges reviewed this period)

- Are third-party applications authorized? (Metric: # authorized [and unauthorized] customer/partner transactions, by application)

There are plenty of additional questions one might want to ask. For example, organizations with extremely high needs for compartmentalization, such as the intelligence-gathering or counterespionage departments of national governments, would typically supplement the basic granting/vetting cycle time metrics with an explicit set that measure the effectiveness of security clearance processes. As it happens, the vetting metric is broad enough that it should cover most uses. The key is determining, up front, what service standards an organization requires, and making sure that application and vetting data are captured properly. In many cases, an organization may determine that *no* vetting is required for certain third parties, because of conditions specified in their contracts.

Most of the third-party metrics I have suggested rely on instrumentation that may not exist in many organizations. For example, few companies possess automated work flow software for vetting and approving requests for access, or for measuring access-granting and revocation cycle times. If no work flow software exists, trouble-ticketing software can serve as a substitute, albeit a slightly clumsy one.

Defining third-party "transactions" is more difficult, because they are almost always application-specific. In most cases, organizations need to write custom code to capture the number of units of work performed by third parties on systems they have access to. For a simple website, a page-view could be considered a transaction. For more complex commerce sites, the definition of a "transaction" might instead mean record-insert or change operations. On the plus side, the code required to record transactions need not be very complex. Simple log-parsing utilities will do the trick for static websites. Database-based applications may require more complicated changes, but these need not be invasive. External database monitoring tools, such as those available from vendors such as IPLocks, Guardium, and ASI, can help, too.

MONITORING

In a chapter devoted to measuring control activities, it is not surprising that at some point we would discuss the act of measuring the measurement processes themselves. Abstract as that might seem, that is what this section—metrics for the Monitoring control domain—focuses on.

COBIT defines the Monitoring control domain as governance activities an organization performs to understand how well its processes operate:

> *"All IT processes need to be regularly assessed over time for their quality and compliance with control requirements. This domain addresses performance management, monitoring of internal control, regulatory compliance and providing governance."*[27]

Thus, monitoring processes determine how well the organization's controls work by "instrumenting" oversight functions such as external audit and security assurance. The processes also include measuring the effectiveness of long-running technical monitoring activities over time, like security monitoring tools. Table 4-9 presents representative monitoring metrics.

Table 4-9 Monitoring Metrics

Control Objective	Metric
Monitor the process	% systems with monitored event and activity logs
	% customer-facing and Internet-facing systems with monitored event and activity logs
	% systems monitored for deviations against approved configurations
Monitor and evaluate internal controls	% critical systems reviewed for compliance with controls
	% third-party relationships reviewed for compliance
	% controls working as designed
	% systems with at least one serious deficiency
	Cost of assurance activities, per system
Ensure regulatory compliance	# regulatory audits successfully completed
	# pending audit items, and estimated time/cost to complete
	# pending customer-related audit items, and estimated time/cost to complete

---

[27] Ibid, p. 23.

Control Objective	Metric
	% key external requirements compliant per external audit
	% security compliance reviews with material weaknesses
	Time/cost spent on audit activities
	Time/cost spent on remediation activities

MONITORING THE PROCESS

Organizations wishing to have effective security controls need to monitor critical elements of their infrastructure to detect security events, create alerts, and control changes to their state.

With respect to events and alerts, the increasing popularity of security information management (SIM) systems has greatly enhanced IT's view of security events within their computing environments. By "security event," we mean actions taken whose consequence changes the security state of an actor or information resource: logins/logouts, requests to access restricted information, privilege-granting activities, and the like. Effective security requires that organizations know the sources and consequences of security events as they happen.

Likewise, as mentioned previously, security effectiveness and change control share a natural affinity. A critical component of any effective security program is the process used to monitor information systems for deviations against standards. These standards include not just the defined security policies an organization might have, but also the accepted threshold for controlled change within the organization. Without change controls, security monitoring processes become much less effective.

Therefore, to monitor the effectiveness of monitoring processes, organizations should strive to answer these key questions:

- To what extent does the organization monitor the security of its information systems? (Metric: % systems with monitored event and activity logs)
- Is the organization monitoring systems that contain customer data? (Metric: % customer-facing and Internet-facing systems with monitored event and activity logs)
- To what extent are systems monitored for changes to their configuration? (Metric: % systems monitored for deviations against approved configurations)

For security measurement purposes, we concern ourselves chiefly with determining the extent and span of the security management régime. Thus, these metrics predominantly answer "coverage and control" questions rather than measuring impact or severity of issues found.

MONITORING AND EVALUATING INTERNAL CONTROLS

Monitoring and evaluating system security often centers around assurance activities. Oxford's defines *assurance* as "a positive declaration intended to give confidence; a promise." In the context of information security, then, independent assurance denotes declarations made by third parties that security controls work as advertised. Assurances are another form of "trust but verify" in action.

Not all companies feel they need independent assurance; many companies with deep pockets and a strong security team prefer to perform assurance activities themselves. Probably the most extreme example is the U.S. National Security Agency, which regularly stages electronic war games to test the agency's internal and external defenses. The "Red Team" tries to break in, while defenders try to keep them out.[28]

Few companies possess the wherewithal and dedication to staff their own internal penetration testing teams. Thus, for most organizations independent assurance activities can provide powerful evidence that a company is doing the right thing by its security program. Assurance activities often include nontechnical activities like reviews of process documentation, system walkthroughs, data-center tours, and interviews with systems owners, business units, and IT operations. Technical assurance activities—control testing—commonly include penetration tests and system vulnerability scans. Key questions answered by independent assurance activities, and the metrics related to them, include these:

- On systems for which independent assurance is needed, are security controls working as designed? (Metrics: % critical systems reviewed for compliance with controls, % systems with at least one serious deficiency)

- Are electronic communications with third parties secured from tampering, interception, and attacks? (Metric: % third-party relationships reviewed for compliance)

- How effective is the process for independently testing security controls? (Metric: % controls working as designed)

- How much money is the organization spending on assurance activities? (Metric: cost of assurance activities per system)

Control assurance metrics, in my view, ought to indicate at a high level the relative success or failure of the assurance activities themselves. They need not necessarily include much detail on the actual deficiencies found in particular security controls.

---

[28] In a previous job I worked with several ex-NSA security experts. At one point I attempted to goad one of my colleagues into verifying that the war game defense teams were called the "Blue Team." He turned to me, smiled cryptically, and quietly said, "They are called many things."

The diagnostic metrics such as the ones I described in the preceding chapter can quantify these. A much simpler "threshold" metric, such as the percentage of systems with at least one serious deficiency, should suffice.

ENSURING REGULATORY COMPLIANCE

Most enterprises are subject to regulatory guidelines and statutes:

- Public Company Accounting Reform and Investor Protection Act of 2002 (also known as Sarbanes-Oxley)
- Health Insurance Portability and Accountability Act of 1993 (HIPAA)
- Gramm-Leach-Bliley Financial Services Modernization Act of 1999 (GLBA)

Organizations are also often bound contractually to adhere to certain industry standards such as the Payment Card Industry (PCI) Data Security Standard 1.1.

To comply with regulations and contracts, organizations in many industries typically commission (or find themselves receiving) formal *audits*. In contrast to assurance activities, which target the verification of particular technical controls, audits examine how well an organization implements those controls in compliance with the statute or contract. They also look for evidence of people bypassing controls. Audits differ primarily from assurance activities in that they reside squarely within the legal realm rather than the technical.

A defining characteristic of audits is that in most cases, only certified parties can conduct them. For example, in the case of Sarbanes-Oxley, only public accounting firms that have registered with the Public Company Accounting Oversight Board (PCAOB) are authorized to conduct audits.[29] In practice, this has meant that the largest accounting firms (PricewaterhouseCoopers, Ernst & Young, Deloitte and Touche, and KPMG, often referred to as the "Final Four") and a collection of second-tier firms have garnered the lion's share of Sarbanes-related audit work.

Accountants speak a different language than IT security people. Instead of policies and processes, they speak of "key controls" and "general controls." And instead of vulnerabilities and violations, they refer to "material weaknesses" and "deficiencies." These terms carry special meaning for auditors (and therefore, for company boards of directors).

With respect to IT security, it is not relevant or necessary to understand all of an auditor's terminology. However, organizations should understand the degree of success of

---

[29] Sarbanes-Oxley Act of 2002, Section 109(d).

audit processes overall, and can understand and correct deficiencies that apply to IT security. Thus, when measuring audit processes, try using metrics oriented toward process questions like these:

- How much time and effort are security staff spending on audit-related activities? (Metrics: # regulatory audits completed, time/cost spent on audit activities)

- Have audits uncovered serious weaknesses in existing controls? (Metrics: % security compliance reviews with material weaknesses, % key external requirements compliant per external audit)

- How much time and effort are security staff spending fixing problems uncovered by audits? (Metrics: # pending deficiencies and estimated time/cost to complete, time/cost spent on remediation activities)

- Have audit activities uncovered problems with controls that would affect customer trust or privacy? (Metric: # pending customer-related deficiencies and estimated time/cost to complete)

As with my comments on internal controls, metrics for regulatory compliance need not verge too far into the realm of technical control verification. It is more important that managers understand the nature and kind of effort associated with assisting with audit and compliance activities. Doing so can help with workload planning and staffing, and in many cases can justify technological investments to automate IT security controls.

SUMMARY

In information security, trust is good, but control is better. Security program metrics help organizations understand the performance of their security processes. They underpin the essential process disciplines that companies need to "verify" those things that they already "trust."

Using the COBIT framework as an organizing taxonomy, this chapter presented metrics for measuring processes for four domains:

- **Planning and organization:** Defining strategic security plans, scoping overall program budgets and levels of investment, assessing risk, and managing organizational and human resources

- **Acquisition and implementation:** Identifying, acquiring, developing, and installing security solutions

- **Delivery and support:** Defining service levels; managing internal and third-party access; training end users; handling incidents; and operating programs to secure data, facilities, and operations
- **Monitoring:** Monitoring systems, assessing the effectiveness of security controls, and supporting audit processes

These domains correspond roughly to typical stages in the system development life cycle: strategy, planning, implementation, maintenance, and support.

So that firms do not spend forever and a day boiling the ocean, I recommend that most enterprises simplify certain assumptions about their risk assessment, asset valuation, and accreditation activities. For purposes of program metrics, specific risk scores matter less than the simple act of counting which assets have had risk assessments performed on them. Likewise, until the broader IT world converges on a formula for precisely valuing IT assets, enterprises should use a coarse-grained, Occam's Razor approach—an asset is either critical, or it is not. And finally, regardless of the complexity of an organization's accreditation processes, the metric for measuring the relative penetration of accreditation activities is much simpler: do system owners sign off on the security of their information systems, or not?

Process metrics should measure activities that an enterprise feels are important for promoting correct security behaviors. Security training attempts to encourage certain behaviors, such as "good passwords." These behaviors can be measured with tools like password-breakers and by analyzing physical security data against observed technical behaviors.

Allocating security costs is an important objective for security organizations. Cost allocation is, for most organizations, a black art. Regardless, security organizations should try to associate specific expenditures with business initiatives whenever possible—for example, by estimating built-in security costs during the launch of a new business application. For infrastructure security line items that cut across the organization, like security awareness training, directory synchronization, and antivirus, pro rata allocation to each business unit based on head count represents a fair and transparent method.

Understanding data's direction, magnitude, and sensitivity is an important discipline for information security programs. Security metrics for data should measure the amount of data flowing into and out of the organization. They should also identify the amount of potentially "toxic" data that must be monitored, handled properly, and contained.

Third-party risks require companies to understand the performance of security processes devoted to granting, reviewing, and revoking access to assets by outside parties.

Key metrics include vetting and revocation cycle times, and access rights review frequencies.

Organizations should measure monitoring, internal, and independent audit processes. Key areas for metrics should include understanding the nature and kind of effort related to preparing for and conducting audits, tracking effort related to remediation activities, and measuring the extent of coverage of testing activities. High-level metrics need not necessarily include detail on deficiencies found in particular controls. When simplicity is desired, "threshold" metrics such as the percentage of assets with at least one serious deficiency can serve as an indicator of how widespread security weaknesses might be.

This chapter, and the preceding one, described in colorful detail everything you wanted to know about particular security metrics (but were afraid to ask). If this book were reimagined as a lesson in studio art, these chapters would signify the trip to the art supply store. Specifically, this would be the point at which I roll the shopping cart up to the checkout counter, fully laden with every tube of pigment in the place.

Assuming we wish to make something other than an expensive finger painting, a short course in technique would be nice, wouldn't it? Thus, the next chapters, "Analysis Techniques" and "Visualization," represent the next part of the lesson. The former presents formal methods for analyzing data; the latter shows how to present them in imaginative ways.

Analysis Techniques 5

You are what you are.

—Bill Parcells, on football won/loss records

If the numbers are boring, then you've got the wrong numbers.

—Edward Tufte, *Envisioning Information: Narratives of Space and Time*

As demonstrated in the preceding chapter, organizations seeking to measure their security operations can draw from many potential sources of data, including systems, people, and process controls. So, aren't metrics as simple as collecting data from these sources and letting them speak for themselves? No. In almost every case, analysts need to filter, sort, analyze, or transform the data so that they appear in a useful form. In this chapter, we will talk about some common analytical methods for making data "pop" so that the headlines practically write themselves.

Many companies take the science of data analysis seriously. Earlier in my career I had the privilege of working for a transportation and logistics provider that served as an outsourcing partner for General Motors. We were invited to bid on a piece of business that would have required us, as part of the contract, to store and analyze vast amounts of transportation data. I represented the technical side of the bid team that was summoned to Detroit (and when a supplier deals with General Motors, "summoned" is the operative word).

At the bidders' conference, our hosts at General Motors opened the day by discussing the firm's philosophy toward information analysis—or, properly speaking, toward data warehousing. As our hosts explained, for a data-warehousing program to be successful, one starts with raw data gathered from various sources. Raw data must first be processed into useful *information*. After examining the information, further hard work and analysis yield the ultimate goal: *insight*. Figure 5-1 represents the essential process of developing insight from raw data.

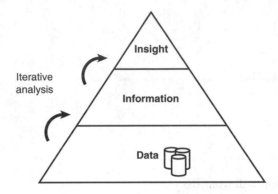

Figure 5-1   Data, Information, and Insight

I do not know whether General Motors invented this concept, but because I have seen it expressed in similar terms in other organizations, I suspect they did not. The origin of the concept is less important, though, than the point that raw data is not enough; one gains insight only through consistent, thoughtful, and iterative analysis. Putting this point a bit differently, George Forrester Colony, the founder of Forrester Research, once stated that any idiot can tell you what something *is*; it is much harder to say what that thing *means*. A corollary for security vendors might be this: when a security vendor pitches you a product that promises "reporting capabilities," expect information but not insight.

This chapter describes several common techniques for analyzing security data:

- Average (arithmetic mean)
- Median
- Standard deviation
- Grouping and aggregation
- Time series analysis
- Cross-sectional analysis

- Quartile analysis
- Correlation matrices

I will describe core concepts of each technique: what they mean and how they are constructed. The techniques themselves are generic and not specific to security. In addition, I will provide some guidance in the form of use cases (situations in which a technique can be used profitably). I will also describe a few "abuse" cases (situations in which the technique might be better left in the toolbag).

The careful, numerate reader will note that few of the statistical techniques covered in this chapter qualify as especially advanced. Most students taking introductory statistics learn these in the first few weeks. This book does not attempt to teach statistics per se; rather, it describes a simple subset of analytical techniques that help show off data in the best possible light—and I hope in a way that should not frighten off prospective analysts or their intended audiences.

MEAN (AVERAGE)

The tried-and-true arithmetic mean (or "average," as it is popularly known) serves as a standard aggregation technique. Means underpin core statistical concepts such as standard deviation, variance, covariance, and correlation, two of which (standard deviation and correlation) I will discuss later in this chapter.

Any reader who has learned elementary pre-algebra knows how to calculate the mean: add up the elements in a data set, and divide by the number of elements in the set. What could be easier than that? Because means (averages) are both easy to calculate and easy to understand, many of the statistics passed off as "metrics" in the popular press tend to be dominated by averages. For example, the annual Computer Security Institute/FBI cyber-crime survey typically includes an "average spending per employee" metric.[1]

Means present problems for several reasons. They often:

- **Obscure richness in the underlying data.** Suppose we see a statistic stating that the "average security spend per employee is $200 for financial services firms." What does this mean? We don't know how well this figure represents spending for, say, a particular investment bank versus a reinsurance company, even though these two types of firms tend to have vastly different attitudes toward security spending. The data set likely contains much more granularity than the mean might otherwise imply.

---

[1] For example, see the 2004 CSI/FBI Computer Crime and Security Survey, which includes statistics, broken down by industry sector, called "Average Reported Computer Security Expenditure/Investment Per Employee."

- **Give a false impression of what is "typical."** Rookie analysts who employ arithmetic means believe that the results ought to imply some sense of what is typical based on the underlying data. But averages distort easily. Two data sets containing {5,5,5,5,5,5} and {0,2,4,6,8,10} both yield a mean of 5—even though the second set varies significantly from the mean. Because most "the average of . . ." statistics presented don't bother to include standard deviations, readers cannot tell how varied the data might be.

For these reasons, means are a poor choice for aggregating highly variegated data sets. They tend to distort or obscure hidden insights and often steamroll over spikes and valleys that an analyst might consider interesting.

That said, arithmetic means are acceptable in certain circumstances when the scope of data represented by the average is narrow. For example, cross-sectional analyses (discussed later in this chapter) often aggregate each subset of the data using arithmetic means. It is perfectly fair, and much more interesting, to compare average spending for, say, small, medium, and large investment banks (and commercial banks, and insurers, and credit card companies . . .) rather than just "financial services" as a whole. In these cases, the sacrifice in analytical rigor is worth it. Readers can easily grasp the context represented by the mean (the scope is sufficiently narrow) and will not scratch their heads, wondering if it glosses over something important.

MEDIAN

As mentioned, most analysts employing arithmetic means do so in an attempt to characterize what is "typical." In many cases, they might have been better off using the *median* rather than the mean.

The median of a data set is the number that separates the top 50% of elements from the bottom, when sorted in order (typically, descending order). In other words, a data set's median indicates the point where half of the elements lie above it and half below. For example, consider the following data set of eleven elements:

Sample Data Set

9	17
22	3
13	25
19	15
23	12
2	

The median of this data set is 15. You can determine this yourself by sorting the numbers and picking the sixth element—15. If you are using a spreadsheet tool such as Excel, you can do this easily using the =MEDIAN(*range*) formula.

Like the arithmetic mean, medians help aggregate data sets into smaller sets by summarizing a range of records. However, medians offer more insight for understanding the "80/20" rule for performance-related data, particularly if outliers at either end of the data set skew the data.

For example, consider a password-auditing tool that determines the number of seconds needed to crack user account credentials. What added value does the statement "It takes 1,344.8 seconds on average to crack 1,000 end-user passwords" provide? Very little. To begin with, the tool output's unit of measure (seconds) has plenty of precision already. Using an arithmetic mean might tempt an analyst to indulge in unnecessary subsecond precision, which is not needed here. Second, suppose the more security-conscious users chose very difficult-to-guess passwords. The time required to crack these might take days, thus skewing the mean sharply upward. Using the median instead of the mean offers better insight into how effective the user passwords are, because it identifies how long it took to break the weakest 50% of them. If the mean time to crack 1,000 passwords was 1,344 seconds, but the median was 822, that would tend to suggest that outliers might have distorted the average and therefore painted a rosier picture.

In short, medians offer some significant advantages over means, particularly with respect to measuring performance.

STANDARD DEVIATION

Standard deviation measures the degree of statistical dispersion of a data set from its mean. Put in plain English, standard deviations tell analysts whether data tend to cluster or are "all over the map." The smaller the standard deviation, the higher the degree of clustering. High standard deviations suggest that the data may be highly irregular or unpredictable.

Mathematically speaking, we calculate standard deviations by first calculating the mean of the data set. Then, for each element in turn, we square the difference between the element and the mean. After adding up the squares of the differences, we divide by the number of elements in the set (or the number of elements minus 1, depending on the implementation). The resulting number, known as the *variance* and symbolized by the Greek letter sigma squared (σ^2), provides a raw measure of dispersion. The square root of the variance produces the result we want, the standard deviation. Sigma (σ) symbolizes the standard deviation.

This may sound complicated, but it really isn't. For example, in the sample data set shown in the preceding section, the mean is 14.54. Table 5-1 works through the standard deviation calculation manually.

Table 5-1 Calculation of Standard Deviation for a Random Data Set (n=11)

Element I	Value (x_i)	Square of Difference from Mean $(x_i - 14.54)^2$
1	2	157.38
2	3	133.30
3	9	30.75
4	12	6.48
5	13	2.39
6	15	0.21
7	17	6.02
8	19	19.84
9	22	55.57
10	23	71.48
11	25	109.30
Sum of squares of differences:		592.73
. . . divided by (number of elements − 1) = variance (σ^2):		59.27
Standard deviation (σ):		7.70

All of this probably sounds like a lot of bother. Fortunately, most mathematical and statistics tools provide a shortcut function to do all this for you. In a spreadsheet such as Excel, the function is =STDDEV(*range*).

Incidentally, when I was learning a bit about statistics, I wondered whether the Greek symbol sigma (σ) bore any relationship to the "Six Sigma" phrase often seen in the quality assurance literature. Indeed, it is the very same sigma. It turns out that standard deviations have some very interesting properties when data sets resemble a typical "bell curve," otherwise known as a *normal distribution* or *Gaussian distribution*. When modeling manufacturing and other processes, manufacturing companies typically assume that defect rates on manufactured goods will follow a pattern that looks like a bell curve.

For normal distributions, the set of data elements that lie within one standard deviation from the mean comprise just over two-thirds of the set (see Figure 5-2). If the range is extended to two standard deviations, the percentage goes up to 95%; for three standard deviations, it is approximately 99.7%. "Six Sigma," then, denotes the percentage of data elements that fall within six standard deviations of the mean—99.9997%. In manufacturing terms, that represents just over three defects per million.

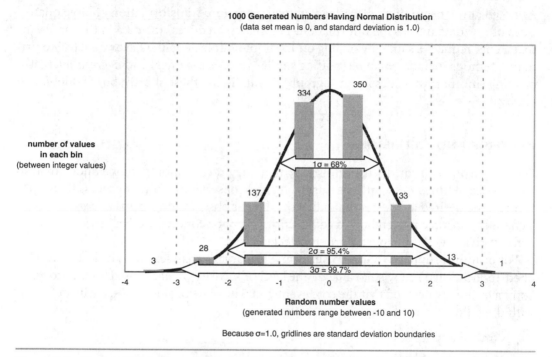

1000 Generated Numbers Having Normal Distribution
(data set mean is 0, and standard deviation is 1.0)

Figure 5-2 Normal Distribution and Standard Deviations

Standard deviations tend to suggest whether the underlying data are relatively sane or crazy. In the example shown in Table 5-1, notice that the standard deviation is fairly large—7.70 suggests that the data points do not cluster to a significant degree around the mean (14.54). In fact, two standard deviations ($7.70 \times 2 = 15.4$) encompass the entire data set! In truth, though, this is not particularly surprising for a small data set. That said, if these data represented a bona fide security process, would the high standard deviation tend to indicate anything unusual? Perhaps. It might make sense to check the data sources and methods of data collection.

Skeptical analysts should always sniff for the standard deviation when reviewing a report or vendor claim that contains arithmetic means. If the author does not provide the standard deviation along with the sample size ("n-size"), be suspicious.

GROUPING AND AGGREGATION

As noted at the beginning of this chapter, metrics require transformation of large quantities of raw data into useful information. The analyst "reduces" the data in the same way that a chef reduces a sauce: by boiling off the liquid but leaving the flavor intact. Two primary methods include *grouping* (putting similar records together) and *aggregation* (calculating summary statistics for each group). I will discuss these shortly, but first let me clarify a few terms.

RECORDS AND ATTRIBUTES

For the purposes of the discussion, assume that any process or data source under analysis has a series of *attributes* worth measuring. A single observation of that process that captures all the desired attributes (including the date of observation) forms a *record*. Generally, most records embody a core security event or concept, such as a security defect, privacy violation, open port, or detected virus.

For example, suppose your firm performs regular risk analyses on its in-house developed applications. You wish to analyze the level of security of all assessed applications. You have already decided that the core event you will be recording is a "security defect" with the following attributes:

- Name of application
- Department of business owner
- Name of defect
- Date detected
- Exploitability (index score; for example, based on CVSS[2])
- Impact if exploited (index score based on asset value)
- Business-adjusted risk (index score; product of exploitability and impact)
- Cost to remediate (estimated engineering hours)

---

[2]   A cross-industry proposed standard, CVSS intends to provide a consistent method of "scoring" the seriousness of computer security vulnerabilities. Coauthors of CVSS include security researchers from Cisco and Qualys.

A sample record (stored in a spreadsheet or relational database) might appear similar to Table 5-2. Table 5-3 shows a sample (if trivial) complete data set containing 27 records from a single quarter (Q1 2005).

Table 5-2 Sample Record (Application Defects)

Attribute	Value
Application	Nantucket
Owner	Accounting
Defect	ICMP ECHO Broadcast Replies Enabled
Date	5-Feb-05
Exploitability	3
Impact	1
BAR	5
Engineering Fix Hours	6

Table 5-3 Sample Data Set (Application Defects)

Date	Application	Owner	Defect	Exploitability	Impact	BAR	Engineering Fix Hours
3-Jan-05	Nantucket	IT	ICMP ECHO broadcast replies enabled	3	1	5	6
3-Jan-05	Nantucket	IT	Open vulnerabilities in third-party software	3	3	9	6
3-Jan-05	Nantucket	IT	Usernames and passwords are written to an unencrypted log file	5	5	25	6
3-Jan-05	Backoffice	Operations	Passwords and credit card numbers are stored unencrypted in the application database	5	2	10	20
6-Jan-05	Antivirus	IT	Viewer key	4	5	20	11
7-Jan-05	Nantucket	IT	Installation of rogue software	1	3	3	6
10-Jan-05	Nantucket	IT	The administrative role does not appropriately restrict account management	2	1	2	6
10-Jan-05	Antivirus	IT	Failed logins reveal too much information	4	4	16	11

continues

Table 5-3   Sample Data Set (Application Defects) (Continued)

Date	Application	Owner	Defect	Exploitability	Impact	BAR	Engineering Fix Hours
10-Jan-05	Redwood	Sales	Strong requirements for account credentials are not being enforced	2	5	10	4
10-Jan-05	eCommerce	Sales	All-or-nothing access to the back end	2	5	10	25
10-Jan-05	Backoffice	Operations	Information is leaked unnecessarily	5	1	5	32
10-Jan-05	Backoffice	Operations	File systems are not mounted with optimal security settings	3	3	9	32
19-Jan-05	Backoffice	Operations	Unauthenticated users can shut down the JRUN server	3	3	9	32
22-Jan-05	Antivirus	IT	Overflow of the InstallDir Registry key	3	3	9	11
10-Feb-05	Nantucket	IT	Acrobat plug-in architecture	5	5	25	6
10-Feb-05	Antivirus	IT	System spoofing	4	5	20	11
10-Feb-05	Redwood	Sales	Application source code is publicly viewable	2	5	10	4
19-Feb-05	Backoffice	Operations	WebLogic and Netscape server processes run as root in a non-chrooted environment	5	5	25	32
22-Feb-05	Redwood	Sales	Sensitive information stored in .inc files	1	5	5	4
22-Feb-05	Backoffice	Operations	TCP sequence numbers are predictable	5	1	5	32
27-Feb-05	Redwood	Sales	EEPROM security settings not enabled	1	5	5	4
27-Feb-05	Backoffice	Operations	Executable stack	5	3	15	32
1-Mar-05	eCommerce	Sales	Network multicasting enabled	3	3	9	25
6-Mar-05	Backoffice	Operations	Memory access	5	3	15	32
14-Mar-05	Backoffice	Operations	Internal attack on the EDS-hosted server	5	3	15	32
14-Mar-05	Backoffice	Operations	Default IIS extension mappings	1	5	5	20
24-Mar-05	Backoffice	Operations	Authorization of administrative users is not strictly enforced	5	3	15	32

GROUPING

After collecting the data for the desired observation periods, the first step involves deciding how to group the records. For the purposes of this discussion, *grouping* means placing together all the records within a particular scope of analysis, such as by department

("Sales," "Operations"). That is, if you sorted the data set by the group's attributes, all the records in the group would follow each other.

Groupings should include any attributes that could serve as a unit of measure. It is useful to fast-forward to the exhibit: do you expect to present numbers as being "per" something? For example, we may wish to express statistics on a "per-application" or "per-department" basis. If so, you should group on these attributes. In addition, with time-series analyses (see the next main section) one typically groups on broad time intervals such as month or quarter.

AGGREGATION

Once the analyst groups the records, the next step is *aggregation*: consolidating the records into summary statistics for each group. When creating a "summary statistic," for all records in each group we perform one or more of the following operations on each attribute and include the results in the output set:

- Sum
- Mean
- Standard deviation
- Highest
- Lowest
- Count

In most cases, aggregation typically involves summing or averaging numeric attributes and counting nonnumeric ones. This allows us to reduce the number of records while preserving valuable information about each group.

How do you know if you have grouped and aggregated correctly? Here is a good rule of thumb: examine the nonnumeric record attributes. Would combining any two records force you to merge or drop any of these attributes (because they cannot be summed or counted)? If so, consider grouping on the nonnumeric attributes as well. If, upon consideration, you realize that you do not need the subgroups, you should simply count the number of unique instances instead, or drop the attribute.

Consider the data set shown in Table 5-3. A simple aggregation strategy for this data set might be the following:

- Name of application: COUNT UNIQUE
- Department of business owner: COUNT UNIQUE
- Name of defect: COUNT UNIQUE

- Date detected: DROP
- Exploitability (index score; for example, based on CVSS[3]): MEAN and STANDARD DEVIATION
- Impact if exploited (index score based on asset value): MEAN and STANDARD DEVIATION
- Business-adjusted risk (index score; product of exploitability and impact): MEAN and STANDARD DEVIATION
- Cost to remediate (estimated engineering hours): MEAN and STANDARD DEVIATION

Ignoring the time/date aspect for a minute, because the data set is small we can calculate statistics using just a few spreadsheet formulas: =COUNTA(*range*), =AVERAGE(*range*), and =STDEV(*range*). Table 5-4 contains the results. A more sophisticated strategy might group by department, or by application, rather than simply aggregate them.

Table 5-4   Aggregation Example (Application Defects)

Attribute	Aggregate Value		
	Count	Mean	Standard Deviation
Applications	5	—	—
Owners	3	—	—
Defects	27	—	—
Exploitability	—	3.4	1.5
Impact	—	3.5	1.5
BAR	—	11.5	6.8
Engineering Fix Hours	—	17.6	11.9

Notice how we aggregated the nonnumeric attributes: by counting them. In addition to aggregating these records, we could have grouped them first by department. That would have produced three sets of aggregate results (one for each group).

---

[3] A cross-industry proposed standard, CVSS intends to provide a consistent method of "scoring" the seriousness of computer security vulnerabilities. Coauthors of CVSS include security researchers from Cisco and Qualys.

For larger data sets, simple formulas will not do. If the data set is small enough, an Excel PivotTable should work fine. Figure 5-3 shows a sample configuration screen that produces results equivalent to those in Table 5-4.

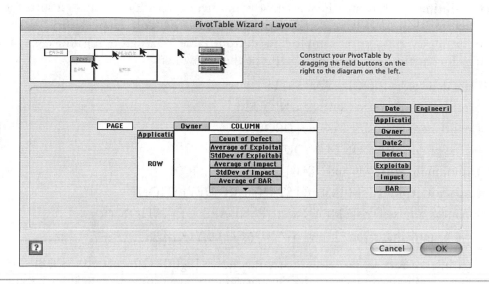

Figure 5-3 PivotTable Example (Application Defects)

For large data sets, consider more sophisticated tools such as SAS, SPSS, or a business analysis tool combined with relational database storage. That said, for most casual data analyses spreadsheets provide plenty of headroom, especially when the process for calculating metrics is neither regular nor automated.

Time series analyses, quartile analyses, and correlation matrices rely heavily on grouping and aggregation techniques. Discussions on these techniques follow.

TIME SERIES ANALYSIS

Time series analysis refers to the technique of attempting to understand how a set of data behaves over time. More specifically, a *time series* contains a series of observations for a particular attribute, measured at regular intervals; the analysis refers to the steps taken to measure performance over that interval.

Time series are generally grouped and aggregated by a desired *analysis interval*. The interval should be sufficiently precise that it lends insight, but not so precise that the detail overwhelms the reader. For example, with relatively infrequently collected metrics such as application security defects, monthly or quarterly intervals make sense. In fact, most security metrics worth measuring do not require more precision than this.

Thus, the first step involves grouping and aggregating all the records within the desired interval of time, be it by month, quarter, or year. After aggregation, the analyst sorts the result set by date, generally in ascending order so that earlier entries appear first.

For example, consider the sample data set from Table 5-3. A grouping and aggregation strategy for the time-series analysis might be the following:

- Date detected: GROUP BY MONTH
- Name of application: COUNT UNIQUE
- Department of business owner: DROP
- Name of defect: COUNT UNIQUE
- Exploitability: MEAN and STANDARD DEVIATION
- Impact if exploited: MEAN and STANDARD DEVIATION
- Business-adjusted risk: MEAN and STANDARD DEVIATION
- Cost to remediate: MEAN and STANDARD DEVIATION

Aggregating the data set produces the results shown (lightly reformatted) in Table 5-5. Note that Excel requires a little extra persuasion to create a suitable PivotTable because it does not know how to group dates into month intervals. But an inserted column whose cells provide the "group name" (such as a formula that generates a text string containing the year, followed by the month) works well.

Table 5-5   Time Series Analysis (Application Defects)

Metric	Jan-05	Feb-05	Mar-05
Defects	14	8	5
Mean Exploitability	3.2	3.5	3.8
StdDev of Exploitability	1.3	1.9	1.8
Mean Impact	3.1	4.3	3.4
StdDev of Impact	1.5	1.5	0.9
Mean BAR	10.1	13.8	11.8
StdDev of BAR	6.4	8.8	4.6
Mean Engineering Fix Hours	14.9	15.6	28.2
StdDev of Engineering Fix Hours	11	13.8	5.5

Cursory examination of the data suggests several key "headlines":

- The number of security defects identified declined from 14 to 5, suggesting that application security improved overall during the period.

- Although the overall number of defects decreased, those detected in later periods were of higher impact and were slightly easier to exploit (3.1 average impact in January increased to 3.4 in March; 3.2 exploitability increased to 3.8).

- The amount of engineering time required to fix defects increased over time (from 14.9 to 28.2), as did the standard deviations of the estimates. This in turn suggests that the easy-to-fix problems were likely fixed early; estimates for the remaining, harder problems have become more consistent over time.

This example, of course, is a cooked one, and alternative explanations for the results exist. But it is always a good idea to examine the numbers; what you find might surprise you!

Time series analysis is an essential tool in the security analyst's bag of tricks. It provides the foundation for other types of analysis. When combined with cross-sectional analysis and quartile analysis, it provides the basis for benchmarking.

CROSS-SECTIONAL ANALYSIS

If time-series analysis attempts to understand how an attribute varies over time, cross-sectional analysis asks how the data vary over a cross section of comparable observations. That is, if we "slice" a set of records by a particular attribute, what happens to the other attributes? The idiom "comparing apples to apples" applies here.

Cross-sectional analysis involves three steps. First, the analyst selects an attribute to use for creating the cross section—that is, an attribute to slice with. Typically, textual attributes such as department, industry, or categories make good cross-sectional attributes. After selecting a suitable attribute, the analyst groups and aggregates the data. Finally, the real fun begins: analyzing the results.

For example, consider the sample data set from Table 5-3. Suppose we want to analyze the performance of each department. Using the owner attribute as the cross-sectional attribute, a suitable grouping and aggregation strategy for the cross-series analysis might look like this:

- Department of business owner: GROUP
- Name of application: COUNT UNIQUE PER GROUP
- Name of defect: COUNT UNIQUE PER GROUP

- Date detected: DROP
- Exploitability: MEAN and STANDARD DEVIATION
- Impact if exploited: MEAN and STANDARD DEVIATION
- Business-adjusted risk: MEAN, STANDARD DEVIATION, and SUM
- Cost to remediate: MEAN and STANDARD DEVIATION

In addition to these items, we also wish to calculate two other summary statistics: MEAN DEFECTS PER APPLICATION and MEAN BAR PER APPLICATION. Both of these metrics help us understand how well each department writes code: the average number of defects per application, and a relative measure (BAR) of the mean aggregate risk carried by each. But wait, you protest: aren't averages a bad idea? Not in this case; the scope of the subset of records is sufficiently narrow that readers should be able to grasp the context easily.

Grouping and aggregating the data set produces the results shown (lightly reformatted) in Table 5-6. Excel PivotTables, by the way, are not quite sufficient to produce all the data we need. In particular, Excel cannot properly produce the result rows for "Applications" (count unique), "Mean Defects Per Application" (for each owner, divide applications by defects) and "Mean BAR Per Application" (for each owner, divide BAR by defects). I have calculated these statistics manually.

Table 5-6   Cross-Sectional Analysis (Application Defects)

	IT	Operations	Sales
Applications*	2	1	2
Defects	10	11	6
Mean Defects Per Application*	5	11	3
Sum of BAR	134	128	49
Mean BAR Per Application*	67	128	24.5
Mean Exploitability	3.4	4.3	1.8
StdDev of Exploitability	1.3	1.3	0.8
Mean Impact	3.5	2.9	4.7
StdDev of Impact	1.6	1.3	0.8
Mean BAR	13.4	11.6	8.2

	IT	Operations	Sales
StdDev of BAR	8.9	6.1	2.5
Mean Engineering Fix Hours	8	29.8	11
StdDev of Engineering Fix Hours	2.6	4.9	10.8

What interesting headlines pop out of the cross-sectional analysis? Several things should seem fairly obvious:

- Operations appears to be worst off, based on the number of defects per application (11) and the risk carried by each (BAR score of 128). Compare this to Sales, whose applications contained just three (on average) and a BAR score 80% lower (24.5).

- In addition to having fewer defects per application overall, Sales' defects tended to be consistently less serious. Note how the Sales department's mean BAR per defect (8.2) was considerably less than those of Operations (11.6) and IT (13.4) and had a lower standard deviation (2.5 versus 6.1 and 8.9).

- Although IT sits between Operations and Sales with respect to average defects and BAR scores, its defects tended to require the least amount of engineering time to fix (8 hours compared to 29.8 and 11). This suggests that IT has more "quick hit" opportunities and may have more potential to improve its scores in the future relative to its peers.

Trivial though this example may seem, it should demonstrate to you that cross-sectional techniques provide a powerful way to compare security effectiveness by organization, security topic, or other attributes. One could certainly improve on the example. For instance, suppose the sample data set contained an attribute that classified each security defect (such as authentication, encryption, and user input validation). A cross-sectional analysis might compare the incidence rate by department for each type of defect. Managers could use knowledge of the "trouble spots" to better target developer training. Departments could also "compare notes" and share knowledge of best practices.

This last point bears repeating: one of the main benefits of cross-sectional analysis is *discussion*. Because cross-sectional analyses naturally highlight differences in outcomes based on certain factors, people will want to know *why* the differences exist. That is what humans tend to do—attempt to explain things they do not initially understand. The need to explain typically leads to a discussion of root causes—and from there, people will want to discuss solutions.

QUARTILE ANALYSIS

Of all the techniques described in this chapter, quartile analysis may be the most power-ful. Quartile analysis is an old management consulting technique. I learned about it much later than the previous techniques I have mentioned, and even then, almost entirely by accident. I was reading an article in the *McKinsey Quarterly* about e-commerce website performance measurement,[4] and the article's use of the technique was a revelation to me.

Quartile analysis shares several traits in common with cross-sectional analysis. The two techniques require the analyst to select a collection of attributes to examine. For both techniques, the analyst must identify a suitable grouping and aggregation strategy. And finally, in both cases insight springs directly from the contrasts uncovered by attribute-by-attribute comparisons.

In contrast to a pure cross-sectional analysis, which considers all records in the aggre-gated result set equally, quartile analysis takes an extra step and, for each attribute based on the desired sort order, ranks the results into four "bins" or *quartiles* (hence the name). The first quartile represents the best 25%, the second quartile cuts off the best 50%, and the third quartile cuts off the top 75%. The fourth quartile represents the worst 25% in the result set.

In case you were wondering, the top and bottom 50% are divided by—wait for it—the median! The *top quartile* separates the first and second quartile; you can think of it as another median between the first element and the median. The *bottom quartile* divides the third and fourth quartiles.

Let us see how this works for a single attribute using a sample data set of sixteen ran-dom numbers. Figure 5-4 shows an unordered set on the left, and on the right, the same set after ranking into quartiles.

By ranking each attribute into quartiles, the analyst gains a broad understanding of which "buckets" each record falls into: best, worst, or somewhere in between.

---

4   V. Agrawal, L. D. Arjona, and R. Lemmens, "E-Performance: The Path to Rational Exuberance," *The McKinsey Quarterly* (2001), Number 1.

Unsorted ➝ Arranged into quartiles

```
98          98
 8          90   First
38          89
48          89
33          ————————————————— top quartile
89          87
86          86   Second
90          84
 5          80
32          ————————————————— median
46          48
84          46   Third
89          38
24          33
87          ————————————————— bottom quartile
80          32
            24
             8   Fourth
             5
```

Figure 5-1   Sample Quartile Data

QUARTILE SUMMARY STATISTICS

If you want to understand how a specific data record ranks relative to others in the set, the analytical process I have just described works well. But for analysts seeking to understand more macro-level behavior, we add another level of refinement: quartile summary statistics. Put simply, after the data are ranked into quartiles, a final aggregation step calculates metrics for the quartile as a whole. Typically, the arithmetic mean works well as a metric. Summary statistics provide excellent insight into how well each quartile is performing relative to the others.

For example, a few years ago I coauthored a study of network security defects based on the hundreds of clients my firm had assessed. One of our signature exhibits included the quartile summary data shown in Table 5-7.

Table 5-7   Quartile Analysis of Network Vulnerability Data[5]

	First Quartile	Second Quartile	Third Quartile	Fourth Quartile
Network Vulnerability Count	5.5	7.75	16.67	65.3
Network BAR Index	25.5	57.3	96	313

[5]   Sample exhibit data from unreleased study by A. Jaquith, K. J. Soo Hoo, @stake, Inc., 2002.

Notice how the table nicely summarizes how the four quartiles of clients performed relative to each other for both vulnerability counts and BAR index scores. Now *that* is macro-level behavior.

FIRST-VERSUS-FOURTH ANALYSES

Quartile summary statistics "cluster" performers with similar characteristics into a small, discrete set of buckets. As such, quartile statistics possess a great deal of analytical power and play an important role in benchmarking.

Sometimes, though, management does not want to analyze all the data—they simply want to make decisions. First-versus-fourth-quartile analysis—that is, discarding the middle two quartiles—permits extremely rapid conclusions to be made based on the data at hand. Discarding the middle quartiles sharpens the contrast significantly by focusing on the outliers; the message comes back reflected as if through a fun-house mirror.

For example, the data from Table 5-7 reveal vast disparities between the first and fourth quartiles: nearly twelve times the network vulnerabilities, and an even larger differential in business-adjusted risk. When presenting first-and-fourth analyses across a large number of attributes (for example, six, ten, or more), root causes pop out almost immediately. In almost all cases, healthy discussions—and action plans—follow the presentation.

I discuss graphical examples of first-versus-fourth analyses in the next chapter.

CORRELATION MATRICES

So far, the methods presented in this chapter have focused on reducing, aggregating, grouping, and summarizing large data sets into smaller, bite-sized nuggets of insight for management. Some of the latter techniques, particularly quartile analysis, help analysts understand implicit relationships between attributes—that is, how each attribute influences the others. However, these techniques tell us nothing *explicit* about the relationships. For instance, do instances of higher security defect rates in software correlate with the amount of time spent assessing the code base?

Understanding the explicit relationships between attributes helps analysts uncover hidden patterns in data. Strictly speaking, the statistical concept of *covariance* refers to the tendency of one set of values to move with (or in the opposite direction of) another set.[6] The related concept of *correlation* normalizes the covariance number to a scale

---

6   For an accessible explanation of covariance, see Wolfram Research's public website: http://mathworld.wolfram.com/Covariance.html.

ranging from −1 (the two sets move in the exact opposite direction relative to each other) to +1 (the sets move perfectly together).[7] A correlation of 0 indicates that the two data sets have no apparent relationship to each other. Note that a highly positive correlation between two data sets need not imply a cause-and-effect relationship; it simply means that the two sets move together. I will not get into the math behind covariance and correlation; you need only remember that these concepts measure how strongly two data sets relate.[8]

Figure 5-5 illustrates three pairs of data sets that are, respectively, positively, weakly, and negatively correlated with each other. The chart on the left shows two attributes that are moderately correlated (0.52); you can see how the X and Y values move together. The chart on the right shows the opposite: the X and Y values move in opposite directions (−0.64). The middle chart shows two attributes that have no apparent relationship (0.06).

Knowing how well two data sets correlate is a fine way of understanding the relationship between two attributes. Security attributes, however, do not just come in pairs. Most analysts want to explore relationships between more than one pair of attributes at a time. For this, we need a correlation matrix.

Correlation matrices provide a structured and compact way to analyze many pairs of attributes at once. They help analysts understand which variables tend to move together, without needing to know up front which pairs to look at. A correlation matrix is a simple grid, typically hand-implemented in a spreadsheet that correlates each attribute with every other. That is, for every attribute n, the grid contains a row of cells containing the formula =CORREL($range_n$, $range_{1\ldots m}$), where m represents the number of attributes under test.

For example, imagine that We Hunt Bugs LLP, an application security consultancy, wishes to understand prevailing patterns and trends with its client engagements. The company has kept a scrupulous record of each engagement's defect statistics. The defects database's record attributes include:

---

[7] For an accessible explanation of correlation, see Wolfram Research's public website: http://mathworld.wolfram.com/StatisticalCorrelation.html.

[8] Securitymetrics.org colleague Chris Walsh, who has a deeper statistical background in statistics than I, points out that correlation measures bivariate relationships where the data sets are both on linear scales. He urges readers to note that "correlation is appropriate for linear relationships. Where a relationship is logarithmic, it can lead you to mistakenly think that the variables are much more weakly related than they are."

- Assessment contract value
- Assessment duration
- Assessment effort
- Number of defects found
- Mean risk score
- Mean impact score
- Business-adjusted risk (BAR) score
- Number of full-time equivalents (FTEs) performing assessment
- Defects found per FTE

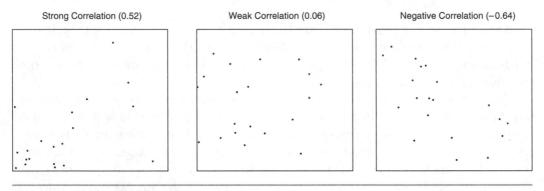

Figure 5-5   Strong, Weak, and Negative Correlation

We would like to understand whether any of these attributes relate with each other in any way, to uncover patterns and detect potential sources of bias. To do this, we construct a correlation matrix with a cell entry for each attribute vertically arrayed on the left side of the grid. The same cell entries are repeated in a horizontal array across the bottom. At each intersection point on the grid, the formula $=CORREL(range_x, range_y)$ calculates the correlation between the attributes. Note that a range always correlates perfectly (1.0) with itself, so the matrix need not include these intersections. Ditto for the upper-right intersections above the diagonal, because correlations are commutative—$CORREL(range_a, range_b)$ equals $CORREL(range_b, range_a)$.

Table 5-8 displays the correlation matrix for a sample data set (which, by the way, derives from a real example). Note that for the reader's convenience, the darker shaded text highlights the strongly correlated attributes; the lightly shaded text, strong negative correlations.

Table 5-8 Correlation Matrix Example

	Duration	Effort (Days)	Contract Value	Number of Findings	Mean Risk Score	Mean Impact Score	BAR	Number of FTEs
Duration								
Effort (Days)	0.84							
Contract Value	0.82	0.78						
Number of Findings	0.11	0.10	0.19					
Mean Risk Score	−0.02	−0.13	−0.17	0.00				
Mean Impact Score	−0.28	−0.20	−0.29	−0.22	0.03			
BAR	0.02	0.01	0.06	0.89	0.28	0.02		
Number of FTEs	0.13	0.62	0.26	0.09	0.20	−0.03	0.05	
Findings Per FTE	0.06	−0.13	0.05	0.90	0.16	−0.20	0.85	0.75

Notice how certain attributes correlate with others. Duration, effort, and contract value strongly correlate, as one would expect. The number of findings strongly correlate with the BAR score. Nothing shocking so far, right? Look closer. Two things should surprise you.

First, there appears to be only a very small correlation (0.11) between the number of findings and engagement duration. This *might* suggest that the client applications exhibited a wide range of defects and levels of code quality. However, an alternate explanation exists. The lack of correlation could simply mean that longer testing yields no extra benefit in terms of the number of defects found!

Second, there appears to be no correlation (0.09) between the number of consultants (FTEs) on an engagement and the number of defects found. This implies that there may not be any extra benefit to a large assessment team; a small team with a core of highly skilled consultants should suffice.

Correlation matrices help validate the data analysis by discovering attribute relationships. As Table 5-8 shows, they can help validate assumptions in the data-gathering process—or debunk them. To provide an extra level of analytical rigor, analysts should get into the habit of making correlation matrices part of their repertoire.

SUMMARY

Metrics start life as raw data, refine themselves into information, and, when presented in the correct analytical contexts, manifest themselves as insight. Analytical techniques are essential to finding the insights that hide inside your data. The analyst's toolbag includes:

- **Average** (**arithmetic mean**), a simple method of understanding the central tendency of a data set. It is calculated by summing all items and then dividing by the number of items in the set.

- **Median**, which identifies the member in a data set at the 50% percentile.

- **Standard deviation**, which quantifies how dispersed a data set tends to be relative to its mean. Data with smaller standard deviations tend to be clustered tightly around their mean, whereas those with high standard deviations are "all over the map."

- **Grouping**, which collects all data records in a set that share a common attribute, such as a category name, department, or defect type.

- **Aggregation**, which calculates statistics on a grouped set of records, such as the sum, mean, standard deviation, minimum, or maximum.

- **Time series analysis**, which shows a series of values juxtaposed over time so that analysts can understand how they vary over the period of observation.

- **Cross-sectional analysis**, which aggregates and contrasts groups in a data set. Each "cross section" or group is compared with all others, which throws the differences between each in sharp relief.

- **Quartile analysis**, a technique that rank-orders a data set by a single attribute, such as risk score, and then divides the data set into four groups, each of which contains 25% of the records. The top 25% of the records are known as the first quartile; the bottom 25% are the fourth. Aggregated statistics between the first and fourth quartiles are almost always dramatic and revealing.

- **Correlation matrices** allow analysts to understand which attributes in a data set move together by calculating a matrix of correlations between pairs of attributes. The matrix allows an analyst to quickly spot two factors that may be related.

Using techniques such as these, analysts can examine large data sets and quickly spot patterns. Spreadsheets can support the basic analysis needs, but for larger data, tools such as SAS and SPSS work much better.

Data analysis techniques help analysts isolate the most important messages that hide within data sets. Once these key insights pop out, they must be presented in the best possible light. Chapter 6, "Visualization," shows how to graphically depict data in effective ways.

Visualization

One picture is worth ten thousand words.

—Fred R. Barnard (1927)

Graphic design which evokes the symmetria of Vitruvius,
the dynamic symmetry of Hambidge,
the asymmetry of Mondrian;
which is a good gestalt,
generated by intuition
or by computer,
by invention
or by a system of coordinates,
is not good design
if it does not communicate.

—Paul Rand (1985)

Security is such a complex topic that it defies easy description. In addition to the natural camouflage afforded the subject by its often-esoteric terminology and concepts, the sheer scope and volume of available security data overwhelms practitioners and laypeople alike. Because of these two facts, most information security professionals have no real idea how to "show security," either literally or figuratively.

It is fair to say that one of the reasons security professionals have so much difficulty dealing with their bosses is because they lack simple and clean metaphors for communicating priorities. Astute analysts recognize—correctly—that visual representations can dramatically enhance managers' abilities to understand security issues. Unfortunately, few analysts have received any formal training on the subject of presentation graphics or (more generally) graphic design. In addition, product vendors generally provide poor or inflexible graphical reporting tools.

This chapter is all about how to get your point across—that is, how to present your hard-won data in a clean and elegant manner that informs, illustrates, and illuminates.

In my view, information security urgently needs fresh thinking about data visualization. Most of what passes for information graphics in the security field generally takes one of two tired forms:

- **Simple bar and pie charts** showing samples of a single coarse-grained metric, such as the number of vulnerabilities found on BugTraq or the number of undesirable e-mails caught by an organization's spam engine
- **Traffic lights** that show the "health" of a range of analysis topics, typically built by hand-coloring reds, yellows, and greens into a grid or thermometer bulb

I find both of these approaches problematic. Bar and pie charts tend to be graphically inefficient; pie charts in particular take up a great deal of space relative to the number of distinct data points they show. In addition, they tend to include only a single metric or data range, rather than (for instance) juxtaposing several ranges.

Traffic lights are worse, because they oversimplify issues too much. In the same way that arithmetic means dilute important points by steamrolling over the outliers (see Chapter 5, "Analysis Techniques"), traffic lights obscure the variation, exception, and detail that lead to insight and smart decision-making.

"But wait," wail fans of traffic lights. "Senior management likes nice graphics. They want something simple. They don't understand the rarefied world of information security. If we give them anything more complicated, they won't understand it!" A former colleague of mine once made a statement like this to me, apparently seriously. I have met many information security professionals who agree with him. But the statement is pure rubbish, and arguably condescending. Want proof that the boss is not a simpleton? Consider a typical stock index chart in the *Wall Street Journal* or *New York Times*. Most charts of the Dow Jones Industrial Index contain these features:

- A time-based horizontal axis, often the last 30 trading days
- High, low, and closing positions for the dates in the range

- Trading volumes for each day in the range
- Often, a 30-day moving average

Doing the math: 4 data points per day, times 30 days, equals 120 pieces of data. These data appear in a compact, two-or-three-square-inch graphic. The boss understands this quite well, thank you very much. Compare this to a traffic light graph that shows exactly *one* data point that is neither accurate nor precise, or with the low-resolution "DefCon"-style bar charts espoused by the likes of Symantec[1] and ISS[2].

As an industry, we can do better than simple pie charts and traffic lights. We need to treat viewers of security metrics data—managers, regulators, and the general public—with more respect. In this case, "respect" means recognizing that intelligent people can, with a minimal amount of training, learn powers of discernment that go beyond nodding and smiling at low-resolution, brain-damaged exhibits.

We need to think of graphically representing metrics as an information visualization challenge, not simply as a "reporting issue." The term "information visualization" is relatively new to the business landscape. Broadly defined, it refers to the practice of using high-resolution graphics and related exhibits to display sets of data, particularly when the sets are large. If the analytical techniques reviewed in the preceding chapter describe ways to uncover patterns in data, information visualization provides methods of showing them off to maximum effect. Visualization concerns include composition, color, typography, arrangement, and use of space (both positive and negative).

Many readers might perk up their ears here and say, "Ah, so you mean making charts!" Yes and no: while information visualization does indeed often mean creating charts, these are means but not ends. Charts are often one part of the larger process of carefully evaluating the best way to present the information at hand.

As mentioned previously, this chapter discusses ways to graphically show off data to their best advantage, without losing the richness and texture that best facilitate deep understanding. Unfortunately, some of the most compelling examples described in this chapter cannot be easily reproduced with standard off-the-shelf office productivity packages. In these cases, I'll describe ways to create the exhibits yourself using custom tools.

A warning to the reader: as if you could not tell already, this chapter is heavily flavored with the strong tastes of my own opinions. If the taste seems excessively bitter, that is because I find more affinity with the aesthetic tastes of graphic designers and high-end management consultants than those of information security vendors and professionals.

---

[1] Symantec DeepSight™ Threat Management System, http://tms.symantec.com.

[2] Internet Security Systems AlertCon™, https://gtoc.iss.net/issEn/delivery/gtoc/index.jsp.

A relative latecomer to security, in my early years I was part of a business team that contracted Boston Consulting Group (BCG) for a seven-figure management consulting engagement. Believe me, several million dollars buys you a hell of a lot of management-grade graphical excellence. Since then, I have been a fan of the management consulting "house style" in general, and of McKinsey & Company in particular. Certain business magazines strongly influence my worldview, notably *The Economist*. Needless to say, the sophistication of visualization used by the organizations I have just listed could not be more different from the sorts of things we have been seeing in information security lately.

This chapter contains three major sections:

- Design principles—six basic rules to live by
- Guidelines for various exhibit formats—theory and practice for sixteen ways to visualize security data
- Thinking like a cannibal—three real-life examples showing how to rework existing exhibits

DESIGN PRINCIPLES

Before diving into the fun bits (the graphics!), I'd like to lay down some fundamental design principles that will help you create high-impact exhibits. These principles apply equally to all charting and data analysis packages: Microsoft Excel, Keynote, SAS, SPSS, JFreeChart, and others. However, the most common tool used for prototyping business graphics is the spreadsheet. What I am about to say will make the most sense to readers in that context. You can also apply these principles to automated exhibit generation, too, although I leave that as an exercise for the reader.

Generally speaking, mainstream software packages do not serve the cause of information visualization well. The default chart exhibits produced by spreadsheets are far too loud, colorful, and needlessly decorative. Excess chart bloat buries data in an avalanche of shininess, tick marks, unnecessary grids, irrelevant backgrounds, and other foolish bits of graphical frippery. But wisdom, as P.J. O'Rourke one put it, is "knowing the difference between *can't* and *shouldn't*." Just because an analyst can use a program to pollute charts with distracting visual noise does not mean it is a good idea to do so.

This chapter does not attempt furnish a treatise in graphic design. Others, notably the great Edward Tufte, have written beautifully and extensively on the subject already. You should, instead, see this chapter as a summary of effective presentation principles—part *Envisioning Information*, part *How to Lie With Statistics*.

Effective visualization of metrics data boils down to six principles:

- It is about the data, not the design
- Just say no to three-dimensional graphics and cutesy chart junk
- Don't go off to meet the wizard
- Erase, erase, erase
- Reconsider Technicolor
- Label honestly and without contortions

Following these six principles will result in exhibits that are clean, clear, and visually attractive. Let us start with the first one.

IT IS ABOUT THE DATA, NOT THE DESIGN

Good information visualization is like good graphic design. If the reader does not notice anything amiss, it succeeds: the audience pays attention to the data, not the decoration. But if the reader sees something that prompts a gawk or a head-scratch, the exhibit design may be overwhelming the data.

Data should stand on their own, without extra supporting props or bangles. Forcefully and reflexively check any urges to "dress up the data."

JUST SAY NO TO THREE-DIMENSIONAL GRAPHICS AND CUTESY CHART JUNK

I have never understood the fascination with three-dimensional pie and bar charts. I am continually astounded at how otherwise respectable security software companies insist on shipping reporting modules that sport ridiculous, gratuitous 3-D graphics. Unless your professional duties include preparing exhibits for the Department of Energy's nuclear weapons simulation program, few conceivable data sets genuinely merit a 3-D exhibit.

Simple, clean, "flat" charts make the same points a faux 3-D chart does, but with less ink. Certainly, ordinary bar charts and pie charts do not require them; the artificial depth only distracts the viewer from the data.

Recent versions of Microsoft's ubiquitous Excel spreadsheet software allow users to add photographs and flashy wallpapers to the backgrounds of charts or to the colored portions of area charts. Avoid these unless the exhibit serves some theatrical purpose. For example, a flashy photo background might feel right at home as part of a sales-oriented slide deck containing scads of music and the obligatory slide transitions. Nobody will take the exhibit seriously anyway, so the extra flash will not matter. But for situations in which the presenter intends to inform, persuade, or present results of analyses, charts should use white or translucent backgrounds and should omit 3-D.

DON'T GO OFF TO MEET THE WIZARD

Thanks to the profusion of "wizards," "assistants," talking paper clips, and other assorted digital menservants, modern desktop applications have made it easier than ever to create incredibly busy and tasteless graphics. It *is* helpful that Excel's wizards speed users through the process of selecting data series, titling charts, and labeling axes. However, the results disgorged at the end are, at best, overeager. Even the humblest line chart is festooned with a Technicolor palette, distracting axis tick marks, unnecessary grid lines, and a drab gray background. All these aspects distract the reader from the data.

An additional downside is that Excel's default layout wizards produce a particular, immediately recognizable style, one that screams "amateur"! (For me, spotting Excel punters is an admittedly snobbish, and slightly guilty, pleasure.) Use digital menservants carefully, and only as a starting point for exhibits. Generally speaking, graphics created for all but the most casual personal uses require cleanup.

ERASE, ERASE, ERASE

Most charts produced by desktop software default settings contain a profusion of superfluous ticks, grid lines, plot frames, and chart frames. There is a good reason why most mainstream business publications use them sparingly: they look clumsy, and they distract attention from the data. You can eliminate all these ornaments without losing any meaning. In fact, your chart will look cleaner as a result.

The general rule: *if you do not need it, erase it.* Start getting into the habit of eliminating the tick marks immediately after creating a chart. Generally this involves formatting the axes with "No major tick marks" and "No minor tick marks." Likewise, eliminate the plot frame and chart frame by formatting each with "No border." These are not needed; the axis lines provide all the framing the chart needs. For bar charts, eliminate the enclosing borders for the bars; the bars themselves provide all the information needed.

Grid lines are trickier. Although I usually erase them, they do have appropriate uses. For sparse exhibits in which subtle comparisons are neither possible nor desirable, omitting the grid eliminates visual noise without sacrificing readability. For dense exhibits containing large data series, however, muted grid lines help readers compare individual data points. When using grid lines, always draw them in a light color (20 to 25% gray) or in black as sparse dots. They should not intrude on the data and should sit in the background.

In fact, other than those required to plot the data, good charts contain no lines other than the x- and y-axes, and (perhaps) some muted grid lines. Even the axis lines can be muted further: try choosing a thin line (1-point) and softer color (50% gray).

The cumulative effect of these erasures results in a crisp chart with few distracting lines. Although my recommendations may seem Spartan—severe, even—the results are worth it.

Reconsider Technicolor

Make no mistake—when used judiciously and appropriately, color can add tremendous depth and richness to charts and graphs. The eye's ability to make sense of, and discern between, wide ranges of colors is one of the great wonders of the human physiognomy. It is what enables us to discern objects in our peripheral vision or spot a blazer-wearing deer hunter from a long distance.

Tufte has previously noted that small, saturated spots of color are often the best way to draw attention to key points or to outliers in data sets. By that rationale, it stands to reason that many large swatches of saturated color are almost certainly overwhelming to the human eye.

In that light, the default Technicolor palette for Excel charts is less than ideal; the colors are far too saturated for most uses. The default palette includes Lemon Pledge Yellow, Kermit the Frog Green, Ticket-Me-First Red, and Cobalt Blue. For charts with multiple data series, that is quite an eyesore.

To prevent your exhibits from looking like an irradiated piece of luggage as it goes through an airport metal detector, consider these two suggestions:

- **Mute the color palette.** Reds, blues, greens—beautiful colors, all. But they need not saturate the screen. Consider replacing red with burgundy, blue with navy, and "Kermit" green with hunter or forest green. Readers will thank you for it; their eyes will relax rather than twitch. That said, if you need to emphasize a particular data point or series, use a small, focused swatch of saturated color.

- **Use a monochromatic palette.** An alternative to a less saturated palette is one that uses only black, white, and shades of gray. Monochromatic palettes work well when the target output device cannot be guaranteed, *and* when the number of data series is about five or less. A reasonable monochromatic palette includes white (with a black border), 20/25% gray, 50% gray, 75% gray, and black. Use pure colors; avoid fill patterns because they tend to "vibrate." On a related note, because photocopies of good exhibits (like the ones you will produce after reading this book!) tend to proliferate mysteriously into unforeseen hands, get into the habit of printing all exhibits in black and white *first*, before finalizing designs. By "proofing" exhibits this way, you can catch potential reproduction problems before they become an issue.

While I'm on the subject of color, be careful with yellow. There is nothing intrinsically wrong with yellow, but it tends to wash out in printed work and presentations. Use it as a "highlighter pen" accent color, but *not* as a data series color unless the background is very dark.

LABEL HONESTLY AND WITHOUT CONTORTIONS

Labels matter. Labels convey an exhibit's intent; lack of proper labels leads to loss of clarity and meaning. Label honestly so that readers understand the units of measure, time intervals, and data series—and do it in a professional manner that does not cause torticollis.

A few guidelines are in order. First, *pick a meaningful title* that summarizes the exhibit's main point. A plain title like "Application Security Defects" is fine. More-forceful titles can help too; for example, "Decreased Risk from Applications" succinctly provides the main takeaway message. For charts that display data over a range of time, subtitles help establish the data source and context. For example, a good subtitle might be "Defects reported per application, 2001–2004."

Second, *label units of measure clearly*. Although this sounds simple enough, you might be surprised to see how many people forget to label either the independent or dependent axes, as if the thing being measured were somehow self-evident. Nothing is worse than a beautifully formatted line chart that insightfully points out that over time, a company observed a clear and definitive increase in the number of . . . uh, something.

Axis labels should succinctly describe the unit of measure and scope of each data point and should typically include one of these magic words: "of," "per," "by," or "from." For example:

- Number of defects per application
- Percentage of passwords
- External attacks, by source
- Median number of days per patch

Exception: axes containing units expressed in years do not require labels, since the unit of measure is self-evident.

Third, *do not tilt text toward the vertical* if you're running out of axis room, or, in fact, for any other reason. With apologies to my East Asian and Middle Eastern readers, Western-language text was meant to be read left to right. Slanting x-axis labels or turning them 90 degrees forces viewers to crane their necks. You don't want to be responsible for unwanted chiropractor bills, do you? Of course not. In all seriousness, though, tilted text tends to indicate deeper problems with the exhibit format itself, generally in the orientation. In such cases, try switching the x- and y-axes.

Spreadsheet software (Excel is a notorious offender) often rotates text by default because it believes it is being helpful. Do not let it. Instead, always position chart axis labels with 0° rotation—that is, exactly horizontal.

Fourth, for multiseries charts, *consider eliminating series legends* if you can get away with it. Place the series labels directly on or near the data series themselves—that is, at the point of use. This practice works especially well with line charts.

Fifth, *do not abbreviate*. Although it may seem more efficient to label axes with "nmbr.," "app.," and "bus," doing so forces readers to unconsciously pause while reading the chart, an unnecessary distraction from the data. Also, abbreviations look sloppy. Of course, any rule has exceptions. For example, most people understand that % stands for "percentage" and that *IT* denotes "information technology." In most cases, though, try expanding all abbreviations. If narrow space on the y-axis forces an abbreviation, try giving the axis more breathing room by widening the left margin.

Sixth, *use simple and consistent fonts*. Charts are not the place to trot out that new typeface downloaded from the Internet. Use classic sans-serif typefaces like Helvetica, Franklin Gothic, or plain old Arial. In addition, keeping text the same size throughout the chart helps readers focus on the data, rather than the labels. Therefore, as a general rule, all labels other than the title (axes, data, subtitles) should be the same size and font. For printed documents, I recommend 9-point Helvetica plain or 9-point Arial plain. For space-constrained exhibits, the "narrow" versions of these fonts work pretty well, too. Opinions differ on correct formatting of titles; I prefer to make them the same size and font as the other labels, but in boldface.

Finally, *cite any data sources used to make exhibits*. To make a citation, place a small, short caption at the bottom of the exhibit. A simple "Source: Security Metrics Study (1999–2004), Andrew Jaquith Institute" in 6-point type (or something similar) works nicely. In addition to making the exhibit look more official, the caption provides valuable information to readers about sources and methods.

EXAMPLE

Although my suggested design guidelines may seem onerous, when followed they can dramatically improve the look and feel of metrics exhibits. For example, consider the very basic password-quality data set in Table 6-1.[3] The analyst has decided to create a graphical exhibit for management showing the results of the latest password audit. He fires up Excel and selects a standard bar chart (formatted in 3-D because it "looks cool"). Figure 6-1 shows what Excel disgorges when using default settings.

---

[3] This example is deliberately simplistic; normally, very small data sets should be presented in a table format, *not* a chart.

Table 6-1   Sample Password Data Series

Department	Value
IT	230
Account.	22
Ops.	129
Sales	40

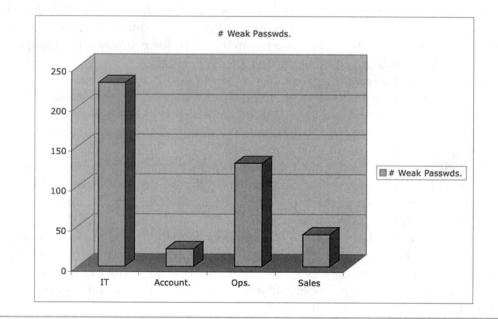

Figure 6-1   Initial Exhibit for Password Data Series

What is wrong with this picture? All sorts of things:

- Gratuitous 3-D effect
- Abbreviated category names
- Unnecessary legend
- Grid lines add no value
- Distracting shadows and background
- No data labels

Let's clean this up. Figure 6-2 shows a redrawn version of the exhibit. I made quite a few changes:

- Specified a sensible chart title indicating what the exhibit signifies—"Results of Password Audit by Department"—and a relevant time interval—"March 2005."
- Added a y-axis label, "Number of Weak Passwords."
- Eliminated the horizontal grid lines.
- Removed the series legend.
- Added data labels above each bar.
- Removed the tick marks from both the x- and y-axes.
- Removed the series border around each bar and changed the color from lilac to navy blue.
- Harmonized all labels to use the same typeface (Arial instead of Verdana), size (9-point), and style (plain, except for the title in boldface). Also, cleared the "auto-scale" check box for all text items.
- Removed the plot area border and background fill.
- Removed the chart area border and background fill.

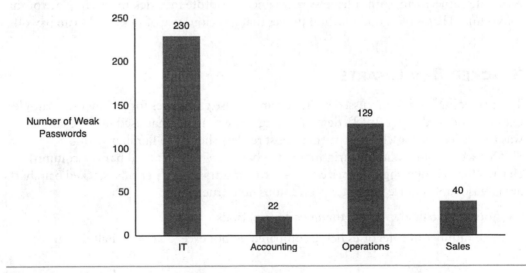

Figure 6-2 Redrawn Exhibit for Password Data Series

We can still improve this exhibit further by making some additional changes to the format. First, switching the axes provides additional flexibility for the department names and looks more professional. In addition, sorting the departments in descending order of the data points strengthens the exhibit's message. Finally, reducing the exhibit's overall size saves some space. Figure 6-3 shows the chart in its final form.

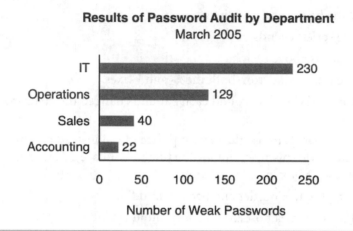

Figure 6-3   Redrawn Exhibit for Password Data Series (2)

As an alterative form, some business magazines substitute thin tick marks in place of the x-axis line. That looks good too, and proves that judicious use of tick marks can pay off.

STACKED BAR CHARTS

The preceding section discussed some commonsense guidelines for redrawing a sample exhibit produced using Excel's default settings. The chart format used in the example was the venerable bar chart—a format most readers should be familiar with.

This section introduces a variation on the bar chart—the stacked bar (or column) chart. When comparing categorized data across multiple time periods, stacked bar charts are a reasonable choice, when two conditions hold true:

- You need to analyze more than two time periods
- The number of categories being compared do not exceed about a half dozen

Two variants of the stacked bar chart exist—one that normalizes all values relative to their percentage share of the total, and one that does not. Readers of *The Economist* should recognize the former. Figure 6-4 shows a sample "normalized" stacked bar chart created using a spreadsheet package.

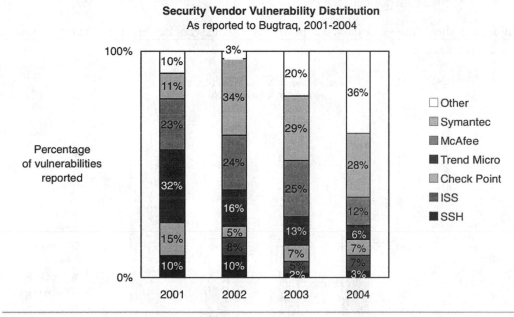

Figure 6-4 Stacked Bar Chart (Normalized)

To increase readability, I tweaked the chart as follows:

- Grouped all data rows after the top six into a catchall category called "Other."
- Removed the background fill and all tick marks.
- Simplified the y-axis labels so that they show only the minimum (0) and maximum (100%) values.
- Manually reversed (and put in boldface) the series labels that lie on dark-colored backgrounds.
- Stretched the chart legend vertically to better align the legend labels with the bar positions. Note how the chart legend items line up, horizontally, with the items in the stacked bars.

- Manually added an opaque white background to the "3%" label.
- Changed the color of the "Other" category to white (so that it is less noticeable than the named categories).
- Tweaked the color scheme so that the shades of gray alternate between light and dark (to improve contrast between categories, and thus readability).

Figure 6-5 shows the same data, but plotted using the second, non-normalized stacked bar chart variant.

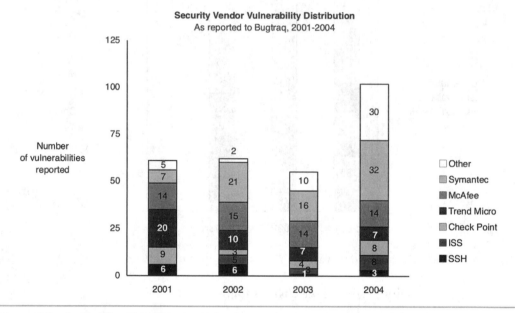

Figure 6-5   Stacked Bar Chart (Nonnormalized)

I do not use stacked bar charts often, but they can be useful when the number of data series and corresponding points are relatively small. The primary advantage of stacked bar charts is that readers recognize them fairly readily.

WATERFALL CHARTS

Popularized by McKinsey and Company, the "waterfall chart" provides a flashier alternative to the stacked bar chart. It is best used in relatively simple exhibits where the analyst is trying to show the relative contributions of different factors to a larger total.

For example, in the past I have used waterfall charts with executive audiences to illustrate how particular categories of security vulnerabilities contribute to an overall risk score.

A typical waterfall chart (see Figure 6-6) contains the total number at the top, represented as a horizontal bar. Bars arrayed underneath "explode" the component numbers onto separate rows. Numbers for each row appear to the right of the bar. A dashed line typically separates each bar.

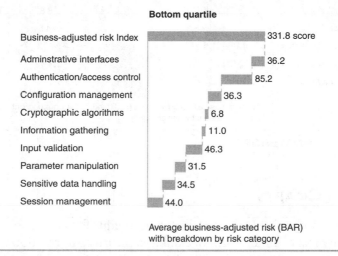

Figure 6-6   Waterfall Chart

Waterfall charts tend to be more readable and less claustrophobic (or space-efficient, depending on your point of view) than bar charts. Waterfall charts look neater, and facilitate comparisons better, than the equivalent stacked bar chart.

A side benefit of waterfall charts is that they can be used in small-multiple exhibits, but only when done with care, and with multiples of perhaps two at most. Figure 6-7 shows a "side-by-side" small-multiple variation of the waterfall chart that looks good and tells its story well.

Few software packages exist that can create waterfall charts; in most cases, analysts must hand-draw them using a graphics package like Visio, ConceptDraw, Adobe Illustrator, or (in a pinch) a presentation package such as PowerPoint. As an alternative to hand drawing, waterfall charts are also good candidates for automation. A few lines of Perl or Java, for example, can easily generate vector graphics for waterfall charts.

Waterfall charts are good for high-end management presentations, but that is about it. Their legibility degrades quickly after about a dozen rows. For data sets that are highly dense, consider treemaps instead. I discuss treemaps later in this chapter.

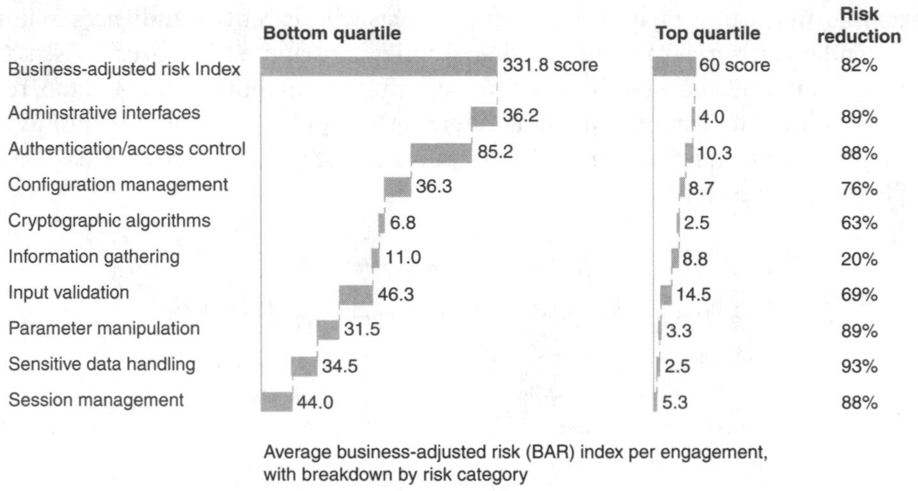

	Bottom quartile		Top quartile	Risk reduction
Business-adjusted risk Index		331.8 score	60 score	82%
Adminstrative interfaces		36.2	4.0	89%
Authentication/access control		85.2	10.3	88%
Configuration management		36.3	8.7	76%
Cryptographic algorithms		6.8	2.5	63%
Information gathering		11.0	8.8	20%
Input validation		46.3	14.5	69%
Parameter manipulation		31.5	3.3	89%
Sensitive data handling		34.5	2.5	93%
Session management		44.0	5.3	88%

Average business-adjusted risk (BAR) index per engagement,
with breakdown by risk category

Figure 6-7   Small-Multiple Waterfall Chart

TIME SERIES CHARTS

Time series charts are probably the best-known technique for visualizing security metrics. They remain the most common form of exhibit in security information reports, and they figure prominently in products for measuring compliance or tracking vulnerabilities.

BASIC TIME SERIES CHARTS

Chapter 5 discussed how a *time series* captures a set of consistently measured data records over an interval of time. Each record contains a number of data attributes. Time series charts simply graph an attribute (or set of attributes) over a time interval. The time interval (generally days, months, quarters, or years) serves as the independent variable and usually appears on the horizontal axis. The attribute(s) that vary over time serve as the dependent variable(s) and appear on the vertical axis.

Variations on the basic time series chart exist. Clever analysts occasionally add a second vertical axis on the right side of the exhibit to display a contrasting attribute in the same exhibit. Most readers are likely familiar with financially oriented time series charts (*The Economist, Business Week*) that show, for example, interest rates on the left and money supply on the right.

Time series charts accommodate a number of formats, depending on the preferences of the security analyst. Formats that work well include

- Line charts
- Area charts
- Bar charts

Each format has strengths and weaknesses. Personally, I prefer line charts for exhibits used in isolation. In an individual exhibit, the direction and tendency of the series line matters most; bars and colored chart areas distract the reader. But for small-multiple exhibits (discussed later in this chapter), area charts can help imbue individual exhibits with stronger "shapes" that are better distinguished by the eye.

Figure 6-8 depicts a sample time series graphic, drawn as a line chart. It shows the number of infections for the 2001 Slammer worm, based on data from the Cooperative Association for Internet Data Analysis (CAIDA).[4] When I prepared this chart, I wanted the infection trend line to be the most prominent characteristic. Note how the x- and y-axes are relatively plain and thin, while the data series itself appears as a thick line drawn in saturated blue.

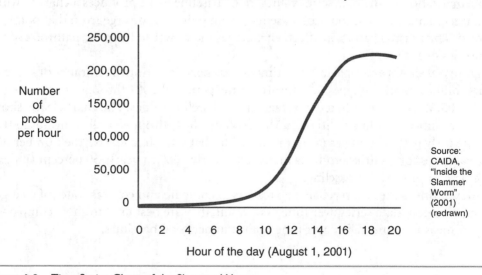

Figure 6-8   Time Series Chart of the Slammer Worm

---

[4]   See CAIDA's examination of the Slammer worm at http://www.caida.org/outreach/papers/2003/sapphire2/sapphire.xml.

Time series charts are perhaps the most easy-to-understand form of information graphics. Everyone—managers, staff, and laypersons—knows how to interpret what they mean. Every graphics package worth its salt supports one or more of its forms. And unless the analyst commits a horrible labeling blunder, they are nearly impossible to screw up.

INDEXED TIME SERIES CHARTS

Popularity and wide tool support mean that time series charts make a good starting point for visualizing security metrics. One of the more common applications of time series charts is for displaying improvement over time against a baseline. By "baseline" I mean a set of measurements taken at a particular point in time. A twist on the venerable time series chart, therefore, is an "indexed" version that charts each data series relative to the baseline.

To create the baseline, the analyst selects a starting point in time and normalizes all dependent data series values at that point to some "base" index value. I prefer normalizing to the number 100 because it corresponds to the "report card" or "IQ score" scales that most people are familiar with. As a side benefit, it displays fairly nicely and can show up to two significant digits of precision if required.

Normalization of the data series values to the baseline value produces a chart in which all values emanate from a common baseline origin point and diverge from that point forward. The normalization, in effect, encourages the viewer to trace the pathways of each series over time.

Figure 6-9 shows a sample indexed time series chart depicting the number of security vulnerabilities in several types of software for the period of 2001 through the first quarter of 2005. It uses 2001 quarterly averages as the baseline values. The chart clearly shows that the number of vulnerabilities for Microsoft products dropped well below its 2001 baseline early in 2003 and has not yet returned to that level. In contrast, the number of vulnerabilities for security products increased in early 2005 to nearly 50 percent (indexed value: 151) over the 2001 baseline.

Indexed time series charts challenge readers to compare and contrast rates of change among divergent data series over time. As a result, they are best used to show comparisons of measurements taken over time against understood baselines.

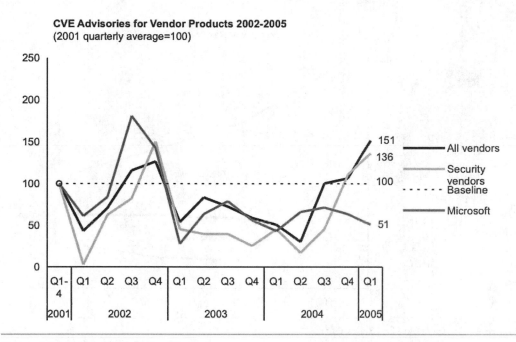

CVE Advisories for Vendor Products 2002-2005
(2001 quarterly average=100)

Figure 6-9 Indexed Time Series Chart

QUARTILE TIME SERIES CHARTS

Indexed time series charts showcase one way to revisualize sets of time series data by normalizing to a baseline. Another variation on the time series chart, which I refer to as the "quartile time series chart," showcases another technique. It uses quartile information from data sets to show broader measures of performance over time.

As you may recall from Chapter 5, quartiles group data into four bins: the top 25% of the data points in the sample comprise the first or "top" quartile, and the bottom 25% form the fourth. The last element in the second quartile, in fact, is the *median* data point in the set.

To create a quartile time series chart, the analyst calculates the first, second, third, and fourth quartile numbers for each time interval in the data set. The resulting exhibit simply graphs the first, second, and third quartiles. Figure 6-10 shows a sample quartile time series chart. Notice how the exhibit omits the fourth quartile; since it represents the upper bound of the data set, including it would only add visual noise.

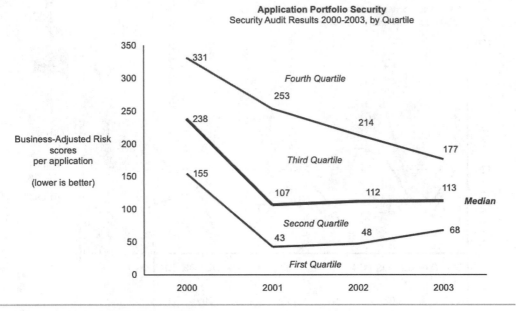

Figure 6-10   Quartile Time Series Chart

The way to read the exhibit is straightforward: the thick line represents the median values that separate the second and third quartiles. The thin line below the median separates the first and second quartiles, and the thin line above the median separates the third from the fourth. Based on the positions of the lines, viewers can quickly identify the correct quartile that any other data point falls into. Although the time series interval in the example I have provided is fairly broad (yearly samples), the broad headlines from this exhibit announce themselves:

- The period from 2000 until 2001 saw the most dramatic improvement (a 50% drop in median scores).

and

- Since 2001, median scores have stayed fairly flat.

but

- The worst applications (fourth quartile) demonstrated continuous improvement through all periods.

and

- All quartiles appear to be converging, which means that application security scores are generally improving across the board (specifically, the difference between the first and third quartile lines decreases over time).

although

- The first quartile has worsened in the most recent year (2003) relative to the previous one.

This chart contains two minor graphical refinements worth mentioning. First, all the quartile lines appear in the same color (black). However, the line that arguably provides the most context—the median—was drawn thicker (a 3-point line instead of 1-point). Second, I have added free-form text labels (italicized) to clearly establish the territories occupied by each quartile and to identify the median (italicized and bold).

In addition to these refinements, analysts can plot additional data points to show which quartiles they fall into. This is extremely useful for answering a common question from management about a particular item (namely, "How did we do?"). In fact, an analyst could combine the quartile time series line plots with a scatter plot showing the scores for selected (or all) data points in the set.

Alternatively, the analyst could create what I refer to as the "You Are Here" benchmarking chart by adding a horizontal line representing the score for a particular data point being benchmarked. The line crosses the y-axis and extends the width of the chart. When I was a consultant at @stake, for example, we used this technique to show how a client's freshly assessed application scored relative to our first/second/third/fourth quartile benchmarks. Clients liked the "You Are Here" chart because it showed how their applications ranked—that is, which quartile they fell into. From the consultant's point of view, the "You Are Here" chart helped drive business because it made the point that the client's application would have ranked better (or worse) in different periods.

Quartile charts excel in revealing how data change over time. They dig below the surface by graphing more than just simplistic averages or means. I rarely see them used, and that is a shame. Make them part of your toolset.

BIVARIATE (X-Y) CHARTS

As noted earlier, time series charts are the most common information security visualization technique. The unadorned time series chart is like an old reliable friend who speaks plainly and always shows up on time. Everyone knows what to expect, and he rarely disappoints. But he is not too bright, and his insights are rarely very penetrating. His slightly more flashily clad brothers—the indexed and quartile-based time series charts—offer a bit more excitement but not necessarily any extra insight.

In contrast, bivariate charts—which show how two variables interrelate—resemble cranky uncles more than old friends. They offer lots more insight and wisdom but require readers to take more time to understand their unique qualities (or eccentricities, if you prefer). You can't just inflict an uncle upon the uninitiated.

Bivariate charts gain their power from the often-unexpected linkages one finds by plotting two variables from the same data set on the same page. Each variable corresponds to an attribute in the data records being analyzed. When charted together, cause-and-effect relationships often emerge. Note that bivariate charts are time-independent; that is, they do not show temporal relations in data the way time series charts do. In most cases, bivariate charts display data for a given time interval; make sure to note the relevant interval in the chart's title.

Let us try a security example. Recall the application security defects data set discussed in the preceding chapter (in Table 5-2). The data set contained instances of security defects in a developed application. Each record in the data set contained these attributes:

- Application
- Owner
- Defect
- Date
- Exploitability
- Business impact
- Business-adjusted risk (BAR)
- Engineering fix hours

An analyst could use a bivariate chart to show how two of these attributes relate. A hypothetical chart might show one of the following:

- Exploitability versus business impact
- Business-adjusted risk versus engineering fix hours
- Business impact versus engineering fix hours

Figure 6-11 shows all three of these charts using the sample data set from Table 5-2. To show the relationship between the x- and y-axis variables explicitly, I have added a logarithmic regression line for the latter two charts.

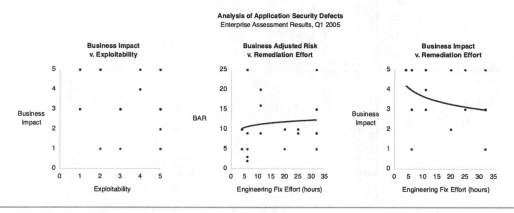

Figure 6-11 Sample Bivariate Charts

Casual examination of the two rightmost charts suggests that a weak relationship exists between remediation effort and either business impact or business-adjusted risk. That fits; one can reasonably expect that more serious security flaws will take longer to fix. In contrast, the left chart suggests that no obvious relationship exists between business impact and exploitability. This, too, seems to align with expectations—exploitable security holes do not possess any intrinsic qualities that would cause them to also be high-impact.

Exploring relationships between variables in a graphical way can help confirm or deny an existing hypothesis. For example, an analyst reviewing the exhibits in Figure 6-11 would not be able to make strong, definitive statements about cause-and-effect relationships between business impact, exploitability, and remediation effort.

Some bivariate charts show much stronger relationships. Figure 6-12 shows a fictitious bivariate chart that displays the relationship between end-user training and password strength, as measured by a password-cracker like John the Ripper. In this case, the relationship between the cause (how long since the last user training session) and the effect (the relative security of passwords) is much clearer. I have added a logarithmic trend line to highlight the relationship; a linear trend line works well also.

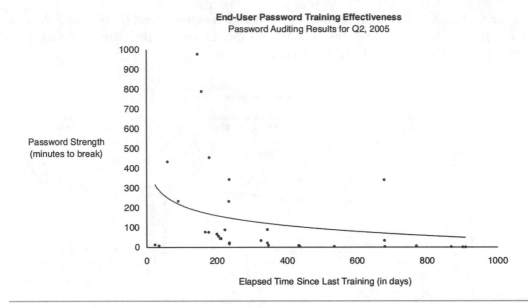

Figure 6-12   Password Effectiveness Bivariate Chart

TWO-PERIOD BIVARIATE CHARTS

Although bivariate charts cannot display temporal relationships as well as time series charts can, they can show comparative data in a limited way. A variation on the standard bivariate chart, the "two-period" bivariate chart, plots each period's data series and connects interperiod points with thin lines. Different markers distinguish the "before" and "after" points. The overall effect resembles a football or basketball chalkboard diagram. Figure 6-13 shows an excellent two-period chart from *The Economist* of a Boston Consulting Group study of investment banking revenues and corresponding value at risk (VAR).[5]

Two-period bivariate charts are a relatively specialized breed; they do not work well with sets larger than about a dozen pairs of data points. In addition, mainstream desktop packages like Excel cannot create them, so they must be hand-drawn.

---

[5]   *The Economist*, "Happy Days," Dec. 29, 2004.

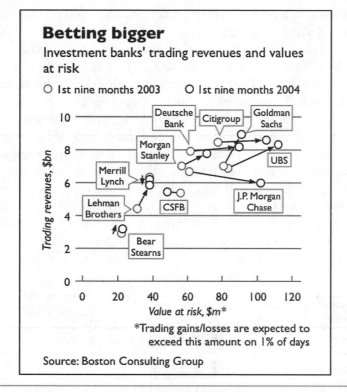

Figure 6-13   Sample Two-Period Bivariate Chart (Redrawn)

SMALL MULTIPLES

Curious people like to probe, ask questions, and understand why something is the way it is. One of the most powerful ways to satisfy a person's curiosity is to provide ways to compare and contrast. People instinctively know how to compare before with after, apples with oranges, and like with unlike. Why do they do this? In part so that they can understand relationships by spotting the differences.

In the field of information graphics, a concept called *small multiples* provides a natural, instinctive way to show how things relate and, more importantly, how they differ. First popularized by Edward Tufte, small multiples plot several cross sections of data in separate mini-charts and then combine them into a single exhibit. As a result, readers can—at a glance—quickly sweep back and forth across the exhibit, looking for patterns, similarities, and differences. An important quality of the small-multiple chart is that the axes remain constant with respect to their units of measure and scales. Only the data cross sections being plotted change.

Figure 6-14, a screen capture from the distributed network intrusion detection project DShield, shows how small-multiple exhibits work. The small multiples are in the column labeled "Activity Past Month." They show the relative number of hostile scans encountered for the network services enumerated in the "Service Name" column. Although the x- and y-axis labels are not shown, it seems clear enough what they must be: the vertical axis scale starts at 0 and increases at a linear—or possibly logarithmic—rate to maxima held constant in all graphs. The x-axis shows how the relative number of scans varies over time. Minor quibbles about labeling aside, the use of small multiples in this exhibit enables the reader to quickly get a sense of which ports are most likely to be scanned. In this case, they are 445 and 135—two ports associated with Windows services that are often prone to compromises. A network administrator running an all-Windows environment, for example, might see this exhibit and decide to push out a group policy temporarily restricting access to these ports.

Service Name	Port Number	Activity Past Month	Explanation
epmap	135		DCE endpoint resolution
microsoft-ds	445		Win2k+ Server Message Block
---	1026		
icq	1027		icq instant messanger
ms-sql-s	1433		Microsoft-SQL-Server
ms-sql-m	1434		Microsoft-SQL-Monitor
radmin	4899		Remote Administrator default port
netbios-ssn	139		NETBIOS Session Service
---	1028		
smtp	25		Simple Mail Transfer

Figure 6-14   Sample Small-Multiple Exhibit[6]

---

6   This chart was obtained from DShield, http://dshield.org/topports.php.

One can easily imagine how this exhibit could be enhanced. Instead of simply showing the "top 10" most-scanned ports, we could show the top 100, or a subset of the most common well-known ports. Doing so would require some graphical nips and tucks. The "Explanation" column would need to vanish, and we would want to combine the "Service Name" and "Port Number" columns. From the point of view of aesthetics, representing the scan results as solid filled area charts on a white background (instead of black) could increase the small-multiple format's readability.

An intriguing small-multiple format that would work well here is the *sparkline*—a minimalist "simple, intense, word-sized graphics" format invented by Tufte.[7] Figure 6-15 shows a fictitious redrawing of the preceding exhibit using sparkline format, constructed using Excel. Each mini-chart includes a dark gray line to show the trend for each cross section, as well as a light gray band denoting the "normal" range—that is, the mean value plus or minus the standard deviation. So that the reader can understand the plot lines in context, the final data point in each series is highlighted with a red marker and numeric label.

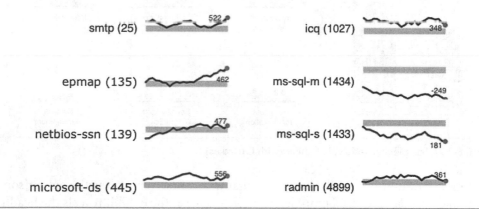

Figure 6-15 Sample Small-Multiple Exhibit (Sparklines)

QUARTILE-PLOT SMALL MULTIPLES

The time-series-oriented small multiples in Figures 6-14 and 6-15 help the reader understand the relative magnitude of activities over time. But time series charts are not the only type of graphic that can be used as a small multiple. Figure 6-16 shows a hand-drawn small-multiple exhibit using bar charts that compares and contrasts the

---

7   See E. Tufte, *Beautiful Evidence*, Graphics Press, 2006.

distribution of security flaws across nine different application security areas for a selected group of applications.[8] Each multiple contains a vertical bar chart displaying the area's first and fourth quartiles in the data set.

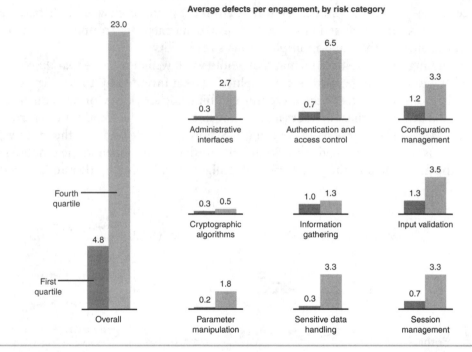

Figure 6-16   Sample Small-Multiple Exhibit (with Quartiles)

The combination of the small-multiple format with a first-versus-fourth comparison yields an extremely powerful graphic. A simple glance at the exhibit reveals the headline: fourth-quartile applications are much worse than their first-quartile counterparts in some areas, but not others. For example, the "best" applications contain 90% fewer authentication defects, have 90% fewer problems related to sensitive data handling, and suffer from 80% fewer session management issues. In contrast, the number of crypto-graphic issues are few across the board, and the difference between the best and worst applications is not large.

The exhibit is interesting for another reason: it sports a "layered" macro/micro design that shows both the overall total (on the left) and the contributions made by individual

8   A. Jaquith, "The Security of Applications: Not All Are Created Equal," @stake, Inc., 2002.

multiples. The scaling factors for the y-axis remain the same for both, and the quartile labels on the "overall total" graph serve as a key. Not all small-multiple exhibits lend themselves to such an elegant format, but it is nice when they do.

Small multiples, while powerful, are not well-supported by mainstream spreadsheet packages. For example, due to lack of better methods, a security analyst would need to hand-draw Figure 6-16 using Visio or a similar drawing package. Some careful spreadsheet jockeying in Excel might also work, although to do so would require the analyst to painstakingly format and align each multiple down to the pixel—and pray that Excel doesn't move or reformat it. However, in most cases analysts would do better to generate the individual multiples using a script and then stitch them together programmatically into a web page or PDF.

TWO-BY-TWO MATRICES

A special form of the bivariate chart, two-by-two (2×2) matrices became popular in the 1960s and 1970s with the advent of modern management consulting. Sometimes also called quadrant charts, two-by-two grids cluster the data in an X-Y plot into four boxes, divided by crosshair-like grid lines at the center of the chart. Two-by-two matrices abound in management circles and have even spread to the lay public. Steven Covey's "Seven Habits" Urgency/Importance grid, for example, introduced the technique to millions of readers. And the Gartner Group's "Magic Quadrant" 2×2 matrix is well known to IT professionals.

As a management consulting device, the 2×2 matrix offers a powerful framework for analyzing business problems. The Boston Consulting Group's Growth-Share Matrix, shown in Figure 6-17, was one of the early 2×2 matrices. Its success with clients helped the firm establish its reputation as a leading strategic adviser. The technique is fairly simple: the analyst plots the company's set of products according to the growth rate of each product's market segment (y-axis) and its share of the market relative to competitors.[9] Products with high relative shares in fast-growing markets are designated "stars." Those in slow-growing markets are considered "cash cows" if they command a significant share, and "dogs" if not. Finally, slow-selling products in high-growth markets are called "question marks" because they could transform into stars if their market shares go up, or wither into dogs if the overall market cools.

---

[9]   Variations of the Growth-Share Matrix include an optional "bubble plot," in which the diameter of each product scales in proportion to its revenues. To keep the example simple, I have excluded this feature.

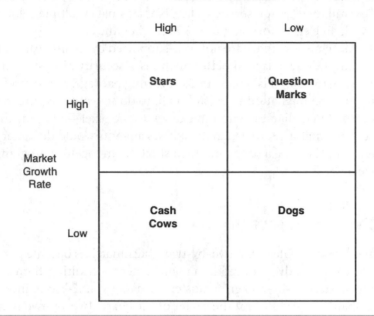

Figure 6-17   The Boston Consulting Group Growth-Share Matrix (2×2 Matrix)

The Growth-Share Matrix might seem simple—deceptively so, in fact. Yet this form of 2×2 grid has proven to be tremendously resilient because it:

- **Speeds comprehension by grouping data into simple buckets.** Most good managers are pattern-finders; they want to make sense of things. Classifying a potentially large data set into quadrants speaks to this natural human impulse.

- **Facilitates cross-sectional comparisons.** Within each quadrant, the reader can perform rapid comparisons among data points as a way of understanding how quadrant members are alike (or different).

- **Exposes the analytical process.** Bivariate plots (plots containing two variables) such as the BCG matrix use two labeled, quantitative axes to display results. The reader understands the explanation for each point's plot position simply by looking at the axis labels.

- **Presents a small, logical set of management options.** In addition to the designated label, each quadrant contains straightforward advice. In this example, the options are to invest in stars, maintain cash cows, selectively invest in question marks, and divest the dogs.

These benefits accrue to all 2×2 grids, not just the BCG Growth-Share matrix. In fact, the logic and power of 2×2 grids have proven sufficiently compelling that authors have devoted entire books to the subject.[10]

In addition to these explicit and obvious benefits, 2×2 grids contain an unintended—rather subtle—consequence. By its nature, the 2×2 grid constrains the decision space. It is a compartmentalized box; all the data in the analysis *must* sit in one of the four compartments. By carefully choosing the quadrant boundary values and labeling scheme, the analyst can literally frame the decision-making process.

I can personally testify to the power of having a constrained decision space by relating a story about @stake's signature exhibit, the Business Impact Matrix. Early in the spring of 2000, I successfully sold and managed @stake's first contract, a $35,000 engagement to assess the security of a business-to-business commerce website. Of course, since this was the first engagement in the company's history, we needed to invent everything from scratch—the document template, the graphic design, boilerplate text, and exhibits. Fortunately, we had budgeted sufficient time to prototype most of the essential parts of the document.

On the day before the due date, my technical team was busily writing up the detailed findings portion of the document per our agreed-upon formats. I took responsibility for writing the Executive Summary. As overall project leader and lead consultant for the firm, I was painfully aware that presentation and conciseness mattered. In particular, I wanted to make sure that the Summary came in under two pages, including a nice snappy graphic that summarized our technical findings. Figure 6-18 shows the final exhibit for the engagement—a classic 2×2 grid that I later named the Business Impact Matrix.

The Business Impact Matrix displays three attributes for each security defect: the degree of exploitability (y-axis), cost to fix (x-axis), and business impact (size of bubble). All attributes are normalized to a 1-to-5-point scale.

Although I am naturally biased on the subject, it is fair to say that the Business Impact Matrix contributed more to the early success of the firm than anything else we did. Of course, it helps to understand what the sleepy security consulting world was like in 1999 and 2000. Most of our competitors—Big Five accountancies—tended to send in kids with network scanners, who would drop off phone-book-sized reports at the end of engagements. Some of the newer, pure-play consultancies like Guardent (now part of VeriSign) and Rampart Security (later renamed Foundstone, now part of McAfee) appeared to do much the same thing.

Against this backdrop, the Business Impact Matrix represented genuine innovation. Our clients loved it; sometimes they would literally tear off the first few pages of the

---

[10] The 2×2 grid proved so ubiquitous that a pair of business consultants decided to write a book on it. See A. Lowy and P. Hood, *The Power of the 2×2 Matrix*.

report (with the exhibit) and send it to their bosses. Prospects loved it, too, because they could instantly see exactly what they would get from an @stake engagement. Although Symantec retired the Business Impact Matrix shortly after acquiring @stake, it proved its worth in hundreds of client engagements.

When creating bivariate exhibits, consider the 2×2 matrix as an alternative method of display. Ask yourself whether the axes can be sliced into quadrants and labeled. If so, you may be on the verge of discovering something innovative yourself!

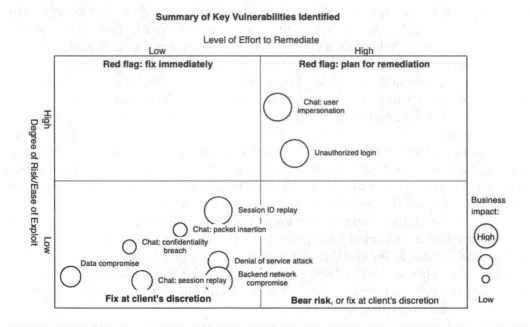

Figure 6-18   @stake Business Impact Matrix (ca. 2000, Redrawn)

PERIOD-SHARE CHART

A clever variant of the bivariate scatter plot, the period-share chart, shows how competitor market shares change when measured at two periods in time, typically on a year-over-year basis. I have seen this technique used only rarely, but its properties make it a natural exhibit format for analyzing security data.[11]

---

[11] The term "period-share chart" is my own designation for this exhibit format. I have not seen it formally named in any business or statistical literature.

To create the chart, the analyst plots each competitor's market shares relative to the leader for both periods, with the previous period on the x-axis and the current period on the y. A position above the diagonal designates the competitor as one who gained share relative to the previous period; below the diagonal, as a share loser. Figure 6-19 shows an exhibit from a Boston Consulting Group study of capital markets.[12]

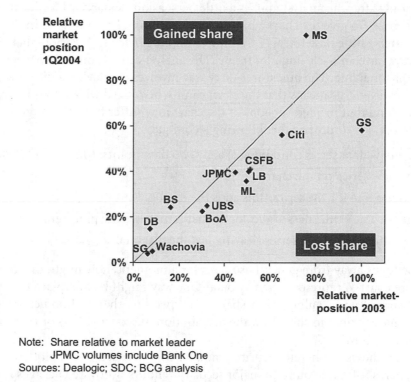

Figure 6-19 Sample Period-Share Chart (BCG Investment Banking Study)

Examine the chart carefully; its simple appearance belies a sophisticated analytical approach. The use of ratios relative to each period's leader is the key. By using these

---

[12] S. Ivanov, L. Kuebel-Sorger, B. Rauls, *Investment Banking and Capital Markets: Fourth Quarter 2004 Edition*, The Boston Consulting Group, 2005, http://www.bcg.com/publications/files/Q4_2004_Market_Report_BR_TM_NYC_10Mar05.pdf.

measures as the x- and y-axis values, readers can clearly see the relative period-over-period increase (or decrease). The beauty of this approach is that firms whose positions change relative to the lead firm "automatically" appear above or below the diagonal. The period leader always falls either along the top or right of the chart. If a firm holds the leader position for both periods, it appears in the upper right, at the top of the diagonal line.

Mechanically speaking, spreadsheet software such as Excel can create period-share charts, but only after the analyst applies a little persuasion. A standard X-Y scatter plot supplies the base. To give the chart a bit of extra headroom, I recommend increasing the axis maximums a little past 100% (1.0)—for example, 110% (1.1). Period-share charts should always have an enclosing plot frame. The analyst can use one of two methods to create the diagonal line. The quick-and-dirty way involves overlaying a diagonal line over the chart. However, this means that the chart cannot be resized without also moving the diagonal line and that printed versions of the chart may suffer from line alignment problems. Therefore, I recommend the following technique:

- Create a new data series containing exactly two data points: (0,0) and (110%,110%).
- Plot the new series on the chart.
- Add a trend line for the series (this adds the diagonal).
- Change the line's thickness and color so that it matches the plot frame.
- Hide the markers for the series (leaving just the diagonal).

Shifting the focus away from general use cases for a moment, how might one use a period-share chart to represent security data? One way might be to replace the concept of "market shares" with "vulnerability shares" or "spending shares." In other words, use the period-share format to show how the distribution of security flaws or spending priorities changes over time.

Figure 6-20 shows a concrete security example. On the chart, I have plotted the "vulnerability shares" of flaws found in major security vendors' software packages for the years 2003 and 2004.

Another security example might be a plot of spending priorities year-over-year, or changes in the types of threats detected by an organization's perimeter controls. I leave these as an exercise for the reader.

Period-share charts efficiently show the answer to a basic question: what's hot this year (quarter) compared to last? In that respect, they work as well as—and maybe better than—stacked bar charts or area charts. But period-share charts work less well in certain situations. For example, the period-share chart (in Figure 6-20) says nothing about the absolute number of vulnerabilities found for either the leader (Symantec) or all companies in the data set.

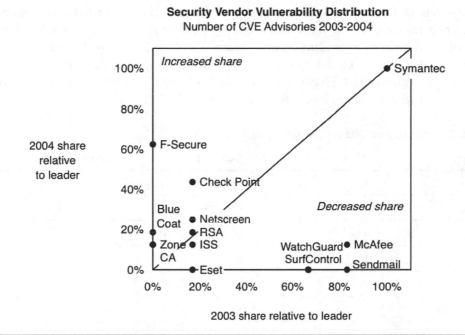

Figure 6-20 Period-Share Chart (Security Example)

Therefore, as a rule of thumb, avoid period-share charts when

- You need to show absolute share values.
- You need to know the absolute size of the market.
- Data sets are thin, leading to a situation where multiple points "cluster."
- The number of competitors exceeds fifteen or more.
- The desired periods for analysis exceed two.

In many cases, alternative chart formats (such as the stacked bar chart or the Pareto chart) are a better choice.

PARETO CHARTS

If period-share charts show how relative leadership positions among data categories change over time, Pareto charts help viewers understand each category's contribution to the total. Analysts commonly use Pareto charts to determine whether a small number of categories contribute disproportionately—that is, whether the data implies an "80/20 rule."

The Pareto chart requires a data set aggregated by category and sorted in descending order. Then, for each record in the data set, the analyst calculates the cumulative total as an absolute number and (optionally) as a percentage. Table 6-2 shows the sample security-related data set used in the period-share discussion, enhanced with calculated values for the Pareto chart. I have sorted the 2004 vulnerability counts and added two calculated columns: "Cumulative" and "Cumulative %."

Table 6-2 Pareto Chart Data Set (Security Example)

Vendor	2004	Cumulative	Cumulative %
Symantec	32	32	28.3%
McAfee	14	46	40.7%
F-Secure	11	57	50.4%
Check Point	8	65	57.5%
ISS	8	73	64.6%
Trend Micro	7	80	70.8%
Zone Labs	6	86	76.1%
OpenSSL	5	91	80.5%
Sophos	5	96	85.0%
Sygate	5	101	89.4%
Webroot	4	105	92.9%
Panda	3	108	95.6%
SSH	3	111	98.2%
Kaspersky	2	113	100.0%
IronPort		113	100.0%
Total	113	113	100.0%

Figure 6-21 shows a naive, sample Pareto chart for this data set, created using a standard combination-chart wizard and heavily reformatted. Even though we've followed our graphics guidelines—the chart looks neat enough—clear readability issues emerge.

To begin with, we needed to stretch the chart horizontally quite a bit in order to fit everything in. But because Pareto charts by definition attempt to show 80/20 distributions, we can safely cut the low-scoring items out of the list and save space. Focusing on the top 10 vendors, rather than including all of them, follows the 80/20 rule. Second, turning the chart on its axes helps quite a bit, although it requires some spreadsheet hackery to do.

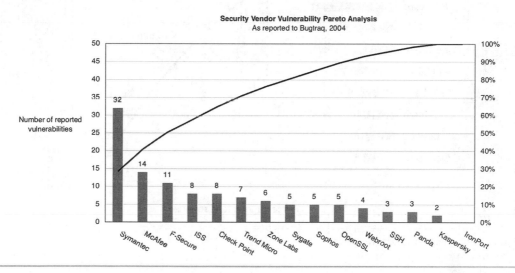

Figure 6-21   Sample Pareto Chart

Figure 6-22 shows the redrawn version of the Pareto chart. To create the chart, I plotted the two data series (one for the absolute vulnerabilities per vendor, the other for cumulative percentages) initially as two horizontal, overlapping bar graphs. The secondary vertical axis (right side of the chart) contains the cumulative percentage bars. I hid the secondary vertical axis' tick marks and labels. Then, I set the fill color and line for the second series to "no fill," rendering them invisible. Last, I added a polynomial trend line with a polynomial regression with an order of "6." This adds the red "cumulative %" line to the chart. Why do this? Because Excel cannot display a horizontally oriented line chart that uses categories (although it will do so with bar charts, which is how the first data series appears). Unfortunately, until Excel's charting capabilities improve, analysts will need to resort to hacks of this sort.

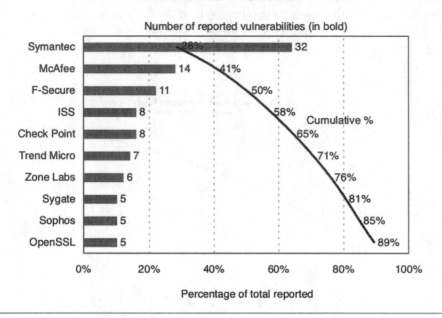

Figure 6-22   Pareto Chart (Redrawn)

TABLES

The last technique I will discuss will probably not seem like much of a technique at all: the humble table. Sometimes charts and fancy graphs are overkill. Tables are typically a better choice when

- **The size of the data set is thin**—less than a dozen data points, and spanning a single series.
- **The data set contains many distinct series,** no one of which dominates.
- **The data are imprecise**—designed to provide relative measures rather than precise, empirical absolutes.
- **The idea conveyed in the exhibit cannot be explained by numbers alone**, and depends on additional, textual exposition.

For example, financial report exhibits typically contain many data series. Each line item (for example, EBITDA) is a series unto itself. The audience might want to first look at

EBITDA, then glance upward at the revenue line, and then back down to the GSA expense line. None of these series dominates, and each one needs some explanatory text (the left column) in order to be understood. Therefore, a table is a natural choice for this type of exhibit.

Evaluation matrices are also a classic table application. Figure 6-23 is an example of an exhibit that shows two data series: degree of trust and data sensitivity. Both are on a 1-to-3 scale. Neither set requires particular precision. Note the use of focused use of saturated blue and thin horizontal rules; they make the data "pop" while allowing the reader's eye to sweep sideways for context.

Network zones: order of implementation
Minimize risks from untrusted sources first, then secure sensitive data.

Zone	Traffic type	Degree of trust***	Risks	Data sensitivity	Dependencies
DMZ*	Many-to-many	●	Unquantified risks, denial of service	●	Feeds from outside Framingham
Data	Many-to-few	● ● ●	IP theft, reputation	● ● ●	Applications, cultural
IT Admin	Few-to-few	● ● ●	Rogue admins, denial of service, eavesdropping	● ●	Hardware upgrades, cultural
Serverland	Many-to-few	● ● ●	Fraud, IP theft, denial of service	● ● ●	App-to-app communications
Userland**	Many-to-many	● ●	IP theft, denial of service	● ●	Cultural, function-specific protections

Implementation order ↓

Figure 6-23   Sample Table

As with other types of exhibits, tables should be relatively free of ornament. In the example in Figure 6-23, created in a presentation package (PowerPoint), all the vertical table lines and margins have been erased. This is in contrast with the default PowerPoint layout, which puts solid black lines around each cell and a 2.25-point black line around the perimeter.

Sometimes decoration has its uses, however. Consider the famous *Consumer Reports* circular icons used in product ratings: black circles for "poor," lightly stroked white circles for "average," and red bull's-eyes for "excellent." In addition to being universally understood (always a good thing), the *Consumer Reports* icons retain their meaning even when reproduced in black and white. This is a subtle but often overlooked property worth emphasizing. Figure 6-24 shows an example done in a similar style, which packs quite a bit of information into a relatively small space.

DRM Protection Effectiveness

Criteria		Myth TV	Macro Vision	MS MP	OMA	TiVo 2	RIM	DTV
Protection against…	Hardware attacks	●	●	●	◉	◉	◉	○
	Software super-cracks	●	◉	○	●/◉	◉	◉	○
	Cryptographic breaks	●	●	○	◉	○	◉	○
Effort for successful attack		●	●	◉	◉	◉	◉	○
Quality of extracted content		●	◉	●	○	●/◉	○	◉
"Water-tightness" of protections		●	●	●	●	●	●	●
Assessment of controls for:	Entitlements (CAS)	●	●	◉	◉	○	◉	○
	Copy control (DRM)	●	●	◉	◉	◉	●	◉

Key message: Hardware-based protections present the highest barriers, and can make conditional access systems very effective. However, even the best protections will not prevent *some form* of medium- or high-quality content leakage, after access has been granted.

Symbol key: low ●   medium ◉   high ○ (Note: Quality of Extracted Content symbols reversed; **h** ● m ◉ l ○)

Figure 6-24   Sample Decorative Table

This exhibit works well for a number of reasons. First, the icons are much easier to read than a sea of numbers, which are not easily distinguished. In addition, the saturated colored circles make the relatively "good" ratings really stand out, which in this case is what we want. Notice the subdued gray grid in the background and the thicker line separating the totals rows from the main table body. Imagine what this would have looked like if it had been done using default settings—that is, with a heavy grid, and with numbers instead of icons. Sometimes, it pays to spend a little extra time redrawing the table.

TREEMAPS

The visualization methods I have described in this chapter show how to effectively display data over time, in cross sections, and using systems of one or more variables.

The vast majority of the security metrics discussed in the preceding chapters lend themselves well to these methods. However, all these methods assume a data set whose records are structured in a relatively simple manner. For example, department *X* has value *Y*, or activity *A* has value *B* at time *T*. We assume that the independent variables—departments or activities—iterate through flat lists of values.

But what if the data set is not flat? Metrics visualization for security often requires the ability to roll up, or drill down into, a data set. In these cases, containment and hierarchy relationships establish vital context for the viewer. Perhaps the best way to view the data is to show the hierarchy as part of the exhibit. For example, one could show the roll-up structure for departments, sites, and business units, or the containment relationships of business processes.

"Hmm," says the IT analyst as he strokes his goatee. "Graphical displays of hierarchy… isn't this what network diagrams do?" Yes, in part. Technology architects have been drawing network diagrams for an eternity, and these show containment relationships quite well. However, network diagrams are rarely suitable for metrics visualization because they are

- **Too technical:** Managers don't care about TCP/IP addresses.
- **Too literal:** Only a small number of security metrics make sense on network diagrams.
- **Space-inefficient:** Lots of white space, low density of nodes per inch.

Fortunately, recent innovations in data visualization outside the information technology field mean that security analysts need not rely on network diagrams to show containment-oriented data sets. There is a better alternative: the *treemap*.

Little known outside of academe, treemaps are used with hierarchical data structures that can be aggregated. The core data elements of a treemap are rectangular nodes that, when rendered, appear as a patchwork of rectangles. The arrangement of the rectangles shows the containment hierarchy, in the same way a Bento box does. The size (area) of each rectangle represents the node's "weight," while its color or brightness displays attributes such as relative importance, criticality, or membership within an arbitrary category. Treemaps possess four properties that make them extremely useful for large-scale data visualization:

- Simple visual paradigm
- Extremely space-efficient
- Naturally suited for aggregation
- Excellent for high-resolution data display

Originally developed by Ben Schneiderman, a professor in the University of Maryland's Department of Computer Science, treemaps are easily the most innovative data visualization technique to emerge from the research world in the last ten years. Although they are not yet mainstream, many companies have created compelling, rich information graphics with them. For example, SmartMoney.com's Java-based Map of the Market applet, shown in Figure 6-25, features a treemap that shows near-real-time stock activity. The size of each block represents the relative market capitalization of the sector or company; the color shows whether prices are increasing (green, rendered here as light grays) or decreasing (red, rendered as darker grays). What is particularly clever about this example is that it precisely illustrates the micro/macro visualization qualities of treemaps. The reader sees the overall sweep and scope of the market, and he or she also sees how the different blocks relate to each other—and can dive into one of the individual data points, too.

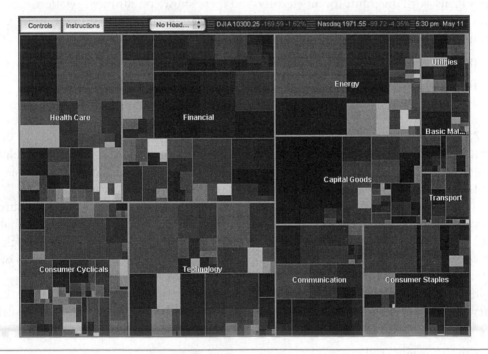

Figure 6-25 SmartMoney.com Map of the Market

CREATING TREEMAPS

Standard office productivity suites cannot create treemaps; instead, analysts must rely on specialized toolkits. Many treemap packages exist, including an open-source implementation I wrote for my own use called JTreemap. Let's walk through a simple treemap example using this tool, available on my website at http://www.freshcookies.org/jtreemap.

To construct a treemap, the security analyst identifies data attributes that supply:

- The size of each rectangle (size of deployed base, dollar value of asset, number of lines of code)
- The saturation value for each rectangle (criticality, priority, business impact)

and optionally

- The containment hierarchy (top-level category, department, business unit)

Next, the analyst formats a data set, loads it into JTreemap, and plots the results. JTreemap accepts a tab-delimited input file; after parsing the input, it creates a graph of the treemap. Table 6-3 shows a sample input file containing action plan data for an assessment of an e-commerce application. The field order for the file is as follows:

- NAME: Displayed as text within the node. Here, we'll use the name of the action item.
- DESCRIPTION: Displayed in the tool tip when the mouse pointer hovers over the node.
- BRIGHTNESS: The node's relative saturation, ranging from 0.0 (transparent) to 1.0 (fully saturated). In this example, we'll supply the item's priority, with the highest values representing the most important items.
- AREA: The amount of space to allocate to the node, relative to all others in the treemap. For the area, we will specify the amount of effort required to implement the action item.
- CATEGORIES[0..n]: The categories to use for this node (separated by tabs), with the highest-level categories first. An arbitrary number of categories may be specified, although in practice most simple applications will not need more than three or four. Each top-level category will be given its own color; in this example, there is only one top-level category. For this example, we will simply supply the name of the responsible business group ("E-commerce security").

Table 6-3   Sample Treemap Data File

Name (Action Item)	Description	Brightness (Priority)	Area (Effort)	Categories (Application Name)
Password policy	For end users	0.9	4	E-commerce security
Secure coding practices	For developers	1	8	E-commerce security
Identity management	Centralized account management	0.6	12	E-commerce security
Website server configuration	To be done by the systems group	0.7	5	E-commerce security

To ensure that nodes are arranged sensibly and in a manner pleasing to the eye, treemaps typically support one or more *layout algorithms*. The first algorithm, originally developed by the University of Maryland, is the "strip" layout. However, at present prevailing consensus holds that J.J. van Wijk's "squarified" layout algorithm[13] provides the best balance of structural fidelity and aesthetics. This is the one I use in my own package.

A single command from the console produces an interactive dialog box containing the treemap:

```
java -jar freshcookies-treemap-0.3.jar test.tab
```

Figure 6-26 shows the resulting JTreemap dialog for our sample data set.

The preceding example, while simplistic, shows how treemaps work. The "Identity management" rectangle dominates because it requires the most effort to fix; the saturated color of "Secure coding practices" (rendered as a lighter gray) shows that it is the most important priority. Since the business group "eCommerce security" will fix every action item, all items receive the same color (red, rendered as gray here).

Treemaps can support much higher data densities than in our simple example. Figure 6-27 shows action items mapped to the ISO 17799 security framework. In contrast to the previous example, which contained only one level of containment (the group name, eCommerce security), this example contains three. These levels correspond to the first three levels of the ISO topic hierarchy. Each rectangle is equally weighted (all have areas of 1) but contains different saturation values. In all, Figure 6-27 displays 556 data attributes (139 topics times 4 attributes: area, saturation, top-level grouping, and name).

---

[13] See Van Wijk's explanation at his website, http://www.win.tue.nl/~vanwijk/rhd.pdf. The visual style of JTreemap follows the one used by Marcos Weskamp's stunning NewsMap application (http://www.marumushi.com/apps/newsmap/newsmap.cfm).

Figure 6-26   Sample Treemap

Figure 6-27   ISO 17799 Treemap (Displaying Three Levels of Hierarchy)

Figure 6-28 shows the same data again, but aggregated so that the lowest level "rolls up" to the top two.

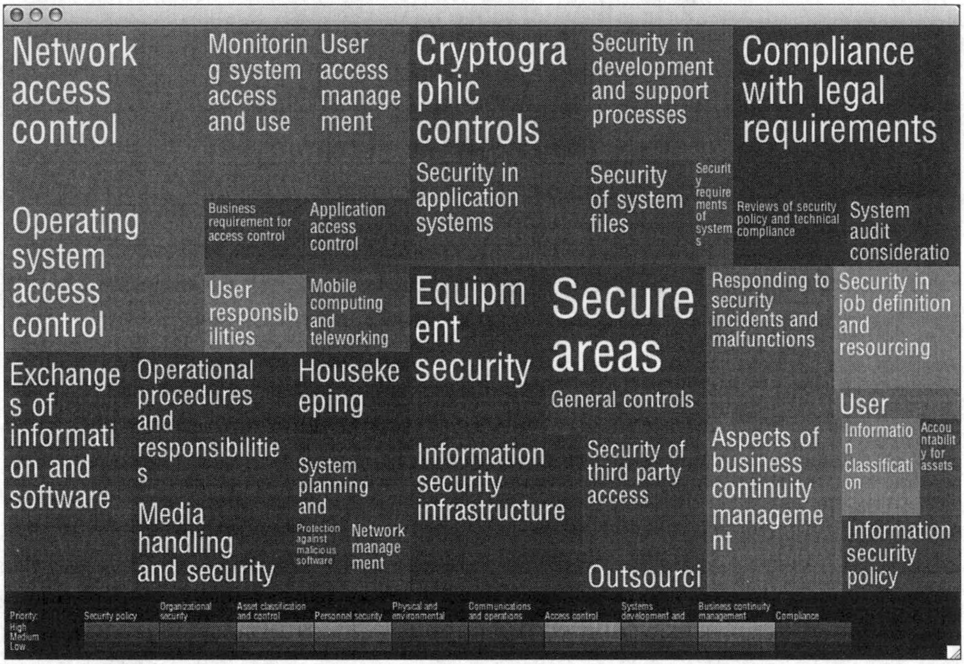

Figure 6-28   ISO 17799 Treemap (Displaying Two Levels of Hierarchy)

Treemap styles often vary from the one I have presented here, which is my own implementation. Some include text in individual nodes; others do not. Other implementations feature clever shading or border-rendering algorithms, drilldown capabilities, and more. The University of Maryland's treemap website (http://www.cs.umd.edu/hcil/treemap-history) contains links to other implementations, including a wide variety of commercial packages.

In summary, treemaps add another tool to the security analyst's bag of tricks. Treemaps provide an effective way of visualizing highly dense, hierarchically structured data. Although treemaps are not yet implemented in commercial office productivity packages, implementations exist that can help you today. Get to know them, and watch your colleagues' jaws drop.

THINKING LIKE A CANNIBAL: THE CASE FOR REDRAWING

Good visualization flows naturally from good design. And good design results from clear thinking about desired objectives; the format should always strive to answer key questions. Analysts should, on a regular basis, revisit existing exhibits to determine whether the questions they answer are the right ones. Equally important, analysts should ask themselves whether the design, format, and details of existing reports answer those questions as well as they could. When an exhibit falls short, consider revisioning and redrawing it.

Redrawing an existing exhibit format requires a certain amount of courage, particularly when an existing process or shipping product depends on it. Let us try an example or two.

A PATCH JOB FOR ECORA

Ecora Patch Manager's Reporting Center produces a patch-management status chart[14] and associated table that summarizes the effectiveness of the patch application process (see Figure 6-29). The chart shows the number of patches available, plus the total number available, and groups these statistics according to the severity of the patch. Unfortunately, the chart does not tell us much other than aggregate statistics, and the exact question it answers seems vague. Questions this exhibit should answer include these:

- What patches are the most troublesome (hardest to apply)?
- How effective or efficient is the patch management solution overall?
- How large is the window of exposure for systems that have not yet applied patches?

We can tell that the chart is not doing its job well just by looking at it. The dead giveaway is that two bars use the same unit of measure (one for total number of patches available, and one for installed patches). Bar charts are typically good candidates for redrawing using a bivariate chart.

Redrawing this chart using two variables improves matters somewhat. Let us assume that effectiveness, or lack thereof, matters most. Therefore, the chart ought not to emphasize applied patches, but *missing* patches—in particular, the percentage of missing patches. Assume for the moment that the number of overall required patches matters to the reader, too, because it implies the overall effort required to apply them. Therefore, the two axes show the number of available patches (on the x-axis) and the percentage of these that were not installed (on the y).

---

[14] Ecora Patch Manager, Installed Patch by Severity Report, http://www.ecora.com/ecora/sample_reports/patchmanager/installedPatch.asp.

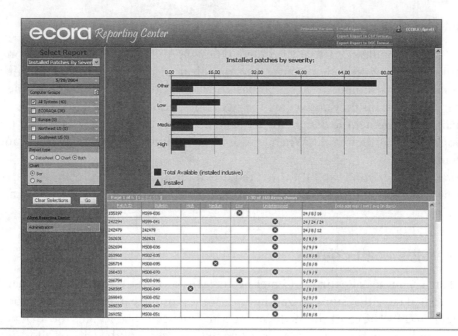

Figure 6-29 Redrawing Candidate: Ecora Patch Manager

An initial redrawing of the exhibit results in the example shown in Figure 6-30. Notice the change in terminology from "available" patches to "required," which better reflects the mandatory nature of patch management; we *want* available patches to be installed, don't we?

Although this bivariate chart improves on the original, it still presents problems: does the reader care about the number of required patches in aggregate? Probably not. The chart becomes more relevant when expressing the number of required patches on a per-machine basis. For the sake of simplicity, assume that the number of affected machines in the sample is five. Figure 6-31 shows the second revision for the chart.

The new chart improves on the two previous iterations, but we are not done yet. Examining the data presented in the table below the original Ecora graph, we notice additional data that might make the exhibit even more relevant: per-patch performance data, expressed in terms of the minimum, maximum, and average days required to apply each patch. A stock-chart style exhibit provides an ideal way to express this concept; a secondary table underneath provides the per-machine missing patch statistics.

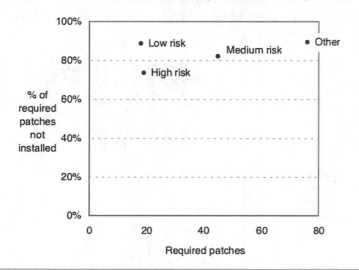

Figure 6-30   Ecora Patch Manager Exhibit (Redrawn)

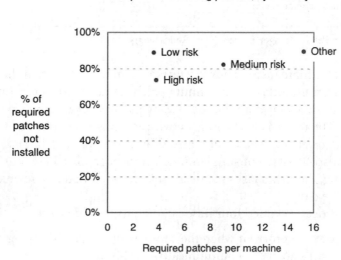

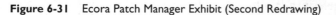

Figure 6-31   Ecora Patch Manager Exhibit (Second Redrawing)

Figure 6-32 contains the final redrawn patch management exhibit (using hypothetical min/max/average data, since we don't have the actual figures). The crossbars for the average patch time appear as opaque white-colored crossbars, which have the effect of "erasing" part of the hi-low bars.

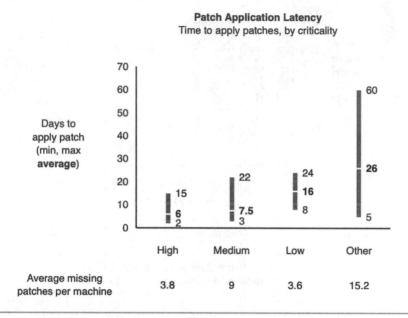

Figure 6-32   Ecora Patch Manager Exhibit (Final Redrawing)

All in all, the final exhibit answers our key questions much better than the original. It shows the average, minimum, and maximum patch latency metrics for four classes of patches, as well as the average number of missing patches per machine in a mini-table below the chart. The revised chart contains twice as many data points as the original, and the data are more revealing. The vertical axes show mean "per patch" and "per machine" performance statistics instead of simpleminded, non-normalized raw numbers. And aesthetically speaking, the new chart's relatively unadorned, functional format focuses the viewer's eye on the data.

The revision process revealed four lessons. Analysts should always:

- **Question the exhibit format** when the complexity of the underlying message exceeds the chart's ability to communicate it faithfully.
- **Dig deeper** for richer, more relevant data to answer key questions.

- **Consider nontraditional formats,** such as our "stock chart" adaptation.
- **Use iterative revisions** to zero in on the right design for the exhibit.

REORIENTING SECURCOMPASS

It seems safe to assume that no security analyst would intentionally create a bad graphic. But sometimes reality challenges even the most cherished assumptions. Consider the "benchmarking" chart shown in Figure 6-33, created using a security assessment tool from Espiria called SecurCompass®. The exhibit, which appeared in the *Computer Security Journal,* shows the average score (and ranges) by industry for security compliance.[15] But you would never know it—the chart is literally incomprehensible:

- **Nondescript title:** The title "Industry Benchmarks" sounds terrific, but what is the "benchmark," and how was it derived?
- **Poor series labeling:** The words "low" and "high" suggest relative measures—but relative to what?
- **Poor axis labeling:** What unit of measure does the vertical axis represent?
- **Mysterious methodology:** From whom was the data obtained, and over which periods?
- **Obnoxious formatting:** Readers must crane their necks sideways to read the category labels, and the data series bars (formatted in 3-D, naturally) seem far too narrow.

This exhibit is a real howler. Ironically, the authors of the exhibit actually have interesting data to present. For example, in the narrative support immediately preceding the exhibit, the reader learns that the "low" and "high" data points refer to the minimum and maximum scores observed in each industry. Four pages prior to that, the reader learns that the numeric scale (0 to 5) refers to scores on a self-assessed security compliance survey. Most significant, the first page of the report—thirteen pages before the exhibit— implies that the sample size for the study exceeded 350 organizations. All these details matter, and should have appeared in the exhibit. It is almost as if the authors were ashamed of their good (?) work, and wanted to bury the evidence.

---

[15] J. Heimerl and H. Voigt, "Measurement: The Foundation of Security Program Design and Management," *Computer Security Journal,* Volume XXI, Number 2, 2005.

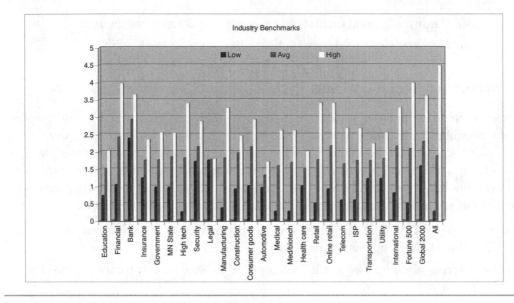

Figure 6-33 Redrawing Candidate: SecurCompass

Cleaning up the SecurCompass exhibit requires a change in format. A "hi-lo-close" stock chart gives us an effective way to show the minimum/maximum/average data points. Changing the format to vertical permits the viewer to read all the industry labels. A few additional chart tweaks help, too:

- More honest chart title (these are scores for self-assessment, not benchmarks)
- Inclusion of sample size (350 companies) and sample interval (2001 to 2005)
- A clearer label for the dependent axis ("mean compliance score and range," plus some minimal examples)
- Data sorted by mean industry score
- Softened grid lines

Figure 6-34 shows the redrawn exhibit. Look at the difference. The headline pops right out. Banks and financial services companies score highest, health care and automotive the lowest. The data also suggest that some industry scores vary more than others; compare insurance, for example, with high tech.

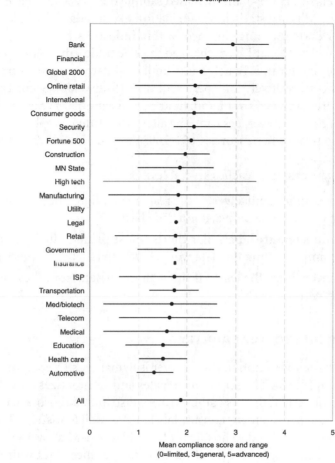

Figure 6-34   SecurCompass Exhibit (Redrawn)

Although redrawing the exhibit provides much more immediacy and impact, it also highlights potential shortcomings in the data. For instance, why do the legal scores vary so little? (Likely answer: a very small sample.) In addition, the total number of companies in the study (more than 350) seems low compared to the number of industries

(25, which equals a mean 14 samples per industry). It would have been better to condense the industries, perhaps by half. Increased sample density would have made it possible to include additional statistical information like standard deviations or quartile ranges—crucial for understanding variances within industries.

Finally, readers will note that I have changed the title to de-emphasize benchmarking. There is a simple reason for this. Benchmarks imply point-in-time measures, but the sample interval covers a relatively long period of time (four years). Security practices change quickly; scores averaged over a four-year period cannot serve as credible "benchmarks"—although one-year averages can. The alternative title I supplied ("Organizational self-assessment scores, 2001-2005) is more honest and sidesteps the benchmarking issue.

The SecurCompass example teaches several lessons:

- **Charts should explain themselves.** If the reader can't figure out a chart without reading the surrounding narrative, it is a bad chart.

- **Not all data points require labels.** For charts whose primary function is to compare cross sections, simply sorting the data works better than labeling every point.

- **Good charts never "bury the lead."** If the interesting data from the chart aren't intuitively obvious, redraw the chart.

MANAGING THREATS TO READABILITY

The final candidate for vivisection in this chapter is Symantec's DeepSight Threat Management System (TMS). The service aggregates and summarizes a wealth of information about Internet-based threats gathered from distributed sensors across the globe. One of the tabs on the management console labeled "Firewall Statistics" shows the most popular network ports subjected to hostile probing. Figure 6-35 shows a sample screen capture taken during the spring of 2005. Nice-looking graphics—but wait! Where is the legend that tells us what the colors on the horizontal bars mean?

Oh, there it is—at the very bottom of the web page, accessible only after scrolling past several completely unrelated tables. Although it is not a fatal flaw, it certainly detracts from readability, because it requires readers to move their heads back and forth between the exhibit (at the top) and the legend (at the bottom).

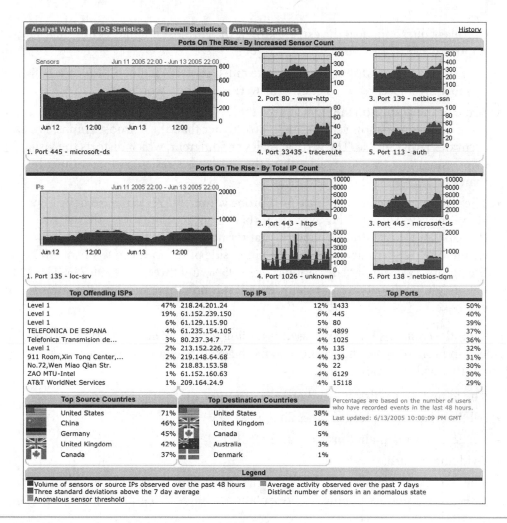

Figure 6-35 Symantec Threat Management System

So what is wrong with this exhibit? Nothing fatal; most readers will find the exhibit—which appears to be a variant of a small multiple—to be perfectly adequate. But upon closer inspection, certain qualities of this exhibit seem odd:

- Why the extra prominence given to the leftmost graphics? Do they summarize the four (times two) small multiples to the right? (Answer: The leftmost graphics are not summaries. They are larger merely because they show the number-one ranked ports.)

- Corollary question: does the extra width of the leftmost graphic signify anything important? (Answer: No.)
- Why don't the legend keys seem to make much sense? What does "Volume of sensors or source IPs observed . . ." mean? (Answer: It is poorly worded.)
- Some of the graphs on the right side of the ". . . By Increased Sensor Count" exhibit, upon first glance, show volumes that look higher than the leftmost graphs. Is this accurate? (Answer: No. The vertical scales are different, which distorts the visual impression. The scale for the graph of the #1 port is a ridiculous eight times bigger than #5.)
- The red horizontal lines indicate port probe volumes three standard deviations above the seven-day trailing average. Is that an appropriate threshold? (Answer: Probably not. Recall from Chapter 5 that for normal distributions, data points within one standard deviation (σ) on either side of the mean covers two-thirds of the points. Two standard deviations covers 95%, and three covers 99.7%. The TMS data might be distributed normally; even if it is not, three standard deviations seems excessive.)

Based on the concerns I have expressed regarding format, scaling, and labeling, the reader can probably guess how I chose to fix the exhibit. Figure 6-36 shows a redrawn version that includes these changes:

- The leftmost graphics' size and scale match those on the right.
- All the small multiples' baselines align.
- Vertical axes maintain consistent scales.
- Grid lines vanish.
- The number of standard deviations in the "threshold" line (red) decreases from three to two, and its graphical representation changes to a gray band extending on *both* sides of the mean.
- Plain-English service names replace the cryptic, IANA-style service names used in the original.
- Chart legend labels vanish; the one relevant legend item (regarding the threshold line) morphs into annotations applied directly to the leftmost multiples.

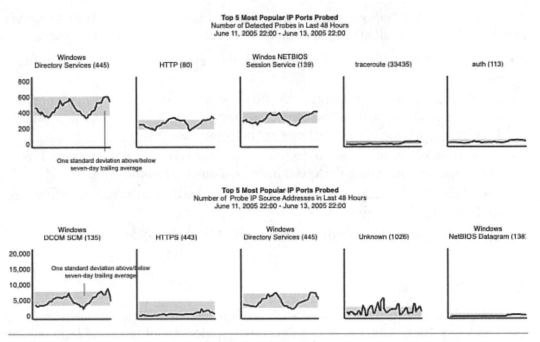

Figure 6-36   Symantec Threat Management System (Redrawn)

The redrawn version communicates the facts more truthfully. Due to the consistent scaling for the y-axis, the reader immediately notices the Pareto-like properties of both the number of detected probes and source IP addresses: after the third port, the numbers drop off sharply. The rescaled version also removes an inadvertent distortion. Instead of an epidemic of traceroute attacks (top row, #4), one sees that the number of detected probes for this port is in fact extremely low relative to the top three.

In addition, the combination of the tightened "threshold line" from three standard deviations to one, and its corresponding extension to below the mean, yields an interesting insight. Most of the time, the levels of probe traffic seem to fall within fairly predictable bands.

The redrawn exhibit could arguably benefit from further improvements. To keep things simple, I omitted time markers on the horizontal axes. Were this exhibit used for forensics rather than (as I imagined) a heads-up dashboard, it would require x-axis markers. And form factor of the exhibit may seem excessively horizontal.

Symantec's Threat Management System provides valuable information, but its slapdash execution makes it less effective than it could be. Its mistakes teach us several lessons:

- To minimize distortions, small multiples should maintain consistent scales for the x- and y-axes.
- Overly wide anomaly thresholds (more than two standard deviations) may not provide enough visual cues to allow viewers to spot unusual behavior. Narrower bands (one or two standard deviations) may provide more value.
- Chart legends should stay as close to the point of use (the charts!) as possible. If possible, consider eliminating the legend in favor of on-chart annotations.
- Superfluous data merely adds clutter. Remove an extra data series not directly related to the main point of the exhibit.
- Small-multiple titles work better when expressed in plain English.

SUMMARY

If a picture is worth ten thousand words, it follows that an ugly picture is worth ten thousand ugly words. With information security graphics, clarity, taste, and restraint can help ensure that an analyst's graphically conveyed *magnum opus* beautifully expresses the story he or she intended.

You can keep your information graphics lean, trim, and elegant by following six basic principles:

- **It is about the data, not the design.** Resist urges to add shiny backgrounds and decoration, or anything else that detracts from the data.
- **Just say no to 3-D.** Fake depth distracts the reader. Unless you are a NASA scientist trying to visualize global warming, you do not need it.
- **Do not go off to meet the wizard.** If using Excel, prepare for radical surgery after clicking Done.
- **Erase, erase, erase.** Get rid of all grids, tick marks, shadows, and superfluous plot frames. Not all data points require labels. For cross-sectional charts, sorting the data works better than labeling every point.
- **Reconsider Technicolor.** Mute the colors, or use a monochrome palette.
- **Label honestly and without contortions.** Pick a meaningful title that summarizes the exhibit, label units of measure clearly, use consistent fonts of the same size, cite the data source, and avoid abbreviations. Chart legends should stay as close to the data as possible; consider eliminating them in favor of on-chart annotations.

Good charts never bury the lead. If the interesting data from the chart are not intuitively obvious, redraw the chart. If the reader cannot figure out a chart without reading the surrounding narrative, it is a bad chart.

The analyst's graphical toolbag includes a wide variety of exhibit formats, each of which has strengths and weaknesses, depending on the nature of the data and the intended message. These formats include:

- **Stacked bar charts,** which show the contribution of each data series over multiple time periods to an absolute total. Stacked bar charts can also be "normalized" to show each series' relative contribution on a percentage basis.

- **Waterfall charts,** which show how multiple categories accumulate to form an overall total, generally for a single period. Waterfall charts are not especially dense but can make for effective management presentation formats because of their association with consulting.

- **Time series charts,** which show how one or more series vary over a given time interval: hours, months, quarters, or years.

- **Indexed time series charts,** which express each data point as a multiple of its starting value. Typically, the starting points are normalized to a value of 100. Indexed time charts work well for analyzing relative, rather than absolute, performance over time for a group of comparable series.

- **Quartile time series charts,** which plot quartile values for a data series over time. Typically, quartile charts plot three series: the median values, the values separating the first and second quartiles, and the values separating the third from the fourth.

- **Bivariate charts,** which show how two variables behave relative to one another. These charts can help analysts understand relationships between pairs of variables, such as potential cause-and-effect relationships. A variation on the bivariate chart, the **two-period bivariate chart,** resembles a basketball chalkboard diagram and helps viewers understand period-to-period changes in relationships.

- **Small multiples,** which plot several identical charts on the same canvas, allowing the eye to quickly sweep back and forth across the exhibit, looking for patterns, similarities, and differences. The axis scales remain constant, but the cross sections change from chart to chart. Small multiples are one of the most powerful ways to visualize cross-sectional data.

- **Quartile-plot small multiples,** which combine the comparative power of small multiples with the insights of quartile analyses. Particularly popular in management consulting circles, this chart format visually isolates factors that separate the best and worst performers.

- **Two-by-two matrices,** which extend the bivariate plot by grouping results into quadrants. Another favorite of management consultants, the 2×2 matrix enables an analyst to frame the terms of debate by categorizing and naming the results sets: for example, "quick hits," "strategic initiatives," "discretionary fix," and "bear risk."

- **Period-share charts,** which plot winners and losers over two successive periods in a square plot. Winners who increase share appear above the diagonal; losers fall below it. Period-share charts work best when the number of participants does not exceed fifteen and where plot positions are dispersed.

- **Pareto charts,** which present as a bar graph a range of sorted values from largest to smallest. On a secondary axis, a line plot shows how the cumulative addition of values converges on 100%. Pareto charts help analysts understand whether a data set follows the 80/20 rule.

- **Tables,** which show data values in a familiar grid layout. Small splashes of color and careful use of icons, such as those familiar to readers of *Consumer Reports,* can enhance table readability.

- **Treemaps,** which show hierarchical relationships in data sets as a series of recursive rectangles. The relative size or percentage of each data point determines the rectangle's size. Importance or criticality determines the rectangle's color saturation; "hot" items appear more saturated.

With all these exhibit formats to choose from, analysts may sometimes find that choosing the right format is not always easy. Analysts should always question the exhibit format when the complexity of the underlying message exceeds the chart's ability to communicate it faithfully. Dig deeper for richer, more relevant data to answer key questions, and use iterative revisions to zero in on the right design for the exhibit.

In the last few chapters, we have discussed what metrics to get ("Diagnosing Problems and Measuring Technical Security," "Measuring Program Effectiveness"), what to do with them once we've got them ("Analysis Techniques"), and how to show them off to their best effect (this chapter). But so far, we have furiously waved our hands over the "getting" part.

I shall wave my hands no longer. Next up is Chapter 7, "Automating Metrics Calculations," which shows you how to obtain and transform raw data from sources such as firewalls, antivirus logs, and third-party reports.

Automating Metrics Calculations

"It takes more than understanding the problem to explain to a computer how to solve it."

—developerdude (anonymous), ca. November 2004

"History may not repeat itself, but it does rhyme a lot."

—Mark Twain

The previous chapters tackled some of the more theoretical concepts related to security metrics: *why* we ought to be measuring security, and *what* sorts of things we ought to measure. This chapter's intent is more practical: to describe *how* to gather the data we are looking for. Because much of the data we seek are, in most organizations, stored inside a vast array of databases, system logs, spreadsheets, and brains, any discussion of "how" must discuss the mechanical processes that enable us to gather data on a large scale. Thus, this chapter concerns itself with one thing: *automation*.

Automation, in the context of scorecards and metrics, has many benefits but can deliver them only when the associated processes and systems are well defined—specifically, well enough understood to tell a machine how to collect data, compute and communicate information, and—we hope—get us closer to the goal of *insight*.

Merriam-Webster defines automation as "the controlled operation of an apparatus, process, or system by mechanical or electronic devices that take the place of human organs of observation, effort, and decision." In our narrative, we will focus mostly on drilling into the issue of "organs of observation and effort."

Toward this end, we will discuss the following topics:

- The benefits of automating metrics computation
- Functional requirements for an effective and efficient automation system
- Logical and physical models of a metrics automation system
- The technologies and interfaces between the software that automates metrics computation and the rest of the security environment
- Phases in the life cycle of an automation program
- The role automation can play, and when it should be tempered with human intervention

To illustrate the process of implementing security metrics automation, at the end of the chapter we discuss a disguised example of one company's experience with setting up an automated metrics management system.

AUTOMATION BENEFITS

I have mentioned the virtues of automation in earlier chapters. Good automation delivers the following major benefits:

- **Accuracy:** The collection, computation, and communication processes are executed precisely to specification.
- **Repeatability:** Any result can be reproduced, thereby enhancing trust that the measurements and scores are not biased or erroneous.
- **Increased measurement frequency:** Having computers do the work instead of humans shortens operations that would normally take a long time.
- **Reliability:** Operations that would normally be error-prone or tedious are more efficient and predictable when computers, instead of humans, perform them.
- **Transparency:** The automation steps used to derive the metrics are readily apparent and accurately documented.
- **Auditability:** The processing associated with each metric as well as any revisions to their definition is recorded and can be reviewed by authorized auditors.

An explanation of each benefit follows.

ACCURACY

Computers excel at following instructions. Automation alone does not automatically result in accuracy, however. The trick, as alluded to by the quote from the anonymous *developerdude* at the start of this chapter, is to understand enough about the desired solution to faithfully translate that knowledge into correct instructions—in the form of object models, work flows, and software. Once the correct instructions exist, computers can effectively and efficiently carry them out over and over again.

Accuracy is a prerequisite for trust. And trust is a prerequisite for effectively leveraging *what* metrics are telling you. Betsy Nichols, the CTO of Clear Point Metrics, relates a story about a meeting she attended whose purpose was to go over a metrics spreadsheet that had been created by one of the participants. Everyone received a hard copy and began to scrutinize the information it contained. After a few minutes, one of the participants pointed to cell M43 and said, "This doesn't look right," at which point the author appeared to be stuck for an answer. This was enough to derail the rest of the discussion—the credibility of virtually every cell in the spreadsheet came under question. The meeting deteriorated into a debate about *how* the spreadsheet was computed as opposed to *what* insight it was designed to facilitate. Trust disappeared and did not come back.

Avoiding loss of trust takes two key ingredients. The first is *consensus* regarding the data, computations, models, assumptions, and possibly even the publishing format of results. The second is *high-fidelity automation* that faithfully captures the essential performance attributes of a process. Automation cannot deliver consensus on the *how* of metrics or scorecard definition, but it can lend structure to the discussion and rigor to the specifications. Trust flows from accuracy once everyone agrees *how* the metrics should be created and are confident that automation can carry out the measurement process in the expected manner. After establishing that the measurement process is accurate, subsequent discussions become about *what*, not *how*.

REPEATABILITY

Repeatability is another key to trust. If two measurements of the same target consistently yield the same result, faith in the veracity of the measurement—both the technique and the result—is sustained. But lack of confidence in the repeatability of a measurement can destroy trust in an instant.

When most people think about automation, repeatability is the thing that gets them excited. Not just because it saves some poor soul from an otherwise thankless task—that is plain enough—but also because it eliminates the "middleman." By automating the measurement of security processes, one can go directly to the primary source of data, such as a server, firewall, or employee directory. One can also pull data from a secondary source that derives its data from multiple primary sources, such as a vulnerability management system.

Repeatability eliminates subjectivity—the enemy of any good metrics program. One enterprise we know implemented a metric regarding adherence to a policy that required shredding of sensitive documents. Their measurement technique consisted of gathering all managers and asking them to grade themselves on how well they felt they had shredded: A, B, C, D, or F. The criteria for receiving a grade tended to change across "grading periods," and there was no way to check if the managers were consistently grading themselves. Subjectivity—that is, the individual bias, mood, mental status, or state of caffeine deprivation of each manager—was baked into each grade, and nobody had any way of distilling it out. Such arbitrariness and lack of consistent scoring criteria are eliminated when data-gathering processes are automated.

But repeatability is not just about making a manual process go faster or without human interaction. Repeatability must also be sensitive to the fact that many security processes are dynamic and that the underlying data change in real time. (One can argue that the attributes of a security process that are the *most* interesting are the dynamic ones.) Change is the enemy of repeatability. So the key to repeatability in automation is to combine the real-time operation of taking a measurement with the ability to remember *when* the result was measured. Given memory of time-stamped and measured values, automation can ensure that repeatability of historical metrics computation is achieved.

In short, we can define metrics "repeatability" as "calculating something using the same data sources and data—over a similar sample period—and arriving at the same result."

But there are often practical limits to repeatability. For example, a Clear Point Metrics customer implemented a Security Event Management system. This system calculates metrics such as "Top Ten Attackers" and "Top Ten Attacked Servers."[1] These metrics are computed on an hourly basis. All of the raw events used to compute these metrics are thrown away after 30 days due to storage limits on the central event repository server. For a given month, the "Top Ten Attackers" or "Top Ten Attacked Servers" for a given hour can be recomputed from raw event data, but computations of these metrics at a time over one month ago are not repeatable. Does the customer view this as a critical defect? No. If it were, the company would add more memory or would redesign the data-gathering process to achieve repeatability for periods longer than a month. For this particular customer's needs, management judged that it was not worth the effort.

---

[1]   I discounted the value of these metrics in Chapter 3, "Diagnosing Problems and Measuring Technical Security." That said, these metrics meant something to the customer.

In summary, automation can deliver repeatability when an adequate storage component is designed into the system. Storage adequacy is defined in terms of time and capacity to be consistent with the goals of the metrics.

INCREASED MEASUREMENT FREQUENCY

A happy by-product of automation is *periodicity*. The benefits of repeatedly and regularly taking measurements and publishing the results are numerous. First, a process that regularly generates a picture of "where we are" facilitates regular review. Data that are always fresh are more likely to be examined regularly. Second, obtaining regular snapshots over time helps people understand trends, uncover potential cause-and-effect relationships, and spot problems more quickly. (This is Twain's notion of poetic history; data rhyme from time to time.) Finally, regular and repeated observations across time can be used to establish an accurate benchmark of current status and to set realistic goals for the future.

Nichols tells of a company that was very proud of its metrics program. Every six months, the security team embarked on a massive manual data-gathering exercise to collect a long list of metrics. The fruit of their labor was a report full of scorecards and metrics, presented at the end of the period. Although this sounds commendable, it is worth noting that all of their information was six months stale as soon as it became available.

Certainly, a cycle time of six months is better than a cycle time of one year. Any information is better than none—usually. However, most companies believe that monthly cycle times are a minimum requirement for most strategic planning—and certainly for tactical and operational planning. In some cases, weekly or daily cycle times are required. Thus, although this company may have had the most ingenious, most insightful security measurement program ever conceived, the staleness of the data diluted its value.

When automation can generate a metric automatically, the process under measurement and the objectives of the metrics dictate the cycle time (or measurement sampling frequency), rather than the capacity of humans to perform the work manually. This is almost always a primary driver to automate—to achieve suitable sampling rates with affordable consumption of human labor.

When processes are particularly volatile, the need for increased sampling frequency become even more critical. The Nyquist-Shannon Sampling Theorem from Information Theory tells us that when a process changes at a steady frequency of F, one must take measurements (or samples) of the process at a rate of at least twice this rate (2F) to perfectly model the original process from the samples.[2] If one is not interested in modeling

---

[2]   See C. E. Shannon, "Communication in the presence of noise", Proc. Institute of Radio Engineers, vol. 37, no.1, pp. 10-21, Jan. 1949

absolutely positively every change, one can measure at much less frequency. But, of course, not all processes change at a constant frequency—far from it. In this case it is often desirable to understand not only the average rate of change in a target process but also the variation in that rate. A high variation in the rate of change indicates that the process may have distinct bursts of change followed by relative stability. This requires sampling rates that are at least twice the highest possible (or burst) change frequency.

In short, automation enables humans to dial up the frequency of measurement processes. For volatile processes, organizations gain additional insights by having the capacity and flexibility to change sampling frequency or adjust measurement cycle time.

RELIABILITY

Reliability refers to the consistent operation of a metrics collection process over time. Consistent, repeated processes in line with specifications increase trust because they allow analysts to derive conclusions from collections of trustworthy results. Reliability guarantees that results are gathered regularly following an agreed-upon schedule, despite the inevitable roadblocks that, without automation, might cause the measurement effort to be postponed or canceled.

Well-managed manual processes can also be highly reliable, but automation often brings a higher level of assurance. Reliability is enhanced via resiliency and failover features built into the automation software. Automation can also automatically retry failed steps or interpolate to fill in missing data.

TRANSPARENCY

I have written about the importance of transparency in previous chapters—particularly with respect to scorecard design. Most humans who read scorecards with a critical eye want to know how the mystery numbers were calculated. Thus, scorecards whose methodologies are relatively transparent help increase the level of understanding and acceptance. This key principle of good scorecard design applies equally to automation. In the anecdote we shared earlier about the dysfunctional spreadsheet meeting, it was not just the seeming sketchiness of the results that bothered the skeptic. The lack of transparency in the spreadsheet itself contributed. After all, spreadsheet printouts display formula results, not the formulae themselves.

Of course, if the preferred metrics automation tool is a spreadsheet, simply printing worksheet formulae will not increase transparency much—they tend to be cryptic to untrained eyes. It is not practical to always publish all of a metric's implementation specifications. However, with other automation techniques, such as an enterprise-class data-management system, one has more flexibility. For more mature automation programs, the system's design should explicitly include mechanisms to publish and distribute metadata about a metric.

By offering an open channel for communication of metrics metadata, there is no mystery as to the details underlying each metric result or scorecard edition. Metadata should describe what data were used to calculate the metric, how they were obtained, when they were obtained, what models and assumptions were used in the computation, what errors were encountered, what version of the business logic was used, and the name of the author of the business logic. Furthermore, the metadata should be easy to read and should be delivered via browsable catalogs of metric definitions.

AUDITABILITY

Auditability applies to all phases of a metric's life. Auditability is what guarantees that all "interesting" events in the life of a metric are memorialized in a chronological log where authorized individuals can see what happened. Examples of "interesting" events include:

- The creation of the metric definition
- Changes or updates to the definition of a scorecard or metric—its business logic or runtime parameters
- The time and date when the metric was put into production to begin generating sample measurements
- The time and date when the scorecard was put into production to begin generating editions for distribution
- Errors encountered when computing the metric
- Changes to the schedules for computing metrics or generating scorecards
- Changes to the external systems used to provide the raw data for metric computation

Because of the pervasiveness of auditability across all phases in the life cycle of a metric, audit requirements can drive lots of decisions about the design and architecture of a metrics automation system. For example, the requirement to audit changes to the business logic associated with a metric drives features into an automation system that are very similar to those for software versioning. A repository for business logic (centralized or distributed) is required that can, at a minimum, assign visible revision identifiers to a metric and be able to associate generated results with the version that created them.

CAN WE USE (INSERT YOUR FAVORITE TOOL HERE) TO AUTOMATE METRICS?

Automation of metrics-gathering processes can bring substantial benefits. To do it right, enterprises need to select their tools with care. As with many "new" data gathering initiatives, it is tempting to view metrics automation as a generic collection activity that can be fulfilled with generic tools: spreadsheets, business intelligence products, and security event and incident management (SIEM) software. These are not good choices, because metrics activities have specialized requirements. Let's talk about each of these in turn.

SPREADSHEETS

In the previous discussion of automation benefits, I noted that spreadsheet printouts do not always offer much in the way of transparency because the printout shows numbers, not formulae. The astute reader might reasonably conclude that I do not think much of spreadsheets as a tool for automating metrics calculations. I do not, actually. The spreadsheet is a fabulous prototyping tool, but it's not well suited to real automation tasks. Anybody who has forced spreadsheet software to do highly unnatural things, as I have, knows that scalability is not its strong suit. Spreadsheets are likewise limited in the areas of external connectivity and data integration, query capabilities, auditing, version control, unattended operation, and automatic exhibit generation. However, spreadsheets are a good choice for:

- Exploring data samples (using, for example, Excel's PivotTable feature) to identify good candidate metrics
- Prototyping a new metric using data sampled from an external table or flat file
- Consolidating data gathered from questionnaires or by other manual collection methods
- Piloting a departmental metrics program

If you would like to realize the full benefits of metrics automation, spreadsheets are a poor option. You will inevitably compromise accuracy, repeatability, increased measurement frequency, reliability, transparency, or auditability. Of course, for smaller-scale metrics automation efforts, some or all of these benefits may not be needed or desirable.

BUSINESS INTELLIGENCE TOOLS

Business intelligence (BI) and data-mining tools such as SAS, Cognos, and Crystal Reports are a better alternative to spreadsheets. But these, too, have limitations. Many companies have tried to use business intelligence and data-mining tools for metrics and scorecard automation, but they concluded they were trying to fit a square peg in a round hole. A key challenge with BI tools is that they are largely oriented toward helping business analysts perform ad hoc explorations of large data sets. They are less well suited for managing metrics collections over time, because they do not necessarily provide versioning and tracking mechanisms for business logic and metadata. For example, individuals with access to the data warehouse can effectively create and change business logic and metrics unfettered, without formal tracking of these changes. And as you might expect, unmanaged changes to formulae might lead to unreliable results—and decrease trust in the overall system.

A second limitation concerns the availability—or lack thereof—of adapters and "glue code" to extract data from external security devices and control systems. Most business intelligence tools have varying abilities to pull in data from general-purpose enterprise systems like SAP, PeopleSoft, and Documentum and also from XML files, relational database files, and flat files. Cognos, for example, can extract data from all these sources; it also provides facilities for merging and scrubbing source data. This is great news, but it does not necessarily help you if the critical data you need reside in, say, the bowels of a Cisco router or in a particular part of your company's Active Directory tree. In those cases, you would need to supplement the standard BI facilities with custom code.

I do not mean to bash business intelligence and data-mining software packages, because they can be tremendously powerful tools for discovering patterns in data. But keep their appropriate uses in perspective. They were not intended to serve as security metrics automation systems—at least in the ways we need them to. Most BI tools were designed to perform ad hoc data exploration and visualization, not to automate and manage collections of metrics.

SECURITY EVENT AND INCIDENT MANAGEMENT (SIEM) PRODUCTS

A third class of tool that can be used for metrics automation includes the software packages used to warehouse detailed security management information from network hardware and security operations. Often referred to as Security Event Management (SEM) or Security Incident Management (SIM) products, or more broadly as SIEM, these packages typically have enterprise-wide scope and keep detailed information about security operations. Leading SIEM vendors include ArcSight, Cisco (Protego), Intellitactics, NetForensics, and Novell (E-Security).

A typical data center is awash in configuration, fault, performance, and usage accounting data. SIEM packages are architected to handle all of these. One SIEM vendor's product that we know of, for example, is designed to accumulate over 100GB of data per day! The reason for this is that operations personnel need to be able to sense "significant" events within seconds or minutes (at worst) of their occurrence. The result is that very high-granularity, high-frequency data is a by-product of normal data center operations. Such data can be leveraged to support strategic metrics, in addition to the minute-to-minute operational role that it supports now.

SIEM systems, in our view, have their uses but are unlikely candidates to evolve into strategic metrics automation systems. SIEM systems are excellent at many things, but they fall short due to some of the things we want to see in an automation system:

- **Real-time focus:** Strategic metric time frames run to days, weeks, and months—rarely hours, minutes, or seconds, which is what SIEM systems typically focus on.

- **Nonaggregated results:** Strategic metrics focus on characterizing behavior to summarize hundreds or thousands of operational observations—not discrete events.

- **Anomaly detection instead of process measurement:** For strategic metrics, mean and standard deviation values are suitable quantities, whereas SIEM metrics deal with individual events or clusters of associated "sympathetic" events.

- **Operational orientation:** Strategic metrics tend to need information from multiple operational subsystems, while SIEM systems often focus on a specific management area such as network performance, server configuration, or event detection and correlation.

- **Lack of connectivity to nonsecurity data sources:** Measurements reported by SIEM systems are based on data collected by the operational system itself. In contrast, strategic security metrics tend to integrate data collected from multiple external primary or secondary data sources outside the scope of SIEM, such as HR management systems. These primary or secondary data sources are often called *element management systems* due to their singular focus on one relatively narrow area.

- **Reporting:** The focus of an operational system is to provide adequate management functionality. Publication of measurements is viewed as a reporting feature that is typically quite limited when compared with more "mainline" management features. But a strategic metrics system's whole purpose is creation, computation, and communication of quantitative data from disparate but related sources; it is much more than mere "reporting."

TECHNICAL REQUIREMENTS FOR AUTOMATION SOFTWARE

This section discusses requirements for both enterprise-class metrics automation software and the supporting management discipline for maximizing the value of security metrics.

The purpose of metrics automation software is to enhance the maturity of an organization's use of measurement and analysis to transform raw data into insight. Such a system delivers on this objective by providing a trusted environment that enforces and perpetuates regular, repeatable, and auditable metric results collection, computation, persistence, and publication. Strategies for improvement are the focus. Disputes over data quality or processing algorithm validity must be minimized, if not eliminated.

The following are key functional requirements for automating metrics:

- **Design environment:** A graphical user interface to design and implement metrics, scorecards, and associated business logic, without programming, is required. Security analysts are the target audience for this design activity, not IT data center operations staff or software developers.

- **Metrics life cycle support:** A robust, standards-based environment is required to ensure that metric results are collected from authoritative sources, run on-schedule, use agreed-upon computational techniques, provide traceable continuity across time, and conform to standards for regularity, accuracy, and auditable change control. This framework must simultaneously deliver trust, reliability, and scalability.

- **Business context mappings:** A facility for placing metric results into the context of the business and business processes under measurement is required. This is a critical prerequisite for strategic application of metric results to yield the insight necessary for improving business process effectiveness and efficiency.

- **Content management work flow:** Metrics are valuable content. Their associated business logic represents one form of content, while metric results and scorecard editions represent another. Both forms of content will expand as time passes—more metrics will be created, and they will be deployed into production to create more metric results and scorecard editions.

- **Flexible results publication:** An adaptable mechanism to support the communication of metric results in the form of scorecard editions is required. Policies associated with metric results distribution include entitlement (who can see what), visualization (what it should look like), dissemination (e-mail, website, static, dynamic), annotation (human-generated interpretation), and subscriptions for automatically "pushed" alerts and notifications. Specifically, media such as PDF files, e-mail messages, and preexisting corporate intranets must be supported while leveraging tools already in place. "Yet another dashboard" is not a desirable solution.

As the use of metrics for security grows, I expect that certain conventions and best practices will emerge, not unlike what has happened in the Network and Enterprise Systems Management disciplines with the establishment of Service Level Agreements and universally accepted metrics for Quality of Service. Automation systems that formally manage the content associated with metrics will facilitate the establishment of "metrics exchanges" that will have the potential to drive measurement across industries and administrative boundaries. This is essential for enterprise business services that span departments, supply chains, enterprises, and business ecosystems.

To meet our functional and usage requirements, Table 7-1 shows the key technical requirements for automation of metrics in detail.

Table 7-1   Technical Requirements for Metrics Automation

Requirement	Description	Benefit
Data portability	Metrics should be data-source-agnostic. The data sources needed to drive them should be defined in a manner that allows "late binding" to the specific provider(s) of this data.	The same metric can be used in more than one IT environment. Thus, partners can share their metrics, despite having different antivirus, vulnerability, HR, and network management products, and so on.
Identity and Access Management (IAM) portability	Identity and access management for metrics should integrate seamlessly with preexisting enterprise directory services.	Administrative overhead of users and entitlements is reduced, and with consequential increase in metric information security.
Abstraction of external dependencies	A metric should be packaged as a self-contained entity. External dependencies such as data sources, computational functions, or scorecard charting capabilities must be explicitly identified in the form of interface definitions, not hard-coded implementations.	Management of metrics is greatly simplified, and sharing of metrics between independent designers is facilitated.
Separation of design from production	The environment for designing metrics should be physically and logically distinct from the environment in which the metrics execute to generate results.	Introduction of new metrics and their resulting data into production operations can be carefully controlled. Specifically, the system should version metrics business logic and should ensure that the collected results are consistently generated.

Requirement	Description	Benefit
Separation of computation from publication	All compute logic for a metric should be encapsulated within the metric business logic and placed under strict version control. Incorporation of computational operations within any publication function should be discouraged.	Separation ensures consistency and auditability of all published metric results. It also ensures that all metric results are available to the widest possible range of publication facilities without any dependence on computational idiosyncrasies embedded in publication logic.
Mining at the edge	Metrics should extract precisely their required data at the point of generation (the data source).	Sensitive data should be isolated, typically to a small number of nodes. Retained data is limited strictly to the results of metric computation—not all the detailed data that may have been used to create it. External data sources are asked to provide precisely the data needed to compute a metric, thus drastically reducing the amount of data used when compared with classical data warehousing extract-transform-load strategies.
Open results	Metric results should be broadly accessible to a wide variety of consumers.	Metric results can drive other related processes, such as risk management, compliance, and audit functions.
View portability	Metric visualization should be publisher-agnostic.	The mechanism used to publish results can leverage preexisting infrastructure such as enterprise intranets or management consoles.

A few of these items merit further explanation. Several of the items in Table 7-1, such as the separation of computation from publication, and of design from production, refer to the need to keep different organizational duties separate. The person operating the production servers used to collect and compute metrics usually isn't the same person who designs scorecards.

On a related note, different system owners have varying needs for confidentiality and integrity of data within the scope of the systems they operate. When gathering data for analyzing password quality, for example, it makes no sense to pull passwords out of individual systems and store them in a central repository. Thus, in many cases organizations should try to "mine at the edge"—do preliminary computations via a process that runs on the source system directly. After initial mining has finished, the rough results can be forward to the automation system's repository. This strategy has an additional benefit of reducing the amount of data stored by the metrics automation system.

A third theme running through the IAM portability, view portability, and data portability requirements concerns interoperability. Most organizations have purchased many systems over the years for managing users, reporting on activities, and storing data. They will undoubtedly purchase more in the future. Thus, an effective metrics automation system should integrate with—but not depend on—the vagaries and idiosyncrasies of particular data sources.

The preceding list of formal technical requirements focuses primarily on the most desirable technical attributes we need. I have deliberately glossed over one of the most important aspects of metrics automation: the data model used to represent security events. Thus, the next section discusses security metrics requirements from the standpoint of the data model. After that, we turn to the external system interfaces (data sources and sinks) involved in metrics collection.

DATA MODEL

To effectively implement a metrics program, we need a model to frame the myriad of quantitative values that threat, exposure, countermeasure, and asset metrics provide. Our model should explain our view of the IT security environment and should help us frame and answer the following questions:

- Which metrics are the most critical to measure?
- Which ones are the drivers or independent variables?
- Which ones are just reflections of changes in the drivers—namely, dependent variables?
- What is the sensitivity relationship between independent or driver metrics and the metrics that reflect results?
- Are sensitivities linear, logarithmic, exponential, or sinusoidal?

Figure 7-1 depicts a logical model of the most basic of IT security processes: describing how threats, exposures, and countermeasures interact as part of a system of controls. My model is largely a synthesis of a model used by Clear Point Metrics and several other models from vendors, educators, and standards bodies. It provides a framework for identifying independent variables, dependent variables, and their relationships. No doubt you have seen something similar to this model elsewhere. Others exist that can be equally illuminating.

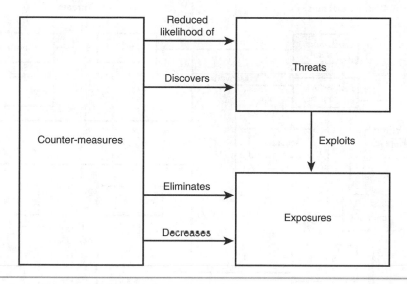

Figure 7-1 Logical Model of IT Security Controls (Level 1)

The model shows a simple block diagram with three interacting forces: threats, exposures, and countermeasures. *Threats* are things that can happen or are the result of proactive acts against one or more target assets. *Vulnerabilities* are characteristics of target assets that make them more prone to attack by a threat or make an attack more likely to succeed or have impact. Threats exploit vulnerabilities, the results of which are *exposures* to the assets. *Countermeasures* are designed to prevent threats from happening or to mitigate their impact when they do. Underlying each of the three preceding concepts (threats, exposures, and countermeasures) are *assets*—namely, the targets of threats, the possessors of exposures, or the beneficiaries of countermeasures. Assets are the things we were supposed to be protecting in the first place.

Merrill Lynch's Alberto Cardona uses a football analogy to explain the differences between assets, vulnerabilities, threats, and countermeasures:

"Your asset is the quarterback. His weak knee is the vulnerability. The primary threat is the other team. Countermeasures include knee-pads, lots of painkillers, and a strong offensive line."[3]

---

[3] Adapted from correspondence between the author and Cardona, October 2006.

To map the data model to metrics automation a bit more formally, let us drill down a bit more. Figure 7-2 shows the model, decomposed further for each of the three areas.

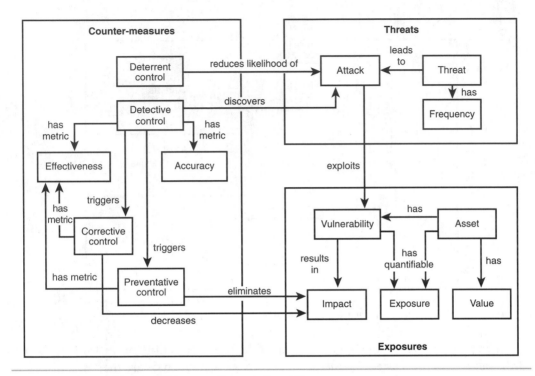

Figure 7-2   Logical Model of IT Security Controls (Level 2)

THREATS

- First, consider the Threats portion of the model. Threats lead to *attacks*. Attacks result in *exploits* directed at specific *exposures*.

- Attacks are *detected* and managed by components within the IT environment, including, for example, commercial products from the SIEM market segment. Managed Security Services Providers (MSSPs) specialize in this part of the ecosystem. (I will discuss the operational aspects of attack detection later, in our discussion of the physical view.)

- For measuring attacks, the most basic quantity is frequency or attack *arrival rate*, measured in terms of number of detected events per unit of time. Other measures include *success* or *failure rates*.

- Simple metrics that can be derived from frequency measurements include the *mean event rate*, variance, standard deviation, maximum, and minimum over several time periods.

For the attacks the model measures, various "dimensions" can be added to these quantities by dividing the observed events into subgroups. These subgroups can be based on event attributes such as event severity, event type, target asset, or attacker. These subgroups can be further refined. For example, target assets can be partitioned by asset value, business service supported, operating system, or owning business unit.

The implications of tagging each attack with asset and event attributes are straightforward. By associating attacks with assets (which are in turn associated with organizations, business services, or business units), we can create metrics that show mean and standard deviation event incidence for:

- Business units, ranked by asset value
- Affected business service
- Targeted operating system
- Severity of attack

Moreover, using forecasting models such as linear regression, one can develop projections for future incident frequency. Using correlation models, one can identify potential interdependencies between attack frequency or severity and other measured factors.

EXPOSURES

Let us examine the Exposures portion of the exhibit. For purposes of discussion, we define exposures as instances of negative characteristics of assets, brought on by a vulnerability that applies to that asset. Exposures can exist for lots of reasons—because of the asset's location (it is Internet-facing, for example), the functions it performs, the technology it uses, its user base, or the workload it is subjected to.

Standards organizations such as Mitre Corporation and First.org, Inc. play an important role in formalizing methods for modeling exposures. Mitre and First.org oversee, respectively, the Common Vulnerabilities and Exposures (CVE) dictionary and Common Vulnerability Scoring System (CVSS). Beyond these two efforts, a broad collection of organizations (some for-profit, some not) maintains vulnerability databases.

In this category are services such as ICAT/NVD,[4] BugTraq,[5] CERT,[6] and the X-Force database from Internet Security Systems.

The Common Vulnerabilities and Exposures website[7] defines the term "exposure" slightly differently. It defines it as security-related facts about an asset that might be classified as vulnerabilities by some, but not necessarily by everyone. (Vulnerability, like beauty or ugliness, is in the eye of the beholder.) For this discussion, let us treat vulnerabilities and exposures as synonymous. The point is that when an attack successfully exploits a vulnerability, there is an impact.

Models that attempt to measure the impact of exposures tend to be quite specific to the asset, the vulnerability, and the attack. Impact is often measured in dollars or in percent degradation. Converting impact into a quantitative measure typically takes additional information, such as revenue per transaction, cost per hour of unavailability, baseline throughput, or mean service time. More complex models take into account the network of interdependencies between assets that commonly comprise a business service.

Many third-party tools map exposures to network assets, including vulnerability scanners like Qualys, Foundstone, and Nessus. Modeling exposures to business services, however, requires higher-order models than a vulnerability scanner can provide.

COUNTERMEASURES

Countermeasures thwart attacks. For the purposes of our model, four types of control techniques are used by countermeasures:

- **Deterrent** controls reduce the likelihood of an attack.
- **Preventive** controls reduce exposure.
- **Corrective** controls reduce the impact of a successful attack.
- **Detective** controls discover attacks and trigger preventive or corrective controls.

ISPs that aggressively block phishing sites are an example of a deterrent control in that they lower the likelihood of identity theft attacks. Firewalls are an example of a preventive control because they block bad traffic. Antivirus software is an example of a

---

4   See the U.S. National Vulnerability Database at http://nvd.nist.gov.

5   See BugTraq at http://www.securityfocus.com/bid.

6   See CERT at http://www.kb.cert.org/vuls.

7   See http://www.cve.mitre.org.

corrective control because it removes detected infections. Examples of detective controls include Intrusion Detection Systems (IDSs) and SIEM systems. However, most companies use their IDS and SIEM systems only to detect attacks; they do not typically use them to trigger corrective controls, other than perhaps updating an event display or cutting a trouble ticket.

For deterrent, preventive, and corrective controls, metrics that quantify effectiveness and efficiency are most important. Both of these ideas can be expressed as percentages—for example, the percentage of attacks thwarted or the percentage of throughput lost. A well-known and hotly debated metric in this space is *accuracy*, defined as 1.0 minus the percentage of false alarms. The term *false positive* is often used to refer to the detection of an attack that turns out not to be one.

ASSETS

The preceding discussion naturally suggests a potential logical model of the IT security environment—essential for automation. If we can model threats, exposures, and countermeasures of the security environment we are measuring successfully, we are that much closer to automating the measurement process.

Although we did not break them into their own section of the diagram, assets are central to our understanding of our logical model. It is worth taking a few moments to elaborate. First, assets are not just targets of attack; they can also be involved in delivering or countering the attack.

As I mentioned in Chapter 4, "Measuring Program Effectiveness," estimating asset value is a difficult, if not impossible, endeavor. No consensus exists on methodology for assigning dollar values to assets. For example, many IT assets are merely part of the infrastructure and are not directly involved in the moneymaking or value-delivering parts of the organization. For example, commodity servers, commercial software products, and networking gear are sold generically to millions of customers. Many security products that provide countermeasures, attack detection, and vulnerability scanning focus on this type of asset. Any individual running instance of these products probably will not have a direct business value, although a collection of these will, in aggregate.

I do not take a particularly hard-and-fast position about the right way to model asset values. However, data models for automation need flexibility for *naming* and *grouping* them. Assets are, in themselves, hierarchies of contained assets that coexist in networks of other, interdependent assets. It is important to allow flexibility for such fuzzy concepts as "aggregate" assets, containment hierarchies, and aliases.

Models exist for understanding basic containment and dependency relationships, but a lot of customization is always required to map metrics about individual components into metrics about the system they comprise. For this reason, tools to compose and tune asset relationships and asset values will always be a requirement for any complete automation system.

The preceding discussion is not meant to be the definitive treatise on security modeling. No one model is appropriate for all companies to use. The security and risk management market has created many alternative versions, and I am sure you have your favorite. This model was intended to get you started. Next, we turn to a discussion about how the metrics model drives requirements for automating metrics collection.

DATA SOURCES AND SINKS

At a high level, security metrics obtain measurements from data produced by a collection of external data *sources*, apply some business logic, and finally publish results (such as scorecards) to an external *sink*. The word "sink" is just a fancy, slightly formal way of saying "destination." The *American Oxford Dictionary* defines sink as "a body or process that acts to absorb or remove energy or a particular component from a system."

Framing sources and sinks in terms of work flow, at one end of the work flow is a collection of data providers (sources); at the other end are results publishers (sinks). The business logic associated with computation and visualization transforms raw data into insight. In this section we focus on the external data providers and data publishers. These are the integration points between an automated metrics and scorecard system and its surrounding ecosystem.

Figure 7-3 depicts the ecosystem in which metrics operate. Notice that, given our focus in this book, we have (naturally) placed Security Metrics at the center of the universe.

Note that the automated security metrics system at the center is both a consumer and a producer of services and data with the other members of the ecosystem. From a technology point of view, this closed-loop symmetry is at the heart of an effective metrics and scorecard automation system.

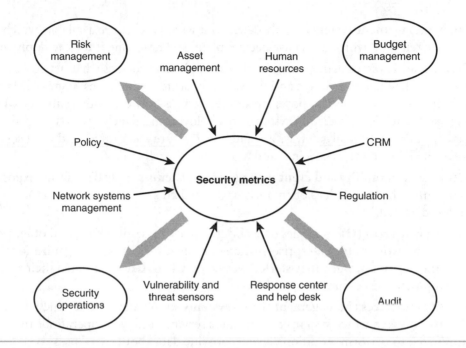

Figure 7-3　Metrics Automation Ecosystem

DATA SOURCES

Metrics automation systems need to *consume* data from external systems to drive the computation of metrics. This is a requirement of many types of software. Most software that requires significant heterogeneous connectivity uses adapters or connectors to form a software bridge to external data providers. The art and science of writing adapters are well developed. Much prior art is available to be leveraged.

When a metric computes, it consumes data from authoritative sources (Figure 7-3 shows just a few possibilities):

- **Asset management systems** supply data such as what classes of assets exist, how many there are of each, where they are located, how much they cost, and who owns them.

- **Configuration management systems** supply data such as what operating system IT assets run, what software is installed, how assets are configured, and what changes have been made to these assets.

- **Patch management systems** supply data about what patches are available, which ones are relevant, which ones have been applied, and how long it took to apply them.

- **Network and system management** systems supply data such as what networks are operational, where the routers and firewalls are located, what access control lists are defined, what protocols and ports are allowed to pass between which subnets, where intrusion detection/protection systems are deployed and which systems are protected, where the e-mail gateways are and how they are configured, and what servers are in the DMZ (Internet-facing) and how they are performing.

- **Security vulnerability and event management systems** supply data about exposure to potential threats (such as open ports or unpatched software) and the actual threats detected.

- **Human resources (HR)** supplies data about employees, contractors, and other personnel who work in the enterprise—where they have offices, what organizational units they work for, when they started work, and when they terminated their relationship with the company.

- **Identity and Access Management (IAM) systems** supply data about which individuals have access to which systems and business services and what operations they are authorized to perform. Additionally, they provide data about users' password strength, how often they change passwords, and whether vendor default accounts are still active.

- **Customer Relationship Management (CRM)** supplies data about customers such as their activity level, satisfaction, and demographics.

- The **Incident Response Center** supplies data about escalated threats and their mitigation, internal user issues and their resolution, escalated customer issues and response time, and staff utilization and workload.

- **Policy information** drives internal best practices, benchmarks, and operational parameters.

- **Regulatory information** informs operational and business requirements.

- **Audit results** contain deficiencies that need resolution.

These data sources, summarized in Table 7-2, produce raw data for a metrics automation system to consume. There may be more than one authoritative system for each of these external sources of data. One example is a company that has multiple copies of Microsoft's Active Directory Service deployed globally. Another example is a company that uses HP OpenView Network Node Manager to manage all its routers, Tivoli Enterprise Console to manage its servers, and Microsoft Operations Manager to manage its desktop and laptop computers. The permutations and combinations of commercial management products in a data center are numerous. This reinforces a critical architectural requirement for metrics automation described earlier—source portability. The business logic associated with a metric must be able to accommodate the wide range of external systems that it relies on for data to drive it.

Table 7-2 Metrics Data Sources and Sinks

Data Source	Data Sink
Asset management systems	Risk management systems
Configuration management systems	Budget management
Patch management systems	Audit and compliance assessment systems (internal or external)
Network and system management	Security operations
Security vulnerability and event management systems	General-purpose reporting systems
Human resources (HR)	Scorecard management systems
Identity and access management systems (IAM)	
Customer relationship management (CRM)	
The Incident Response Center	
Policy information	
Regulatory information	
Audit results	

Figure 7-4 shows the data sources in a conceptual (physical) diagram of a typical data center. Multiple vendors, products, device types, commercial software packages, and homegrown technologies are in the mix. When most people see a diagram like this, they usually start free-associating with products in their own data centers—and can name at least 20 products.

Each of the commercial products shown in Figure 7-4 typically generates data that indicates how it is configured, what workload it is seeing, what connections to other systems it has or is using, what faults it is detecting, and often measurements to characterize the quality of service that it is providing (such as availability, throughput, service time, and variations thereof). All this information is highly valuable to the computation of security metrics.

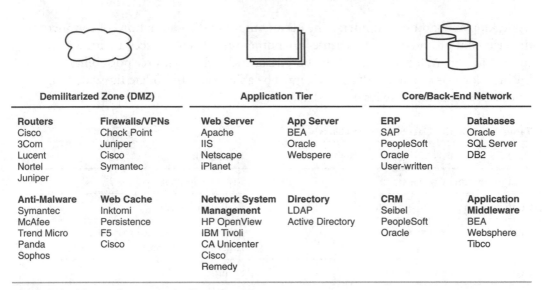

Demilitarized Zone (DMZ)		Application Tier		Core/Back-End Network	
Routers	**Firewalls/VPNs**	**Web Server**	**App Server**	**ERP**	**Databases**
Cisco	Check Point	Apache	BEA	SAP	Oracle
3Com	Juniper	IIS	Oracle	PeopleSoft	SQL Server
Lucent	Cisco	Netscape	Webspere	Oracle	DB2
Nortel	Symantec	iPlanet		User-written	
Juniper					
Anti-Malware	**Web Cache**	**Network System**	**Directory**	**CRM**	**Application**
Symantec	Inktomi	**Management**	LDAP	Seibel	**Middleware**
McAfee	Persistence	HP OpenView	Active Directory	PeopleSoft	BEA
Trend Micro	F5	IBM Tivoli		Oracle	Websphere
Panda	Cisco	CA Unicenter			Tibco
Sophos		Cisco			
		Remedy			

Figure 7-4   Metrics Sources in the Data Center

Of course, so much data are available from these sources that analysts can become overwhelmed. The operational tasks that each system supports function in timeframes of seconds and minutes. Thus, each system can, by itself, generate massive amounts of data—in its own format, and destined for its own storage location. The flood of data can obscure or conceal crucial insights that the data should instead be facilitating.

Fortunately, such fine granularity of operational data can be aggregated and summarized using a handful of techniques. Betsy Nichols notes that "In Clear Point Metrics' experience, gleaned by generating hundreds of metrics, we have discovered only a few patterns—less than twenty—that cover the vast majority of computational algorithms. In the same way that SQL encapsulates a large portion of basic processing requirements for data in relational databases, there are similar operations that accomplish the processing associated with operational data aggregation for metrics."[8]

In summary, the metrics data sources in the typical environment are complex, but we can do much to understand and manage them. There is no shortage of data. Metrics and models from related fields are applicable. And automation can help quickly develop, introduce, and evaluate candidate metrics for standardization or acceptance, as well as facilitate the exchange of metrics, if not data.

---

[8]   From conversation with Betsy Nichols.

DATA SINKS

As mentioned in the preceding paragraphs, metrics automation systems need to collect data from a wide number of sources. They also need to *produce* metric results that can be used downstream by other members of the ecosystem. Most notably, human analysts must produce scorecards for consumption.

Ideally, an enterprise-class metrics publishing system, as a feature of an overall metric automation system, should implement connectors to common report writers, dashboards, charting and graphing packages, relational database management systems, and web content management systems. Some possibilities include:

- **Risk management systems:** Metrics produced by the automation system can compute threat probability, vulnerability latency, and countermeasure coverage. These can be potentially quite relevant inputs for risk-modeling systems.

- **Budget management systems:** Metrics produced by the system measure level of effort, impact, and availability. These can be transformed into dollar values for the purpose of establishing budgets as well as computing return on investment. Budgets are both inputs (How much money did we plan to spend?) and outputs (What did we actually spend?).

- **Audit and compliance assessment systems** (internal or external): Metrics that compute policy compliance for individual resources as well as groups of resources yield results that can enhance reports generated by compliance tools.

- **Security operations:** Metrics that accumulate data over time can help identify trends that suggest specific strategies or best practices for adoption by data center operations staff. Metrics that develop projections based on historical data can be used for planning and what-if analysis.

- **General-purpose reporting systems:** Any results computed by a metric are fair game for being included in operational or ad hoc reports.

- **Scorecard management systems:** Purpose-built software designed explicitly for managing scorecards can visualize metric results. Such systems address both the common functions associated with any modern content management system and several extensions that address the unique aspects of handling results generated by metrics. These include requirements for auditability, repeatability, and consistency across scorecard editions generated over time.

Because many of these technologies already exist in commercial computing environments, it is quite important for a metrics automation system not to replicate any of these technologies. We have heard more than one customer make statements such as

"We have too many consoles—one for each of our products."

and

"If a vendor pitches one more dashboard to us, I'll personally shoot him."

It seems reasonable to assume that some form of adapter or connector architecture is required to produce scorecards—similar but not identical to the familiar connector architecture for consuming data.

External data providers and data consumers can be commercial off-the-shelf software or homegrown applications. The next section looks at the technical requirements associated with exchanging data with external data providers and consumers.

DATA INTERFACES

Integrating disparate software systems is becoming increasingly important as companies continue to become more reliant on information technology to do business. Companies are crossing enterprise boundaries to automate supply chains, share customer credit information, obtain real-time market data, settle trades, run payroll, and on and on. Metrics and scorecard automation are facilitated when the systems that share their ecosystem natively support external interfaces.

So what do these external interfaces look like—technically? The most common interface formats include recent technologies such as XML and web services, and older technologies such as relational databases and delimited ASCII file formats. This section gives a quick sketch of a typical, complex data center environment and the interface technologies that are important for metrics collection.

DATA SOURCE INTERFACES

Important interface technologies for external data sources include:

- XML documents or messages
- CSV files
- Structured ASCII logs
- Excel spreadsheets
- LDAP directories
- Relational database management systems
- Syslog message streams

- Simple Network Management Protocol (SNMP) Management Information Bases (MIBs)
- Web services: Web Service Definition Language (WSDL) and Simple Object Access Protocol (SOAP)
- RSS feeds
- Published software application programming interfaces

DATA SINK (PRESENTATION) INTERFACES

Important interface technologies for scorecards are predominantly associated with systems for data visualization, page layout, publication, and distribution. These include the following:

- For static document definition:
  - HTML
  - Adobe PDF
  - Microsoft Excel spreadsheets
  - XML
  - Image formats such as GIF, JPEG, PNG

- For static document delivery:
  - E-mail
  - Shared file systems and FTP
  - Static websites

- For dynamic document definition:
  - Java-centric: JSP, applets
  - Microsoft-centric: ASP, web parts
  - Interactive data exploration: special "widgets" from companies like Spotfire and ILOG

- For dynamic document delivery:
  - Websites
  - Fat clients

Off-the-shelf commercial data providers can be integrated with a metrics automation system via prebuilt adapters. Most homegrown applications can be integrated via generic interfaces such as SQL/JDBC, LDAP, spreadsheets, or comma-delimited file readers.

Having discussed the myriad of interfaces that an automated metrics system must support, let us now look at the ways in which automation is implemented as part of a larger security metrics program.

METRICS PROGRAM MANAGEMENT

Metrics do not suddenly appear fully formed like Athena from the forehead of Zeus. Metrics are created through an evolutionary process that gains consensus and ensures regular and thorough reviews both before and after publication. This process also includes human analysis and interpretation of results. Key steps include:

- Identification
- Definition
- Development
- Quality assurance
- Production deployment
- Visualization of results
- Analysis of results
- Scorecard layout
- Scorecard publication
- Notification publication
- Scorecard archival

Table 7-3 lists each phase in the life cycle of a metric along with some commentary regarding its suitability for automation. The importance (priority) of automation of each phase varies. Some things (like the Identification phase) need not be automated, but their gathering and distillation steps (Production Deployment) must be.

Table 7-3 Metrics Life Cycle

Life Cycle Phase	Importance of Automation	Description	Automation Measures
Identification	Low	The need for and objective(s) of the metric are established.	None
Definition	Low	A formal definition of the metric is created. This includes authoritative data sources, compute logic, units of measure, assumptions, schedule, draft visualization, and alert criteria.	None
Development	High	An executable version of the metric is created.	Tools to facilitate both the creation of a metric's business logic and integration with authoritative data sources Formal metric metadata models that facilitate categorization, search, and content management
Quality assurance	High	The validity of the metrics is established via testing with a wide variety of data.	Management of test data that provides the needed coverage of potential test cases Tools to track changes
Production deployment	High	The metric is put into production so that it generates computed results on a specified schedule using specified authoritative data sources. Changes to the metric's compute logic as well as input parameters are logged.	Tools to configure the metric Platform to run the metric on a schedule Connectors to external data sources Repository to store computed results
Visualization of results	High	The results are displayed in the form of graphs, charts, or other displays.	Automation can provide a variety of mechanisms and formats. Selection of the most suitable or efficient mechanism cannot be automated.

continues

Table 7-3   Metrics Life Cycle (Continued)

Life Cycle Phase	Importance of Automation	Description	Automation Measures
Analysis of results	Medium	Subject matter experts review results and formulate conclusions and annotations.	None. However, documentation of conclusions or findings can be facilitated via automated content management technologies.
Scorecard layout	Medium	Subject matter experts design what metrics will be visualized and organized, along with textual annotations.	Layout design cannot be automated, but tools can make the process more efficient. Publication of multiple scorecard editions based on changing metric results over time should be automated.
Scorecard publication	High	The scorecards are distributed to authorized recipients.	Publishing mechanisms for websites and e-mail systems
Notification publication	High	When prespecified criteria are met, notifications are issued to authorized recipients.	Subscription management Notifications via e-mail
Scorecard archival	Medium	Historical editions of each scorecard are stored in a manner that allows them to be searched and browsed by authorized users.	Scorecard search and archive facilities

IMPLEMENTING METRICS AUTOMATION: A CASE STUDY

Metrics are most effective when surrounded with institutionalized processes that addresses:

- Framing the problem statement: What needs to be measured, and why?
- Recognizing and gaining access to authoritative data sources
- Achieving consensus on what data to collect and how to compute metrics
- Regular measurement and generation of results according to an agreed-upon schedule
- Consistent compilation of scorecards and a work flow to facilitate review, interpretation, and ultimate publication of regular editions
- Scheduled scorecard reviews that lead to quantitatively based decisions whose effects will be measured by future metric results and scorecard editions

In large companies, the process of reviewing metric results to drive decisions strongly resembles the processes of financial performance and sales performance. Performed monthly, these reviews not only set the agenda for what metrics to collect but also provide a forum for analyzing results to date, making decisions, and then making adjustments in both the processes being measured and the measurements themselves.

The following is an example from a company that Clear Point Metrics has worked with. This example spans the entire life cycle of a metric—from Identification and Definition to Scorecard Archival.

The customer's Security Steering Committee (SSC) includes representatives from each business unit, IT operations, the help desk, and the office of the CISO. In a meeting in October 2004, the issue of purchasing a new centralized IAM system was introduced and a decision made to allocate funds. Additionally, the SSC mandated that a measurement project be established to quantitatively characterize the current state as well as the future state of the IAM after product installation over weekly intervals.

Identification

During the Identification phase, the company asked the following questions:

- What is the efficiency of user management, in terms of how much time and cost (assuming $54 per hour) are required to provision a new user, delete an invalid user, or update an existing user?
- What is the overall investment in the new IAM system annually, including license cost, maintenance cost, and consultants hired to install and operate the system?
- What is the accuracy of user management?

Definition

During the Definition phase, the company determined that the following metrics should be computed:

- User accounts deleted improperly
- Failed password maintenance operations
- User accounts left active improperly
- User accounts that are not policy-compliant (such as passwords over 90 days old)

The company decided to generate these metrics on a weekly basis, starting immediately. In addition, to show that the IAM system was effective, the company resolved to collect "before" metrics for at least 12 weeks prior to the new IAM system "going live" and "after" metrics for the foreseeable future.

Development and Quality Assurance

As part of the Development phase (and in preparation for Visualization of Results), the company laid out and published a collection of scorecards to visualize and interpret results. These were published weekly to a list of designated recipients—around 30 business unit managers, supervisors from the help desk and IT operations, and CISO analysts. Regular reviews were scheduled monthly to coincide with existing regularly scheduled meetings of the SSC.

Production Deployment

After computation of the metrics but before publication of the scorecards, a prepublication work flow was established to:

- Review all metric results for completeness, accuracy, and anomalies
- Develop textual narrative and annotations to clarify any identified issues
- Compile final drafts of the scorecards
- Sign off for publication

This work flow strongly resembled the process commonly used for updating content on an intranet website.

Scorecard Publication

Automation of the Scorecard Publication phase leveraged existing content management technologies that provided:

- Definition of publication projects
- Establishment and tracking of tasks, milestones, and responsible individuals
- Online collaboration, revision, and review of drafts
- Work flow tracking
- Management of content objects such as images, ASCII text, static and dynamic web components
- Simple page layout
- Transformation of content into various media types such as PDF, images, or HTML pages
- Version tracking
- Sign-off
- Managing users and entitlements down to the component level

- Web publication
- E-mail distribution lists and e-mail notifications

Effective program management helped ensure that each weekly scorecard represented the most accurate possible characterization of IAM process performance to-date. Because the scorecard results were trusted, the discussion at the monthly review meetings focused on what the metrics meant and what decisions they should drive, not how they were computed or why they should be ignored.

Summary

Metrics automation delivers on the promise of security metrics by making the process of data gathering, computation, and presentation efficient and repeatable. Benefits from automation include accuracy, repeatability, increased measurement frequency, reliability, transparency, and auditability.

Transparency ensures that organizations can easily understand how metrics were derived; reliability allows organizations to derive confidence from the knowledge that computations are being carried out faithfully. Both of these benefits increase trust in the metrics program. Increased measurement frequency allows management to more closely align security metrics with weekly, monthly, and quarterly initiatives.

For large enterprises, the best solution for automating metrics collection is often a purpose-built collection and computation tool, such as that provided by Clear Point Metrics. Spreadsheets are a good choice for prototyping particular metrics, but they suffer from poor scalability, version control concerns, and a lack of transparency. Business intelligence tools offer much more flexibility for data mining and ad hoc discovery but may not always offer the level of required connectivity to specific security data sources. SIEM products can generally connect to most security tools but are often too operationally focused and lack the ability to connect to semi-structured external data sources and nonsecurity sources such as ERP and HR information systems. Regardless of the technology chosen, a good metrics automation system should have a design environment, metrics life cycle support, business context mappings, content management work flow support, and flexible results publication features. Technically speaking, metrics automation systems should feature:

- Data portability
- IAM system portability
- Abstraction of external dependencies

- Separation of design from production
- Separation of computation from publication
- Mining at the edge
- Open results
- View portability

The logical data model for the metrics catalog should model threats, vulnerabilities, countermeasures, and assets. The asset model should support hierarchy, containment, and flexible naming.

Data sources for metrics automation systems include asset databases, configuration management systems, patch management systems, network and system management products, SIEM systems, HR information systems, threat and vulnerability management systems, IAM systems, and CRM systems. Data sinks (output targets) include risk management systems, security operations, scorecard applications, and budget management systems. Common data interfaces and formats include XML, CSV, LDAP, SQL, SNMP, SOAP, and plain old ASCII.

Metrics automation systems should include flexible support for publishing static documents (HTML, PDF, XML, Excel), delivering results (e-mail, FTP), and dynamically generated content (JSP, applet, ASP).

Although there is no canonical way to create, implement, and automate metrics, a life cycle approach to metrics development can ensure that the process flows smoothly. Phases in metrics development include:

- Identification
- Definition
- Development
- Quality assurance
- Production deployment
- Visualization of results
- Analysis of results

After an organization collects and analyzes its security metrics, only one step remains: to create a scorecard that pulls everything together. In the next chapter, "Designing Security Scorecards," I present an approach for designing a "Balanced Security Scorecard" that presents a compact, holistic view of organizational security effectiveness.

Designing Security Scorecards

"How'm I doing?"

—Former New York City Mayor Edward I. Koch, ca. 1978

Keeping score is a natural human activity. We do it in school, with our sports teams, in our personal lives, and with political candidates. Familiar methods of scoring include report cards and test scores, sports box scores and league standings, stock indices, and opinion polls.

There are lots of reasons for scorekeeping: performance measurement, intellectual curiosity, creeping jealousies, and sometimes simple nosiness. Because I am not a licensed psychologist—merely one with armchair credentials—this chapter focuses only the business performance aspects of scorekeeping—in particular, on scoring security performance.

Scorekeeping, when expressed in a tangible form using a communications medium, takes the form of a *scorecard. The Oxford English Dictionary* defines scorecard as "a printed card with a blank form on which spectators may enter the score in a game."[1] The word *score* itself means "9.a. A notch cut in a stick or tally, used to mark numbers in

---

[1] *The Oxford English Dictionary*, Second Edition (1989), Oxford University Press.

keeping accounts; also the tally itself."[2] Then there is this definition: "1.a. A crack, crevice (*obs.*); a cut, notch, or scratch; a line drawn with a sharp instrument."[3]

I find both definitions helpful. The first reminds us that scores are all about grades and tests; in other words, they are based on evaluations of performance against standards. The second definition alludes to "cuts and scratches"—something we all dread when being scored ourselves.

With that caveat in mind, in the pages that follow I discuss the rationales and goals of "good" security scorecards, guided by a set of principles that can help CIOs and senior managers measure the effectiveness of their enterprise security programs in a concise manner.

Metrics scorecards require enterprises to adopt new processes for measurement. Generally, the process includes steps for defining and validating metrics, collecting data, and creating reports. Michael Rasmussen, an analyst with Forrester Research, suggests a simple four-step process:

- Define:
  - Establish metrics team
  - Define metrics and thresholds

- Source:
  - Find metric source
  - Understand accuracy

- Display and refine:
  - Report on results
  - Revise metric definitions

- Collect and enable:
  - Transform data
  - Create manual entry tool if needed

---

[2]   Ibid.

[3]   Ibid. An irrelevant definition of *score* is nonetheless my favorite: "10.a . . . Now chiefly, the row of chalk marks on a door, or of strokes on a slate, which in rural alehouses used to serve to record the quantity of liquor consumed on credit by a regular frequenter." At least half the fun of working in information security are the war stories . . . preferably shared among colleagues over beers.

This chapter focuses primarily on the first step (defining metrics). The bulk of the chapter discusses a proposed design for an information security scorecard using a methodology called the "Balanced Scorecard." Traditionally applied to the business as a whole instead of security, the Balanced Scorecard methodology shows great promise as a way to align information security with business initiatives. I explore this important new frontier by:

- Introducing the Balanced Scorecard methodology
- Attempting to map the Balanced Scorecard to information security
- Selecting metrics for a hypothetical Balanced Security Scorecard
- Identifying potential barriers to acceptance of the Balanced Scorecard by addressing important organizational issues, such as the importance of "mocking up" the scorecard and "cascading" the scorecard to different levels in the organization

THE ELEMENTS OF SCORECARD STYLE

To my knowledge, no Strunk and White guide exists for information security scorecards. I do not propose to create one here. That said, it seems to me that, like a good piece of prose, a security scorecard needs to follow some basic rules of style to maximize its "readability" for the audience:

- **Complete:** It covers everything in the problem space, without overlap.
- **Concise:** It doesn't waste ink getting the point across.
- **Clear:** It communicates simply, without excessive jargon.
- **Relevant:** Topics in the scorecard mean something to the reader.
- **Transparent:** The methods used to derive the scores are readily apparent.

An explanation of each principle follows.

COMPLETE

The most critical quality any security scorecard must have is that it should be *complete*. By complete, I mean what my friends at McKinsey call "conceptually exhaustive": spanning all areas of security. These areas include the classic triad of people, process, and technology issues, as well as higher-level activities like budgeting, innovation, organizational planning, and operations.

Many security software vendors would have you believe that they, and they alone, can build magic dashboards that display a complete picture of organizational security postures and their effectiveness. It is a seductive vision that is easily sold to middle- and upper-level managers. But it is just not true; every software package on the market has biases and blind spots.

Most security software packages can provide very good statistics about the areas of IT infrastructure under their control. But they cannot report on areas not under their control. They also tend to be very weak at the less-tangible issues: organizational policies, budgets, resource allocations, people, and process.

A well-constructed security scorecard needs to take less-tangible issues into account, not just the things that can be easily gathered from an organization's preferred antivirus or endpoint compliance tool. These things can provide important data, but they provide only a small subset of what is needed for a complete scorecard.

CONCISE

Information security practitioners, as a species, are control freaks. Operationally minded security staff, in particular, tend to be voracious devourers of information and statistics. As a result, it is understandable that this trait might manifest itself during an organization's initial attempt at constructing a security scorecard. Some security dashboards I have seen are overloaded with statistical information, of which the vast majority is related to security vulnerabilities or policy compliance. From the perspective of someone steeped in the day-to-day hurly-burly of security operations, all of this detail is invaluable. But from the perspective of nonpractitioners, the flood of detail can seem daunting at first.

It is tempting to report on everything, even the proverbial kitchen sink. But in reality, this temptation masks an unwillingness to make hard choices about which metrics are the *best* ones. Blaise Pascal famously wrote, "I have made this letter longer than usual because I lack the time to make it shorter."

Studies have shown that most people have well-bounded ranges for assimilating information. For example, in the 1940s Bell Labs Research concluded that most people could remember about seven random numbers for a short period of time. It was this discovery, and not limitations on technology, that led AT&T to standardize on a seven-digit telephone numbering system.[4]

Putting the matter more simply, scorecards cannot ask too much of viewers. When constructing a security scorecard, it is wise to scale back the number of selected metrics

---

[4]   Area codes came later.

to the bare minimum needed to convey an accurate sense of where the organization stands. The scorecard should fit on a single-sided sheet of paper, or on a single web page. Clawing back the initial set of metrics is not always easy, but it is a critical step that speeds acceptance and comprehension. For security scorecards, short-and-sweet is a virtue.

CLEAR

Security scorecards work best when they communicate clearly. Clarity does not necessarily imply dumbed-down, but it does imply using plain language and graphics that are easy to understand. Clarity also extends to three areas: exhibits, annotations, and layout.

Scorecard exhibits should be functional rather than festooned with ornate decorations and gratuitous three-dimensional graphics. I made this point fairly forcefully in Chapter 6, "Visualization," but it is one that is especially relevant with scorecards.

Annotations are essential for establishing context in scorecards, especially when that context includes time-series graphics. Nearly everybody has seen historical charts that do this. Many high-school students have seen graphics of, for example, the United States' GDP over the last 100 years. The "Stock Market Crash" annotation that points to 1929 provides extra insight into the sharp drop in GDP that follows. Annotations on security scorecards for major events such as the Slammer Worm can help explain the data on the scorecard. As John Doerr, partner at venture capitalist Kleiner, Perkins, Caufield and Byers, once quipped, "My two favorite words in the English language are 'for example.'"

With respect to layout, scorecards should group similar metrics. For example, a scorecard might have separate sections for perimeter defenses, spending, process measures, and compliance. To keep viewers from confusing themselves, it is best to constrain the number of high-level groupings to a manageable number: not less than three, but not more than about six. More than that will make readers' heads spin.

The goal of a security scorecard is to communicate two things: an organization's security effectiveness, and its related ability to help the business understand and respond to new threats and opportunities in the future. Clear language, sensible exhibits, helpful annotations, and uncomplicated layouts increase the likelihood that the scorecard will get these messages across in the manner you intend.

RELEVANT

Scads of statistics show only that the collector knows how to collect them. They may not be especially relevant to the subject at hand or to the audience. Practitioners should resist the urge to report on everything they can conceive of or collect data on. In the final analysis, metrics mean something only when they assist with decision-making and analysis. Metrics that cause your audience to shrug their shoulders and say "So what?" should be avoided.

Marshalling impressive-looking statistics, in fact, can sometimes be used as a defensive obfuscation technique. My father—an old management consultant, and quite the folksy philosopher—likes to put it this way: "If you can't dazzle 'em with facts, baffle 'em with bullshit."[5]

There is no surer way to tank a scorecard than to lard it with irrelevant metrics. Any data shown on a scorecard needs to pass the smell test. Sensitivity to relevance forces the hanging question, ". . . why should I care?"

An equally important consideration for scorecards is not just the question of why particular data might be relevant, but *for whom*. Not all metrics matter to readers. CFOs will want to know about cost and risk, CEOs care about impact on reputation and profit, and CSOs worry about all of these things and a whole lot more. Operationally focused staff, of course, need details that are much more closely tied to day-to-day risks and problem management.

TRANSPARENT

Many of the security scorecards I have seen are no better than fairy dust: sprinkle enough of it around, and people will feel good—because they have a "dashboard." Consider the common case of the traffic-light-oriented dashboard. As appealing as this might seem on its face, the process used to derive the color is not usually obvious. When people do not understand something, it is easy to dismiss it—especially if that "red" traffic signal describes something that *they* are responsible for. Thus, many traffic-light scorecards subtly provide team members with an incentive to discount their value. Why give readers ammunition to fight over methodology when their time would be better spent discussing specific observed results and outcomes?

Oxford defines *transparent* as "having the property of transmitting light, so as to render bodies lying behind completely visible; that can be seen through; diaphanous."[6] That is an appropriate goal for a scorecard. Effective security scorecards need to help viewers understand what methods were used to derive the metrics they are looking at. In addition, understanding metrics' component parts helps viewers understand how their contributions can influence the scores—positively *or* negatively.

---

[5] Conversation with the author.

[6] *The Oxford English Dictionary*, Second Edition (1989), Oxford University Press.

Concise labels, plain language, and clear units of measure can help make scorecards more transparent. Units of measure are particularly important: the number of "intrusions" isn't useful. But the number of intrusions *requiring investigation* relating to *customer data* might be, especially if the observed *rate* of intrusions increased to a meaningful degree. Measures having more than one unit of measure, such as ratios or percentages, are especially valuable. Absolute numbers should always beg the question: what is the denominator?

Metrics whose unit of measure is an index (a weighted score composed of multiple factors) need special attention. Indices can certainly be effective, but only when their component parts are well communicated and supplemented with annotations. For example, a historical index of PC endpoint compliance scores should have a related call-out, tool tip, or popup that explains how the score was calculated. Annotations could help explain sudden changes in the scores—for example, the acquisition of a new subsidiary or distribution of a new "baseline" configuration.

By the way, averages (arithmetic means) are rarely transparent unless they are broken into multiple cross sections as part of a benchmarking comparison. As discussed previously in this book, averages make terrible analytical devices because they steamroll over outliers in data sets. It's easy to miss the trouble spots when they are averaged out of sight. Dennis Devlin, the CSO of Thompson Financial, summarizes the problems with averages by asking: "If you have one foot in boiling water, and one foot in ice water, would you say that on average you're at room temperature?"

Going beyond simplistic averages, effective scorecards use quartiles, medians, time series, and cross-sectional measures to provide transparency.

THE BALANCED SCORECARD

The world of security scorecarding has long been a halting, approximating, balkanized affair, with few good "role models" organizations can point to. Certainly, the culture of secrecy surrounding security has hindered the creation of a body of practice for security scorecards. But outside of information security, many mature measurement frameworks exist. Scorecard techniques used in areas such as manufacturing and general business administration include Total Quality Management (TQM) and Six Sigma, *kaizen* and the Balanced Scorecard.

Many readers will be familiar with TQM and its related Six Sigma techniques. At its core, Six Sigma describes a set of methods for measuring defects in processes. As discussed in Chapter 5, "Analysis Techniques," Six Sigma denotes the percentage of error-free activities that fall within six standard deviations of the mean—99.9997%, or three defects per million.

Six Sigma makes a great deal of sense for security processes that manage large volumes of data, especially for those where one can associate notions of "flaws" and "defects." Indeed, some security professionals and vendors have begun using Six Sigma for measuring vulnerabilities detected in networked devices, PCs, and servers. Enterprises such as Motorola, for example, use Six Sigma to measure PC workstation and server vulnerabilities. Likewise, vulnerability management vendor Qualys uses Six Sigma techniques to measure how accurate its vulnerability scans are. (In case you were wondering, as of the third quarter of 2005, Qualys measured 129 false positives per 5.1 million scans—that is, its scan accuracy surpasses Five Sigma.)[7]

Incorporation of Six Sigma and TQM techniques into vulnerability management regimes may well be one of the most heartening measurement trends in recent memory. Six Sigma shows great promise as a general-purpose tool for measuring defects in process-driven areas of organizations—and information security is, if nothing else, all about process.

That said, Six Sigma is *just* a tool, albeit a valuable one. As a scorecarding framework, Six Sigma falls short. The Six Sigma methodology says nothing about for what purposes it should be used, and it doesn't offer any organizing principles for framing the security problem per se. For that, we need more than a measurement technique—we need a framework for organizing the problem space. Naturally, it would be dandy if said framework did not just offer some organizing principles, but provided a shared vocabulary that (gasp) businesspeople could relate to.

That might sound like a tall order. Fortunately, a popular business framework for measurement already exists, although it remains relatively obscure in the technology world. Its name? The Balanced Scorecard.

I discovered the Balanced Scorecard several years ago while I was working as a principal at @stake, a digital security consulting firm. @stake specialized in assessing companies' networks and applications for security risks. In late 2000 and early 2001, our consulting business really began to take off. We began receiving inquiries from clients about what to do with all of the risk and vulnerability information they received from us and other consultants. They also began asking us about higher-level services such as helping them create strategies for building security organizations, acquiring new threat-management technologies, and, most importantly, measuring and benchmarking their security programs.

Looking around at the options available to us, I quickly concluded that many of the prevailing perspectives on "scorecards" for information security were incomplete in

---

7 Gerhard Eschelbeck (Qualys), "On-Demand Vulnerability Management and Policy Compliance" (presentation for Yankee Group), October 12, 2005.

some way. The security scorecards I saw, to the extent that companies used them at all, suffered from excesses or deficits in some way:

- Too audit-focused
- Too many metrics, and too technical
- Opaque methodologies, and unclear analytical rigor[8]
- Too focused on vulnerabilities
- No obvious ties to the business

I had seen the Balanced Scorecard cited in several business publications. Curious to learn more, I did some digging. I concluded that the idea was so useful that it was worth mocking up an exploratory scorecard exhibit, based on the Balanced Scorecard, for some of our clients. They liked it very much, but they wanted to know how we would put it into practice. Because @stake was a consulting organization and not a software development house, we could not do it ourselves. And readers may recall that, in 2001, few independent software vendors were thinking of security scorecards in our terms. So the Balanced Scorecard concept stayed put on a dusty shelf.

In the meantime, though, let's take a quick look at what got me, and our clients, so excited.

HISTORY

The Balanced Scorecard was invented over ten years ago by Harvard professors Robert Kaplan and David Norton. Writing in the *Harvard Business Review*,[9] the authors noted that reliance on exclusively financial measures of performance was giving corporations a distorted view of their performance. Put simply, while traditional financial yardsticks offer insight into whether a company is making money, using assets appropriately, or returning value to shareholders, they do not paint a complete picture of organizational health. Among other shortcomings, financial metrics

- Poorly predict future performance—financial measures are trailing indicators.
- May cause management to sacrifice long-term viability at the altar of short-term profits.
- Contain no linkages to organizational strategy.

---

[8] Six Sigma-based scorecards do not suffer from this deficiency.

[9] R.S. Kaplan and D.P. Norton, "The Balanced Scorecard: Measures That Drive Performance," *Harvard Business Review*, January–February 1992, pp. 71–79.

- Reinforce departmental silos.
- Do not measure fulfillment of customer or partner expectations.
- Do not relate to day-to-day activities and incentives of most workers.

The Balanced Scorecard acknowledges that while financial metrics will continue to be used to measure performance, executives need more perspective to understand an organization's true performance. This additional perspective should include nonfinancial metrics that quantify external indicators such as customer expectations and should offer insights into the motivation and well-being of the company's employees.

COMPOSITION

The Balanced Scorecard is "balanced" because it divides organizational performance metrics or *measures*[10] into four primary *perspectives*: financial, customer, internal business process, and learning and growth. The creators of the Balanced Scorecard felt that these four measurement areas, when taken together, paint a more accurate portrait of the organization. Each perspective is defined as follows:

- **Financial:** Traditional measures such as profit and loss, return on invested capital, earnings before interest and taxes (EBIT), earnings per share (EPS), and others.
- **Customer:** Measures that indicate how effectively the organization serves its customer base, such as customer retention, market share, customer complaints, order fill rate, average deal size, and profit per customer.
- **Internal Process:** Measures that indicate how effective the organization's internal processes are at satisfying customers and achieving financial objectives. Typical measures include order-to-cash ratios, product development cycle times, labor utilization, days of sales outstanding, and technology support metrics.
- **Learning and Growth:** Measures that show how well the organization's people are equipped to succeed in the workplace, such as training investment per employee, staff turnover rates, knowledge management metrics, and participation in professional associations.

Figure 8-1 shows a typical diagram of the Balanced Scorecard. In it, you can see the four scorecard perspectives, supported by the bedrock of four important core concepts:

---

[10] The Balanced Scorecard uses the term "measure" synonymously with my term, metrics. The balance of this chapter uses both terms interchangeably.

mission, values, vision, and strategy. In his review of Balanced Scorecard, Paul Niven defines them this way:

- **Mission:** A concise statement of why an organization exists, and benefits it brings to the world.
- **Values:** The qualities and guiding principles that shape how the organization acts and reacts.
- **Vision:** A "word picture of the future" that describes what the organization will accomplish in service of its mission. The "vision" is an image, five or ten years from now, of what the organization will have accomplished.
- **Strategy:** Differentiating activities that help the company achieve its vision.

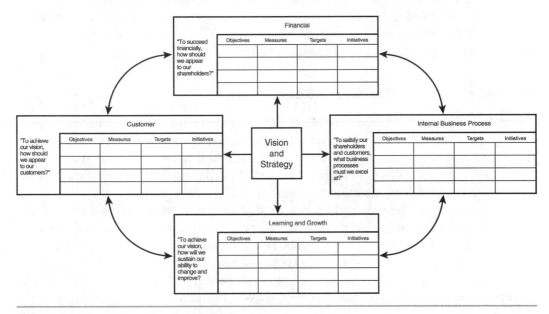

Figure 8-1 The Balanced Scorecard (Redrawn)

Measures chosen for use in a Balanced Scorecard align with an organization's mission, values, vision, and strategy. When implementing a Balanced Scorecard, a significant portion of the up-front planning time is spent ensuring that the measures chosen for the scorecard are in concert with these concepts. I will not get into significant detail here, other than to say that Niven's treatment of the subject is excellent.

Kaplan and Norton stress that measures selected for Balanced Scorecards must demonstrate strong *cause-and-effect linkages*. In other words, the measures in the Scorecard flow directly from the organization's specific objectives, which in turn derive from the corporate vision and strategy.

The strong emphasis on cause-and-effect relationships is not just a nice-to-have feature; it is essential to success. For example, if a firm's objectives include a mandate to offer outstanding customer service, selected measures should indicate how well the organization is tracking toward this objective. Sample "cause" measures might include the number of days required to fill orders or resolve customer service requests. The "effects" could be measured by the rate of customer renewals, number of escalations to management, and net profitability per customer.

Conversely, sometimes an organization cannot identify suitable measures for an objective. In these cases, this means that the objective may be too vague or is inherently immeasurable—and should therefore be discarded or refined. Thus, the Balanced Scorecard penalizes vagueness and rewards practicality.

FLEXIBILITY OF THE BALANCED SCORECARD

The Balanced Scorecard framework is just that—a framework. It is not meant to be an all-singing, all-dancing, one-size-fits-all solution. Rather, the framework recommends that each organization choose measures that best suit its business and are best aligned with its strategy and culture. This gives adopters of the Balanced Scorecard the ability to draw from a deep well of potential measures.

In addition to the wide variety of measures that an organization can choose from, the authors of the Balanced Scorecard point out that even the number and kind of perspectives aren't set in stone. Provided that broad sets of measures are chosen and grouped into a clear set of buckets, organizations are free to restructure the perspectives as they see fit. Thus, an organization that has no customers per se, such as a government agency, might choose to rename the Customer Perspective "taxpayers"—or, more fittingly, "Congress."

CHALLENGES AND BENEFITS OF THE BALANCED SCORECARD

The Balanced Scorecard offers great promise as a framework for measuring organizational performance in ways that go beyond traditional financial metrics. But there is no such thing as a free lunch—all frameworks have caveats. The Balanced Scorecard is no exception. Two problem spots tend to recur: metric saturation and ambiguity.

By "metric saturation," I mean the tendency to try to measure everything under the sun, right off the bat. Balanced Scorecard practitioners caution newcomers not to get too carried away with scorecard measures. It is easy to enumerate a vast panoply of perfect measures that accommodates everyone's wishes and fondest desires. But the desire to please everyone—at least initially—is at odds with the need to get things done. Although I made this point earlier in the chapter, it is worth restating that restraint should overrule enthusiasm, especially with Balanced Scorecards.

A second caution area for would-be Balanced Scorecard implementers lies on the flip side of what would seem to be an advantage: flexibility. Sometimes "flexibility" can be a code word for "ambiguity." Any framework worth its weight in books needs to provide enough versatility to enable champions and practitioners to adapt it to the needs of an organization. But frameworks also need to be practical; they need enough grounding that participants do not spin their wheels endlessly. Exactly what constitutes customers, internal processes, and employee learning is something each organization needs to figure out for itself.

If what I am describing sounds like that gooey, warm, slithering mass known as organizational change, you are right. By virtue of their flexibility and comprehensiveness, Balanced Scorecards cannot simply be taken off the shelf; the perspectives and measures in the Scorecard must be agreed to by an organization's body politic and *adopted*. Adoption implies many things, but for the most part it implies agreement on goals; understanding of what each participant must do to support those goals; availability of work instructions, tools, and support to help each participant do what he or she has agreed to do; and successful execution by all concerned.

In the case of the Balanced Scorecard, organizations must:

- Find an executive who will sponsor the development and implementation.
- Attract a capable and representative team to do the day-to-day development work.
- Achieve organizational consensus on the mission, values, vision, and strategy.
- Agree on a small set of "balanced" perspectives to measure performance.
- Select suitable measures for each perspective.
- Make sure that each measure passes the "So what?" test with executives and the rank and file.
- Develop methods for gathering data and reporting on results.
- Execute, and use lessons learned to make adoption easier.

Done right, the Balanced Scorecard has the potential to help organizations add accountability and a shared understanding of goals and their success criteria. When all levels of the organization agree on suitable measures, the Balanced Scorecard becomes a critical management tool and strategic enabler. We will return to organizational issues later in the chapter.

Everything I have mentioned in the last few pages refers to using Balanced Scorecards in the context of general business administration. For purposes of clarity and brevity, I have left information security out of the discussion. We turn to that discussion next.

CREATING THE BALANCED SECURITY SCORECARD

The Balanced Scorecard provides a holistic view of organizational performance. As a general technique, it balances Financial, Customer, Internal Process, and Learning and Growth Perspectives to arrive at an overall scorecard for an organization. These techniques are fully transferable to the domain of information security.

Some readers may be wondering how the Balanced Scorecard relates to information security. On its face, it probably does not feel like it maps particularly cleanly. The line of reasoning runs this way: it is all fine and good for businesspeople to burble on about "balance," but the Information Security group worries about more pressing issues, such as threats, vulnerabilities, policies, and compliance. Therefore, it would be best to rename all of the Balanced Scorecard perspectives to make them more security-focused.

Right?

Follow that line for a minute. According to Kaplan and Norton, the Balanced Scorecard is not meant to be a straitjacket. For our purposes, it would be perfectly proper to change the number and names of the scorecard perspectives to better match the classical information security paradigms. For example, instead of using the normal Balanced Scorecard perspectives, we could use the four areas I just mentioned to create a "security-centric" scorecard:

- **Threats:** External network risks such as viruses, worms, and DDOS activity in the wild
- **Vulnerabilities:** Weaknesses in enterprise networks or applications, as reported by audits or scans
- **Identity and access management:** The number and kinds of entitlements to data and assets, as possessed by employees and external parties
- **Policies and compliance:** Technical and self-assessed compliance against policy and regulations

We could mock up a pretty nice quadrant-oriented scorecard this way. Each of the four perspectives would have a series of measurements associated with them, with data supplied by periodic surveys and automated electronic methods such as systems management software and antivirus systems.

Sounds good, right?

There is nothing intrinsically wrong with this hypothetical, renamed scorecard. The case for a scorecard framework like this is straightforward and logical. It covers a reasonable portion of the daily operational concerns of security (threats, scans, technical compliance) and addresses several of the longer-range programmatic aspects, too (policies and regulation). In that respect, it would probably provide real value for an operational security manager or CSO.

THE CASE AGAINST "SECURITY-CENTRIC" BALANCED SCORECARDS

The case *against* a security-operations-centric scorecard is equally logical: it is not a "grabber" for the executive crowd. It does not speak their language (dollars and cents, people, time), and it does not align with the rest of the business. We have come up with a fancier set of labels for our security measures, but that is about it. It is really just the same old wine in a different bottle. In short, the case against an operations-centric scorecard is that it is too, well, *easy*.

Likewise, it is tempting to try to morph the Balanced Scorecard into something that maps more precisely into an existing security taxonomy. For example, many information security managers are comfortable with COSO, COBIT, ITIL, or the ISO 17799/BS 7799 taxonomies. These are certainly reasonable taxonomies for defining comprehensive sets of security controls and activities. However, they skate over many difficult questions:

- **How do controls relate to business value?** Security controls don't exist in a vacuum; they must be considered in the context of the business in which they operate.

- **What are the criteria for measuring successful implementation of controls?** Many frameworks document the need for measurement but are glaringly short on practical details.

- **How does the security organization "roll up" metrics for the taxonomy?** The ISO 17799 framework, for example, contains nearly 200 individual control areas. It isn't at all obvious how 10 top-level numbers could meaningfully summarize all the richness and complexity of the underlying controls.

- **Does the taxonomy "bury" essential evidence?** Some controls specified in security taxonomies are more important than others but are "diluted" when rolled up. For example, compliance with password policy is extremely important for sensitive resources. But an abysmal score in this area might roll up into a perfectly ordinary overall "Access Control" score.

- **How well does the taxonomy incorporate both forward- and backward-looking measures** that affect security? To the extent that security taxonomies prescribe metrics at all, they tend to recommend exclusively backward-looking measures, such as the number of security violations or missed patches.

To be clear, security taxonomies are not worthless. Far from it—they provide an essential, shared vocabulary for classifying and assessing security controls. Auditors, practitioners, and regulators alike use taxonomies for evaluation and accreditation. But they do not give us what we need for a Balanced Scorecard: a concise, representative set of measures that link to overall business objectives.

As businesspeople (first) and security professionals (second), we can do better. Confucius once said "Who must do the hard things? He who can." With Confucius in mind, let's try something hard: mapping information security to the Balanced Scorecard without changing any of the perspectives. In other words, using the Financial, Customer, Internal Process, and Learning and Growth Perspectives—straight up.

To map each perspective to security correctly, we need to consider the following issues:

- What does the perspective mean in the general business context?
- Is there a security-related analog?
- What are the prevailing units of measure for this perspective?
- Can we express security-related metrics the same way?
- If not, can we create them by creating composite metrics?

Other security professionals have come close to redefining security measurement along the lines of the Balanced Scorecard. Foster and Chon tiptoe to the water's edge when they acknowledge the Balanced Scorecard's utility to businesses in a paper about justifying security technology spending:

"The effectiveness of nonfinancial approaches can vary depending on the decision tools already in use by a corporation's executives. If executives already use a balanced scorecard, a security scorecard should be a comfortable metaphor."[11]

Thus, it is fair to say that many security professionals have at least passing awareness of what Balanced Scorecards are. The point I would like to make is that we need to extend the concept further to embrace security. It is time to take the plunge.

---

[11]   N. Foster and Y. Chon, "Justifying Security Spending: How to Make a Business Case for Information Security." Published by TruSecure Corporation (2003). TruSecure is now part of Cybertrust.

THE PROCESS OF CREATING THE BALANCED SECURITY SCORECARD

Our attempt at creating a Balanced Security Scorecard adheres to the core Balanced Scorecard formula: defining cause-and-effect measures that align with objectives for the Financial, Customer, Internal Process, and Learning and Growth Perspectives.

Defining metrics for any scorecard, never mind the Balanced Scorecard, is hard work. Organizations must take time to assemble a team, brainstorm ideas, drive consensus, and promote the results. To develop the scorecard, Niven recommends that an organization undertaking a Balanced Scorecard initiative should[12]:

- Identify and agree on the organization's mission, vision, values, and strategy.
- Hold "objective- and measure-generation sessions" with key team members to brainstorm performance objectives and related measures.
- Refine and finalize the measures into a small core set, ideally not more than five to eight for each perspective.
- Identify targets for each metric: short-term (incremental), medium-range, and BHAGs—big, hairy, audacious goals.
- Vet each metric by evaluating the cause-and-effect relationships between objectives and measures, and among perspectives.

At the end of the process, the organization should have a complete set of measures that covers all four perspectives. The measures should relate forward- and backward-looking metrics to the organization's performance objectives. To give you an idea of what this means in practice, Figure 8-2 shows a sample graphical exhibit from Paul Niven that shows the relationships between objectives, measures, and perspectives. Notice how the perspectives relate: the employee Learning and Growth Perspective contributes to internal processes, which ultimately feeds into financial measures.

For the purposes of discussion, the Balanced Security Scorecard outlined in this chapter shortcuts the process a bit. Rather than walk through the initial setup and planning tasks, let's jump right into the objectives and measures, shall we?

In the pages that follow, I will discuss objectives and measures of each of the four perspectives from the classical view of the Balanced Scorecard. The discussion of each perspective focuses on:

- Identifying the perspective's "classic" objectives, from the viewpoint of the Balanced Scorecard
- Discussing how these objectives relate (or not) to information security

---

[12] Niven, Chapters 5 and 6.

- Recasting the objectives from the viewpoint of security
- Identifying a sample set of candidate leading and lagging measures
- Identifying cause-and-effect relationships

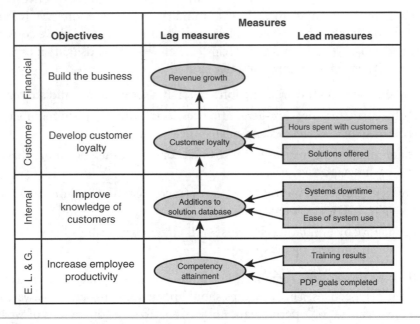

Figure 8-2   Mapping Cause-and-Effect Relationships

Reprinted by permission of John Wiley & Sons. Exhibit from *Balanced Scorecard Step-By-Step: Maximizing Performance and Maintaining Results*, by P. Niven, 2002, p. 167. Copyright © 2002 by John Wiley & Sons; all rights reserved.

After discussing each perspective, I will briefly discuss how to map measures (results) back to objectives (effects). At the end of this chapter, you should have a good idea of what a Balanced Security Scorecard should represent, and how to frame the analytical process. The examples and narrative should provide enough of a framework for you to jump-start your own scorecard initiatives.

FINANCIAL PERSPECTIVE

Summary: the Balanced Security Scorecard's first perspective is the Financial Perspective. It measures how well an organization's security programs support its ability to make money, increase growth, and decrease risk.

Objectives: Balanced Scorecard View

According to the framework for the Balanced Scorecard described by Kaplan and Norton, the goals of the Financial Perspective are to measure areas of financial health that relate directly to an organization's strategy. Accordingly, most objectives fall into the areas of revenues, profits, and growth. Typical objectives for the Financial Perspective include:

- Increasing revenues
- Increasing return on invested capital
- Optimizing usage of capital stock or fixed assets
- Decreasing order-to-cash cycle times
- Maximizing profit
- Decreasing revenue concentration
- Increasing predictability of earnings streams
- Decreasing risk exposure for investment holdings

Typical measures for the Financial Perspective include:

- Return on assets
- Return on invested capital
- Revenue per (billable) employee
- Operating margin
- Net value added
- Earnings before interest and taxes (EBIT)
- Earnings before income taxes, depreciation, and amortization (EBITDA)
- Trailing (and projected) earnings per share
- Percentage of revenue of top x customers ($x = 10, 25, 50$)
- Net portfolio value at risk (for example, at 99% confidence interval)
- Cost of sales as percentage of revenue
- Sales cycle times
- Order-to-cash cycle times

Adjustments for the Balanced Security Scorecard

At first glance, the Balanced Scorecard's Financial Perspective does not appear to share much in common with information security. Many of the financial measures refer to top- and bottom-line concepts like revenue, profit, and cost. Other than cost, security could not possibly have anything to do with revenue or profits, could it? After all, everyone knows that security is "just a *cost center.*"

Security-relevant measures for the Financial Perspective ought to indicate one of these criteria:

- **Promote or hinder the ability to generate, and account for, revenues.** Security is a key component of most companies' technology investments, particularly in operational systems directly related to generating revenues, or accounting for them after the fact.

- **Encourage or retard growth.** Effective security gives customers confidence that they need to do business with an organization; poor security drives them away.

- **Increase or decrease cost.** Spending on security affects organizations' cost structures. Some investments can be tied directly to specific business units; others cannot.

- **Increase or decrease risk.** Information security investments affect organizations' risk postures. Systems with weak controls increase risk; those with appropriate controls reduce risk.

It might seem controversial to try to link security to revenues, but plenty of precedents show that the link is strong indeed.

For example, consider the invention of the Secure Sockets Layer (SSL) protocol by Netscape in 1994.[13] Prior to the invention of SSL, there was no industry consensus on how to ensure confidentiality of HTTP traffic. Specialist companies like Open Market offered solutions, but they were expensive and suffered from the lack of a sizable installed base. But after Netscape unveiled SSL and embedded it in its popular browser, millions of people suddenly possessed the ability to keep their web traffic private. That invention, combined with an act of the U.S. Congress that limited consumer liability for e-commerce credit card fraud, caused e-commerce to take off. We all know the rest of the story: companies like Amazon, VeriSign, RSA, and eBay, capitalizing on consumers' newfound ability to buy goods online, made vast fortunes. These fortunes can trace their lineage to a clever security invention.

Here is a personal example. Several years ago I served as the lead architect and program manager for a collaborative portal for the aerospace and defense industry. Companies in the A&D market have a long-standing practice of building massive data centers, secured like bunkers and firewalled to the gills. The company I consulted for,

---

[13] Kipp E.B. Hickman, SSL 2.0 Protocol Specification, http://wp.netscape.com/eng/security/SSL_2.html.

Exostar LLC, was a joint venture of the five largest aerospace companies in the world—Boeing, Lockheed Martin, Rolls-Royce, BAE Systems, and Raytheon. Exostar had the temerity to suggest that these companies store their CAD drawings, project plans for weapons programs, and other confidential information with Exostar—an *outsider*.

And yet, three years after launch, Exostar's collaboration program has over 5,000 active participants from all five companies. How did they do it? Simple: Exostar implemented exceptionally strong encryption controls for stored data, used multifactor authentication, hosted the infrastructure in an NSA-certified data center, and—most importantly—demonstrated the effectiveness of compliance to its customers through walk-throughs, audits, and periodic assessments. In short, the A&D companies had enough confidence in the security of Exostar's controls that they were not just willing to do business with them—they were enthusiastic. As one customer's CSO put it, "We realized Exostar's security was a hell of a lot better than anything we could ever build in-house."

Exostar's security program cost a king's ransom; it doubled the program budget. But it paid for itself in six months. In other words, security controls increased Exostar's cost of operating its e-commerce systems but enabled the company to generate more revenue.

Pugnacious readers will point out that the SSL and Exostar examples are not especially representative. Their companies are not in the business of working with risk-averse defense contractors, nor of inventing security protocols, they protest. And, of course, they would be right.

But all organizations have customers (paying or otherwise). They manage budgets and risk profiles, too, which security programs can affect. Better security (sometimes) decreases risk, while (usually) increasing cost. The real point of my examples was to provoke readers into exploring the linkages between security, revenues, cost, and risk.

Objectives: Security View

As discussed, the Balanced Security Scorecard's Financial Perspective focuses on revenues, cost, growth, and risk. The Financial Perspective for the Balanced Security Scorecard should measure organizations' abilities to:

- Increase usage of systems that generate revenue
- Increase the integrity of systems that generate revenue
- Increase revenue generated using systems
- Increase the integrity of the process of accounting for revenue
- Decrease the risk of using systems to generate revenue
- Decrease the risk of using systems to account for revenue

- Decrease the cost of securing systems
- Decrease the direct cost of downtime and security incidents

Certain terms require further explanation. To be clear, by "systems that generate revenue" I mean the applications, servers, infrastructure, tools, and people that take customer orders and transform them into receivables and cash. These include e-commerce websites, order-taking software, trading platforms, fund-raising software, EDI- or XML-based order management systems, and payment systems.

By "systems that account for revenues," I mean applications, servers, infrastructure, tools, and people that enable firms to accurately report on the revenues that organizations generate. Systems include accounting packages, spreadsheets, general ledger, and ERP financial modules. These systems also typically account for costs, of course, but for the purposes of discussion we will focus on revenues.

Finally, by "cost" I mean capital and expenditures on people and technology. Major cost categories include hardware, software, maintenance, outsourced services, professional services, direct staff, and shadow staff.

Sample Measures for the Financial Perspective

Measures selected for the Financial Perspective should show how information security promotes or hinders the ability to generate and account for revenues, encourages or retards growth, increases or decreases cost, or increases or decreases risk. Sample measures might include:

- Order or transaction rate
- Order or transaction value
- Number of orders or transactions (total, authorized, unauthorized)
- Number of revenue-generating sessions (total, authorized, unauthorized)
- System uptime
- Downtime cost associated with denial-of-service attacks
- Transaction accuracy (orders, invoices, payables)
- Number of revenue- and cost-accounting events (total, authorized, unauthorized)
- Data flow (customers, vendors, partners)
- Number of controls per transaction
- Number of controls per accounting event
- Cost of security for revenue-generating systems
- Cost of security for revenue-accounting systems

- Cost of security incidents
- Budget allocations for security (new programs, maintenance, discretionary)
- Risk indices for revenue-generating systems
- Risk indices for revenue-accounting systems
- Risk indices for cost-accounting systems

These measures are relatively high-level and could certainly warrant further explanation. We could improve on them by providing further details on the composition of each measure: definition, scope, potential data sources, and performance targets. For the sake of brevity, I leave these tasks as exercises for the reader. If the list I have provided is not suitable for your organization, the examples should be sufficient to get you thinking about other measures.

CUSTOMER PERSPECTIVE

Summary: the Balanced Security Scorecard's Customer Perspective measures how well an organization's security programs permit it to attract, retain, and satisfy customers. These customers may be end users outside the organization, consumers, and regulators.

Objectives: Balanced Scorecard View

Viewed from the point of view of the classic Balanced Scorecard, the Customer Perspective indicates how successful an organization is at satisfying customers. Organizations that measure favorably tend to focus on fostering customer loyalty, increasing market penetration, and improving quality. Typical objectives for the Customer Perspective include[14]:

- Offering value for each customer dollar:
  - Providing competitive prices
  - Increasing choice or convenience
  - Offering wide product selections

- Developing leading products:
  - Bringing breakthrough products or services to market
  - Introducing innovative marketing campaigns

---

[14] Niven, p. 120. Cites Treacy and Wiersema.

- Providing an intimate customer experience:
  - Providing excellent customer service
  - Zero defects

- Acquiring more customers
- Increasing market penetration
- Maximizing share of customer wallets
- Increasing repeat business
- Expanding addressable markets

Typical measures for the Customer Perspective include:

- Market share
- Average transaction price
- Customer churn rate
- Brand recognition rate
- Customer conversion rate
- Sales pull-through ratios for channel partners
- Customer profitability
- Product return rates
- Customer complaints
- Customer service response times
- Number of customer touches
- Service renewal rate

Adjustments for the Balanced Security Scorecard

It is clear from the classical Balanced Scorecard definition of the Customer Perspective that "customers" refers to persons or entities outside the organization that buy goods or services from the firm. Customers include end users, consumers, and business partners.

From the perspective of information security, at first glance it would seem clear that the externally oriented definition of "customer" would not work. After all, most organizations—with the possible exception of managed service security providers—do not sell security per se to their customers. There is no SKU, price tag, or Statement of Work with a line item called "security" that customers pay for. Thus, it would seem that the easiest thing to do would be to redefine "customer" to mean an organization's internal users, business units, and managers who use and consume information security. In other words, Information Security provides security services; everyone else is a customer.

This redefinition certainly seems familiar and intuitive; many IT organizations define their "customers" this way. Entire schools of thought, like the ITIL framework, devote much ink to drawing clear lines between internal technology service providers and their organizational customers. But internal users are not the only customers of information security groups; external entities affected by the organization's security program (positively or negatively) can justifiably claim to be customers, too.

For the purposes of the Balanced Security Scorecard, co-mingling internal and external customers puts us, in my view, in a bit of a bind. Remember that Balanced Scorecards must be concise. By including internal and external customers in the same perspective, we run the risk of diluting the importance of the external constituencies at the expense of internal ones. External constituencies, like consumers and regulators, are too important to dilute.

Recall that Kaplan and Norton's formulation of the Balanced Scorecard takes a similar view: internal members of the organization, while important, are not customers. Instead, the Balanced Scorecard places internal service measurement squarely in the Internal Process Perspective. For the Balanced Security Scorecard, we will do the same. Thus, for "customers," I prefer to take the classical view—external users, partners, and regulators who consume or expect a certain level of security services.

Therefore, security-relevant measures for the Customer Perspective ought to help firms understand how their security program affects external parties. Objectives ought to indicate how information security can:

- **Increase or decrease customers' likelihood of doing business with the organization.** Security measures that are perceived to be effective can play a role in attracting new customers; poor security can repel them in droves.

- **Enhance or hinder an organization's ability to do business with customers.** While security is rarely a commodity or service customers buy, it often plays a catalytic role in enabling business. Security technologies also sometimes enable companies to create new business opportunities that would not have otherwise been possible.

- **Meet, or fail to live up to, security expectations of customers, partners, and regulators.** Trade associations and government agencies often impose security requirements on organizations. Consumers and public interest groups, too, have begun to assert their expectations about how organizations handle security concerns.

- **Burnish or tarnish the firm's reputation in the market.** It's been said the sign of a successful security program is when "nothing happens." Conversely, high-profile hacks can quickly damage a firm's reputation.

A few of these points require further explanation. For starters, the distinction between customers' *likelihood* to do business with an organization (the first point) and their *ability to do so after a relationship has been established* (the second) is an important one. In essence, it is the difference between the run-up to the initial sale and the day-to-day operations that happen afterward. Fully exploring the impact of an organization's security programs on customers requires us to examine both.

Few would argue that security often plays a decisive role in enabling certain types of business opportunities. Virtual private network (VPN) technology, for example, enables partners to keep information private, even when exchanged over open networks; in years past, the parties would have needed an expensive leased line or dedicated modem pool. Likewise, the rise of encrypted and authenticated XML and SOAP messages has largely supplanted traditional EDI as the preferred method of exchanging supply chain information. In both cases, security technologies played a catalytic role.

However strongly one might believe that security plays a role in ensuring the success and continuity of daily operations with customers, the evidence that security plays a primary role in attracting those customers in the first place seems scarcer. In the discussion of the Financial Perspective, I suggested Exostar as an example of a company that successfully attracted customers on the strength of its security program. The pure "enablement" security story is like the Abominable Snowman: it is rarely spotted, but legions of people swear it exists. After all, as my friend Dan Geer puts it, "You don't usually see airlines advertising how their planes fall out the sky less often than their competitors."

But although security is not always a primary attractor, it can play a strong supporting role. For example, consider Internet service provider Earthlink, whose third "feature and benefit" in a recent broadband sales campaign promotes its security thusly:

> *Count on complete protection, for complete peace of mind!*
> *EarthLink protects you against everyday online threats to your privacy and security. EarthLink High Speed comes complete with our full suite of exclusive protection tools—Virus Blocker, Spyware Blocker, and ScamBlocker—to help you block email viruses, sneaky spyware, and online scams.*[15]

Although the first and second items focus on nonsecurity benefits such as time, productivity, and speed, security is not far behind. Interestingly, in September 2005, Earthlink acquired Aluria, the maker of its rebranded Spyware Blocker, for an undisclosed amount.

---

[15] Earthlink High Speed Features & Benefits, September 2005, http://www.earthlink.net/highspeed/features/.

It seems to me that Earthlink felt it could attract substantially more customers by owning the technology itself.

Here's the logic: Aluria claims to have over 35 million customers; if one assumes an average selling price of $10, lifetime revenues would not have exceeded $350 million. If one also assumes that one-third of Aluria's lifetime revenues likely came in 2005, and that a conservative buyout cost equaled exactly one year's revenues, the deal size was probably in excess of $110 million. To put the deal in perspective, Earthlink's 1.44 million broadband customers pay the company an average of $310 per subscriber per year,[16] or $450 million in aggregate.

Clearly, Earthlink would not have made the deal unless it thought the deal would be worth its while in terms of reduced support costs, increased revenues, or both.[17] Assume an equal contribution to each category: that is $55 million, or about 12% of its annual broadband revenues. Although it is a bit slippery and flim-flammy to say so, Earthlink must have believed that Aluria could increase its broadband customer base by at least 12%.

The Aluria deal illustrates the second point from the preceding page: information security protections can enhance an organization's ability to do business with its customers. Recall the $110 million purchase price for Aluria, and my assumption that half of the deal's cost could offset potential savings. Compare the $55 million figure with the approximately $250 million it costs Earthlink to operate its customer support centers;[18] this implies an expected future savings of 22%. This is in line with other estimates of savings that can be attributed to antispyware software; in 2004, spyware accounted for 12% of Dell Computer's technical support calls and for a larger proportion of minutes.[19]

The third point is meant to suggest that security scorecards ought to help an organization understand whether it is meeting the expectations of its customers, partners, and supervising regulatory bodies. Contract law, regulations, agency guidelines, and public lobbying groups all influence the expectations an organization sets for itself. A classic

---

[16] Earthlink 10-Q filing 8/9/2005, http://yahoo.brand.edgar-online.com/doctrans/finSys_main.asp?formfile-name=0001104659-05-037728&nad=. For broadband data customers, Earthlink's average monthly revenue per user (ARPU) was $25.54.

[17] Larry Seltzer makes roughly the same point I do, but with AOL rather than Earthlink. See "Your ISP as a Security Provider," *eWeek*, August 12, 2006, http://www.eweek.com/article2/0,1895,1847799,00.asp.

[18] Earthlink 10-Q filing 8/9/2005, http://yahoo.brand.edgar-online.com/doctrans/finSys_main.asp?formfile-name=0001104659-05-037728&nad=, page 23. For the six months ending June 2005, contact center costs were $120.9 million.

[19] *PC World*, April 19, 2004, "Spyware's Victims Spread," http://www.pcworld.com/news/article/0,aid,115735,00.asp.

example of a failure to meet expectations of partners is CardSystems, a credit card processor for several bank card associations.[20] In early 2004, one of its largest customers (Visa) noticed unusual patterns of activity and realized that someone had stolen credit card numbers. The attacker obtained these numbers from a log file that CardSystems kept on an application server. That data file should not have existed—CardSystems' agreements with its customers specifically forbade keeping credit card data after use. In the aftermath of the breach, customers American Express and Visa announced their intentions to sever their business relationships with CardSystems, citing breach of contract and negligence. Less than three months later, CardSystems was nearly bankrupt. A competitor bought it shortly thereafter.[21]

Finally, the fourth point—that security programs' perceived effectiveness can positively or negatively affect the organization's reputation in the marketplace—warrants discussion. Most examples offered focus on the negative side. Egghead Software, for example, suffered an embarrassing public hack in 2000, was forced to shut down its website for a protracted period, and never recovered.[22] And in 2005, a study by Carnegie-Mellon's Telang and Wattal concluded that 18 public firms that suffered security breaches saw their market values decrease by 0.6 percent on average.[23]

Objectives: Security View

In short, the Customer Perspective of the Balanced Security Scorecard focuses on the impact security programs can have on external actors. The objectives of the Customer Perspective include:

- Increasing the attractiveness of the company's products and services
- Increasing the number of customer orders
- Increasing the volume of electronic business conducted with customers and partners
- Maximizing the number and kind of electronic interchange options

---

[20] My friend Adam Shostack has covered the CardSystems debacle like flypaper. His excellent, privacy-focused blog is at http://www.emergentchaos.com.

[21] *InfoWorld*, September 23, 2005, "Troubled CardSystems to Be Sold," http://www.infoworld.com/article/05/09/23/HNcardsystems_1.html.

[22] @stake, Inc., *Secure Business Quarterly*, L. McCauley, "Anatomy of a Break-In," Volume 1, Issue 1.

[23] Rahul Telang and Sunil Wattal, "Impact of Software Vulnerability Announcements on the Market Value of Software Vendors—an Empirical Investigation," http://infosecon.net/workshop/pdf/17.pdf. I didn't find this study to be particularly persuasive, because the sample sizes are too small and the results too generalized—but it's a start.

- Ensuring the transactional integrity of customer business
- Exceeding customer expectations for availability of systems and data
- Minimizing accidental disclosures of customer and partner data
- Ensuring safe handling of customer and partner data
- Complying with audit requests by customers and partners
- Providing proof of compliance with regulations and statutes
- Preserving the company's reputation for security

Sample Measures for the Customer Perspective

Sample measures for the Customer Perspective should focus on measuring how well the firm attracts and serves customers in an efficient and secure manner, meets expectations with respect to the security and integrity of day-to-day operations, and preserves its reputation. Sample measures might include:

- Percentage of customer wins and losses
- Number of company deals won in which security played a contributing role
- Number (and percent) of customer losses due to security reasons
- Number (and percent) of available electronic interfaces for customers/partners
- Number (and percent) of integrity controls for data exchanged with customers/partners
- Number (and percent) of confidentiality controls for data exchanged with customers/partners
- Number (and percent) of authorized and unauthorized customer/partner transactions, by application
- Number (and percent) of customer/partner employees with access to company systems
- Percentage of strategic partner/third-party agreements with documented security requirements
- Cycle time to grant (or revoke) customer/partner access to company systems
- Uptime percentage for externally-facing systems
- Toxicity rate of customer data
- Volume of electronic customer/partner transactions
- Quantified losses from accidentally disclosed customer/partner data

- Customer/partner ratings of company security effectiveness
- Percentage of externally-facing applications with zero high-risk issues
- Percentage of accredited (signed-off) externally-facing applications
- Number (and percent) of consultations with security teams by externally-facing applications teams
- Number (and percent) of customer consultations with security teams
- Number (and percent) of regulatory audits successfully completed
- Number (and percent) of pending customer-related audit items, and estimated time/cost to complete
- Number (and percent) of pending partner-related audit items, and estimated time/cost to complete
- Percentage of third-party users whose privileges were reviewed this period
- Percentage of systems housing critical assets/functions not accessible by third parties
- Percentage of security incidents involving third-party personnel
- Percentage of third-party agreements requiring external validation of procedures
- Percentage of third-party relationships reviewed for compliance
- Percentage of key external requirements compliant per external audit
- Number of data privacy escalations per thousand/million customers, and estimated time/cost to fix

You will notice that many of the measures I have recommended relate to data privacy and protection of customer information. Although I *am* a privacy proponent and a trifle paranoid to boot, the prominence given to these issues does not reflect a personal agenda. In truth, these measures reflect the old-fashioned idea that when your neighbor loans you something for safekeeping, you ought to take care of it. Measuring the effectiveness of data protection and privacy programs, therefore, might best be seen as a way to put scope, bounds, and expectations on the stewardship of customer data.

In that spirit, consider the notion of a *privacy escalation*, an innovation attributed to Dan Swartwood, the former Data Privacy Officer of Hewlett-Packard and current Data Protection Officer at Motorola. Whenever any HP employee notices an instance where sensitive customer data is at risk of disclosure, he or she files a privacy escalation in a company-wide database. These incidents are tracked and reported monthly. According to Swartwood, privacy escalation measures "give us the ability to measure the extent and cause of privacy incidents to prevent recurring problems .... Additionally, the effort allows us to track and trend areas that may need improvement and show we are meeting our business objectives."[24]

Another idea is the notion of a *toxicity rate* for customer data. This idea comes from Robert Garique, the former CSO of the Bank of Montreal. He treated personally identifiable information from customers as "toxic." The Bank minimizes the risk of leakage by isolating sensitive data in the information security equivalent of concrete drums and mine shafts. Taking Garique's idea a step further, one might compute the toxicity rate by calculating the number of sensitive items in a database (the number of columns and rows containing a customer's name, social security number, and address) over a period of time and dividing it into the number of items overall.

These suggested measures should give you an idea of what the Customer Perspective is designed to accomplish. You will doubtlessly want to develop your own measures.

INTERNAL PROCESS PERSPECTIVE

Summary: the Balanced Security Scorecard's Internal Process Perspective measures how well security programs protect the organization from harm, maximize the availability of IT resources, and enable businesses to respond to new opportunities and threats.

Objectives: Balanced Scorecard View

According to Kaplan and Norton, the Internal Process Perspective concerns itself with supporting operational activities that enable companies to generate revenue and fulfill customer obligations. Successful internal processes lead to happy customers, and happy customers lead to profitability. Typical objectives for the Internal Process Perspective include:

- Developing high-quality products
- Fulfilling customer demand efficiently
- Decreasing the cost of raw materials
- Minimizing logistics costs
- Forecasting customer demand accurately
- Minimizing product development cycle times

---

[24] Nymity, interview with Dan Swartwood, October 2004,
http://www.nymity.com/privaviews/2004/Swartwood.asp.

- Maximizing the availability of internal systems
- Minimizing inventory costs
- Offering prompt and effective customer service
- Invoicing customers and partners in a timely and accurate manner
- Creating innovative products and services

Adjustments for the Balanced Security Scorecard

The preceding discussion of the Financial and Customer Perspectives asked security practitioners to think hard about two concepts they do not encounter very often: customers and money. That may have taken some readers outside their comfort zone—like taking a cat for a walk in the park. But the Internal Process Perspective is more like a nice, comfy living room filled with overstuffed, scratchable sofas and expensive vases begging to be tipped over—in other words, perfect for cats. That is a roundabout and florid way of saying that the Internal Process Perspective is the traditional preserve for all things security-related, and its objectives should present little difficulty for most readers.

Many of the traditional concerns of information security fit right in, without needing additional translation. These include the obvious: minimizing intrusions, managing security vulnerabilities, training and awareness, configuration management, physical security, and so on.

That said, the seeming familiarity of the Internal Process Perspective should not lull readers into a false sense of security (so to speak). It is tempting to simply move traditional security objectives into the Internal Process Perspective and stop there. But remember that internal processes only serve the greater good of satisfying customers and making money. Internal process objectives, therefore, also need to show how security can help other parts of the business achieve their goals.

Therefore, for the Internal Process Perspective, security ought to:

- **Protect the organization from harm.** Successful security programs let trusted parties in, keep unwanted persons out, and reduce the chances that bad things will happen.
- **Grant access to appropriate resources.** Internal users and systems should have access to the resources they need to accomplish their jobs—no more and no *less*.
- **Maximize availability of systems.** Security plays a role in ensuring that critical technology systems can be continuously available to serve the organization, its customers, and partners.

- **Promote technological agility.** Too often security is considered a roadblock to progress; responsive and flexible security teams that engage business units can reverse this perception.

The last point is especially important. I consulted for an organization whose business units saw their security team as The Enemy: filled with niggling naysayers, obstructers of progress, and perpetual paranoids. For their part, the security team would rant and rave about how the business units were filled with reckless cowboys who did not understand the risks they were asking IT to shoulder.

Both parties were wrong—but also right. The security team *did* raise roadblocks at the drop of a ten-gallon hat, but they were not helping themselves, either. They were disinclined to ask questions about what the business units were doing. The business units, on the other hand, disclaimed specific interest in all things security-related and had not been directed to involve the security team at the early stages of initiatives. And so, like a crotchety old married couple stuck in long-established roles, the two parties bickered incessantly.

It did not need to be this way. Setting expectations up front would have led to a dis cussion about the need for responsiveness, flexibility, and agility. This, in turn, would have prompted discussions about realistic service standards for user accounts provisioning, firewall rule creation, and security reviews. The conversations also would have touched on the topics of security policy, accountability, and allocation of responsibilities. In short, the organization needed to take a fresh look at the objectives of its internal security processes and the metrics required to measure their fulfillment.

Objectives: Security View

For the Balanced Security Scorecard, the Internal Process Perspective measures the effectiveness of security program management and its degree of responsiveness to the business. Objectives for the Internal Process Perspective include:

- Protecting information assets
- Ensuring the physical safety and security of people and assets
- Decreasing the damage incurred by security incidents
- Maximizing cooperation between the security team and business units
- Minimizing the risk of attack
- Identifying security vulnerabilities
- Quickly granting or revoking access to systems and users
- Maximizing users' access to appropriate systems
- Minimizing excess privileges granted to users and systems

- Fixing the highest-risk security vulnerabilities
- Maintaining a stable "baseline" for information assets
- Accurately understanding security control gaps and exceptions
- Granting access to assets and networks according to the level of risk
- Verifying the effectiveness of security controls
- Increasing the ability to respond to technological change
- Understanding the organization's risk profile
- Ensuring that security risks are understood and accepted or mitigated
- Maximizing the reach of security controls

Readers will recognize many objectives from the traditional IT security conventions: protecting information assets, minimizing damage from security incidents, identifying vulnerabilities, and the like. Note also the inclusion of objectives that relate to access and agility: quickly granting and revoking access, maximizing cooperation, and accurately understanding control gaps and exceptions. Objectives for the Internal Process Perspectives need to include both viewpoints.

Sample Measures for the Internal Process Perspective

As you might expect, measures for the Internal Process Perspective should provide empirical visibility into how well the organization is protecting itself from harm, granting access, and securing new business opportunities. Sample measures include:

- Percentage of business initiatives with built-in security costs
- Patch latency (mean) by type of technology environment
- Password strength (time to break)
- Percentage of systems with security accreditations (signed off and risk accepted)
- Percentage of security incidents that did not cause damage beyond policy thresholds
- Estimated damage ($) from all security incidents
- Percentage of organizational units with a business continuity plan
- Percentage of IS program elements with operational policies and controls
- Percentage of security compliance reviews with no violations
- Percentage of roles, systems, and applications implementing segregation of duties
- Percentage of users accessing security software who are authorized
- Percentage of users assigning system access who are authorized

- Percentage of highly privileged employees whose privileges were reviewed this period
- Percentage of highly privileged terminated employees whose privileges were reviewed this period
- Percentage of critical assets/functions with documented risk assessment
- Percentage of critical assets/functions with cost of compromise estimated
- Percentage of critical assets/functions with a documented risk mitigation plan
- Percentage of information assets with role-based assignments
- Percentage of critical assets/functions residing on compliant systems
- Percentage of critical assets/functions reviewed for physical security risks
- Number of active user IDs assigned to only one person
- Percentage of systems/applications verifying password policy
- Percentage of terminated user accounts disabled per policy
- Percentage of systems implementing account lockout policy
- Percentage of inactive user accounts disabled per policy
- Percentage of systems implementing approved configurations
- Percentage of systems in compliance with approved configurations
- Percentage of systems monitored for deviations against approved configurations
- Percentage of system configurations compared against the trusted baseline
- Percentage of systems with monitored event and activity logs
- Percentage of systems implementing log size and retention controls
- Percentage of systems with controls to detect anomalous/unauthorized behavior
- Percentage of notebooks/mobile devices checked for compliance at admission time
- Percentage of communications channels controlled in compliance with policy
- Percentage of workstations with antimalware controls
- Percentage of servers with antimalware controls
- Percentage of mobile devices with antimalware controls
- Percentage of systems with the latest patches installed
- Percentage of software changes reviewed for security impact prior to installation
- Percentage of host, subnet, and perimeter firewalls configured per policy
- Percentage of backup media stored offsite

- Percentage of backup media sanitized prior to disposal
- Percentage of downtime of critical services due to security incidents
- Percentage of systems affected by incidents exploiting known solutions/patches/workarounds
- Percentage of security incidents managed per policy/process
- Percentage of systems with critical assets assessed for vulnerabilities
- Cycle time to provision new user security controls
- Cycle time to provision new system security controls
- Cycle time to remove terminated or inactive users
- Cycle time to deprovision users, by system type
- Mean time between failures (MTBF) due to security-related incidents
- Mean time to recover (MTTR) from failures due to security related incidents.
- Number of security team consultations by business units
- Percentage of new systems with initial security consultations

Many of the measures in this list are from the thoughtfully written best-practices guide published by the Corporate Information Security Working Group (CISWG).[25] I have also added quite a few of my own suggested measures. Most companies develop their own measures.

When selecting measures for the Internal Process Perspective, try to achieve a balance between backward-looking measures (lag indicators) and forward-looking ones (leading indicators). As Thomson Corporation's Dennis Devlin puts it:

> *"Things fall into two camps. You either quantify what happened or didn't happen, which is OK—it's the easiest thing to measure, but not terribly relevant—or you quantify an estimation of what the risk footprint looks like, and whether it's getting bigger or smaller. From a practitioner's standpoint, that's more interesting."*[26]

---

[25] Corporate Information Security Working Group Report of the Best Practices and Metrics Teams, November 2004.

[26] Personal interview with Dennis Devlin, May 5, 2005.

LEARNING AND GROWTH PERSPECTIVE

Summary: the Balanced Security Scorecard's Learning and Growth Perspective measures how well an organization equips its employees with appropriate security skills and training. It also shows whether business units and IT are exhibiting behaviors that enable future success.

Objectives: Balanced Scorecard View

In the traditional Balanced Scorecard, the objectives of the Learning and Growth Perspective focus, in general terms, on developing an organization's workforce. Kaplan and Norton spend considerable effort describing why this is important. Simply put, employees with appropriate tools, skills, and knowledge exhibit behaviors that enable them to execute their organization's core internal processes better. Typical objectives for the Learning and Growth Perspective include:

- Developing skilled employees
- Providing a friendly and productive work environment
- Developing an open company culture
- Furthering professional development of employees
- Increasing productivity
- Giving employees the tools they need to do their jobs
- Improving the quality of internal communications
- Promoting business unit collaboration
- Encouraging cultural diversity
- Fostering functional cross-training

Adjustments for the Balanced Security Scorecard

The Balanced Security Scorecard's view of the Learning and Growth Perspective is arguably the least prescriptive of the four. That is, the objectives and measures offered by Kaplan and Norton either are excessively vague or provide exceptional flexibility—depending on your point of view. From the point of view of security, flexibility is a good thing.

For the purposes of our Balanced Security Scorecard, the Learning and Growth Perspective focuses on the requisite behaviors and skills required to ensure that the organization's security processes meet expectations. Most of the Learning and Growth objectives are forward-looking and fall into one of these four themes:

- **Spreading responsibility for security:** Security teams cannot do everything themselves. The business has a role to play in protecting the organization and should be accountable for its security decisions. Security needs to be integrated into business processes.

- **Ensuring that team members possess the right knowledge and skills:** An organization can trace its security effectiveness, in part, to the skills and experience of its team members. Employees require training; for security teams, the "right skills" typically include professional certifications and technical training.

- **Exhibiting behaviors conducive to security:** Effective organizations create environments in which it is easy for employees to act and work securely. To use Dan Geer's formulation, security ought to be "no load" and "inescapable." Effective security engineering should make it easy for employees to make the appropriate security decisions.

- **Encouraging adaptability:** The ever-changing threat landscape requires organizations to maintain eternal vigilance. Organizations' security programs should strive to understand new threats as they emerge, and investigate new countermeasures as they become available.

Several of the themes deserve further comment. Because most of the Learning and Growth Perspective concerns itself with relatively "soft" issues that are not directly related to outcomes, we need to provide specific guidance to keep the discussion grounded in reality, rather than shrouded in generalities.

For example, consider the first issue in the previous list: spreading responsibility for security. It is often taken as gospel that security "is everyone's business." This would seem to suggest that, in the context of the Balanced Security Scorecard, we ought to be able to define specific objectives that organizations can measure. More to the point, the notion of "shared responsibility" implies delegation, which in turn implies that staff other than the security team has primary ownership of large portions of the security program. Would this be a suitable objective for the Learning and Growth Perspective? Most organizations would hesitate to make that leap in logic, because they operate large, monolithic security teams that operate every aspect of their security programs.

Taking the contrarian's view, what if spreading responsibility for security *does* imply that one of an organization's Learning and Growth objectives should be devolution of responsibilities? Indeed, some of the more advanced security organizations are already making the leap. For example, a customer of mine is a prominent investment bank in New York. The firm has long had a large, centralized security team—about 60 people—and maintains sophisticated security systems and processes. However, the managing director in charge of security is actually *decreasing* the team's size rather than increasing it. Specially trained "local security coordinators" in business units are increasingly assuming many of the responsibilities related to training, approvals, and incident response. In today's security climate, why would the managing director do this? Although shrinking the team may seem counterintuitive, it's part of a larger plan to devolve security decisions back to the firm's business units—and spread responsibility for security more widely throughout the company.

A more difficult concept, in practice, is the notion of inculcating correct security behaviors among employees. By "behaviors" I mean both the day-to-day actions that constitute their activities that have security consequences, and the environmental context that might predispose them to act in particular ways. Most organizations place far too much emphasis on the former, without examining potentially significant positive impact of the latter.

For example, security organizations commonly burden employees with increasing mandates to "make security their business" through active behavior modification. Typical user responsibility guides enumerate long lists of best practices and verboten activities that employees must actively practice or avoid. There is nothing wrong with these guides, and every organization should have them. But the longer the list, the harder it is to get users to exhibit correct behaviors.

It is easy, and popular, to blame users for making mistakes. I have done it myself—and in print, even.[27] Microsoft reputedly, in a similar fashion, blamed patch-avoiding administrators for the virus problem.[28] It is convenient to flog employees for failing to adhere to a long list of "dos and don'ts." But it is more difficult to engineer environments in which employees will nearly always make the right choices, without having to think about it.

In the best organizations, it is easy to start secure, and equally easy to stay secure. For example, it is common knowledge that a key reason why the Microsoft Windows security pandemic of the last five years scourged corporations wasn't just pervasive (and continuing) design weaknesses in the majority operating system. The long-rolling wave of virus outbreaks and worm infestations was also made possible by mistakes made by humans—in particular, employees' susceptibility to clicking unknown file attachments or reading HTML-formatted e-mails with embedded JavaScript.

---

[27] S. Gaudin, eSecurityPlanet.com, "Five Years After LoveLetter, Are We Smarter or Safer?," http://www.esecurityplanet.com/best_practices/article.php/3504731, May 12, 2005. "Jaquith says company users are the big problem when it comes to securing a network, adding that most users would probably give up their password to a stranger for a piece of chocolate. 'P.T. Barnum had it all wrong,' he says. 'There are dozens of suckers born every minute.'"

[28] "Microsoft blames laidback sys admins for IIS breaches," 2001, http://software.silicon.com/security/0,39024655,11028169,00.htm.

One can (and should) blame Microsoft for designing operating systems with shabby security designs. One can (and should) blame users for clicking attachments in contravention of policy. But one might also look hard at environmental factors. Was an e-mail client that supports embedded JavaScript—a known threat vector—used? Did the e-mail system allow malicious attachments to get through? Did affected employees possess "administrator" privileges that allowed viruses to spread without restraint? Any one of these environmental preconditions, had they been present, would have increased the risk of infection. The converse is also true: organizations could have reduced risks by removing JavaScript parsing for e-mail clients, scrubbing unknown attachments, and limiting runtime user privileges. Creating conditions that automatically and invisibly induce the correct behaviors, therefore, is as important as the behaviors themselves.

As Ross Anderson and others have noted, security engineering is hard to get right. Good security engineering draws favorable comparisons to application development. In both cases, the project team spends most of its energy and labor figuring out how to best interact with the end user. In the Exostar example I described earlier in the chapter, we spent the majority of the custom application development dollars on usability testing and the security user interface. We felt that security features that were also highly usable would drive adoption and result in higher levels of security.

Apple Computer's Human Interface Guidelines for Macintosh developers, for example, recommend that developers can help people use applications correctly by using clean, simple designs to subtly constrain the range of choices available. Their guidance on user experience testing for applications could easily apply to security engineering, and is worth repeating:

> *"As you observe, you will see users doing things you may never have expected them to do. When you see participants making mistakes, your first instinct may be to blame their inexperience or lack of intelligence. This is the wrong response to have. Remember that the purpose of observing users is to learn what parts of your product might be difficult to use or ineffective because of faulty product design."[29]*

These are wise words. Apple's guidelines stress the importance of usability engineering in fostering correct behavior. This concept applies to security as well. Thus, for the Balanced Security Scorecard, we need to measure not just employee security behaviors, but also the processes used to engineer them.

---

[29] Apple Human Interface Guidelines, "Involving Users in the Design Process," 2005, http://developer.apple.com/documentation/UserExperience/Conceptual/OSXHIGuidelines/XHIGDesignProcess/chapter_3_section_2.html.

The third item that merits explanation is the notion of adaptability. New security threats emerge regularly, so organizations should plan to adapt their defenses accordingly. Thus, an entire set of objectives for the Balanced Security Scorecards' Learning and Growth Perspective relates to creating conditions that allow new threats to be identified, understood, and handled. One might say that this is the security equivalent of Steven Covey's seventh habit, "Sharpening the Saw."[30] Thus, organizations striving for adaptability might choose to contract a security intelligence service or ask its security staff to regularly monitor vulnerability lists. Threat intelligence can take other forms, too; end users are often the best source of emerging threat information. For example, a recent study by security investigations firm Red Cliff noted that of 54 distinct malicious executables discovered on compromised machines, antivirus software detected only eight of them. Employees, noticing nothing more than erratic PC behavior, were the initial method of notification for the rest.[31]

In addition to receiving visibility into new security threats, a second aspect of adaptability concerns emerging security *requirements*. Adaptive organizations need to know what security requirements their business units will need in the future. Business unit heads rarely express security requirements formally. Instead, the security group generally needs to infer what the requirements might be from the context of planned business initiatives.

Regular collaboration and planning sessions can help create a culture of adaptability. For example, suppose a manufacturing company announces its strategic intent to deepen the electronic supply chain linkages with its partners. At collaboration meetings, the security group might begin to hear rumblings from the application development organization about SOAP and web services. Even if no definite plans have been announced, the security group should take said rumblings as its cue to begin investigating web services security technologies and standards such as WS-Security, XML-DSIG, and federated identity management. Thus, when formal development begins, the security group will not be caught flat-footed. Not only that, but by having a solution at hand, the security group bolsters its credibility as an ally and partner.

Objectives: Security View

As discussed in the preceding section, the Learning and Growth Perspective of the Balanced Security Scorecard contains four main themes: spreading responsibility for security, equipping employees with the right security knowledge and skills, encouraging

---

[30] Steven R. Covey, *The 7 Habits of Highly Effective People*, 2001.

[31] Kevin Mandia, "The Evolution of Incident Response" presentation for the Black Hat Briefings; from oral narrative accompanying presentation. (2005)

and engineering correct security behaviors, and promoting adaptability. These themes imply the following typical objectives:

- Delegating responsibility for authoring user activities to business units
- Increasing collaboration between IT security and business units
- Ensuring effective levels of security certifications for security staff
- Promoting security awareness throughout the organization
- Integrating secure behaviors into employees' everyday activities
- Ensuring that security features are easily understood and adopted
- Heightening awareness of emerging security threats
- Exploring discretionary security frontiers
- Giving employees theskills needed to properly handle security incidents

Sample Measures for the Learning and Growth Perspective

To meet the objectives for the Learning and Growth Perspective, security organizations should identify a set of measures that show relative progress toward delegated responsibility, skills acquisition, behavioral engineering, and an increased understanding of future security threats and requirements. Sample measures include:

- Ratio of business unit (shadow) security teams to security team staff
- Percentage of staff with security responsibilities
- Percentage of new employees completing security awareness training
- Percentage of existing employees completing refresher training per policy
- Percentage of position descriptions defining information security roles, responsibilities, skills, and certifications
- Percentage of job performance reviews with evaluation of information security responsibilities and compliance
- Percentage of business unit heads with implemented operational procedures
- Percentage of users who have undergone background checks
- Number of security team consultations by business units
- Fulfillment rate of target external security training workshops and classroom seminars
- Percentage of security staff with professional security certifications

- Number of security skills mastered, average per employee and per security team member
- Percentage of new systems with initial security consultations
- Percentage of business programs with built-in security costs

ORGANIZATIONAL CONSIDERATIONS FOR THE BALANCED SECURITY SCORECARD

We have spent the preceding sections discussing the composition of the Balanced Security Scorecard as the focal point of a security measurement program. I hope that I've persuaded you that its potential utility and power can provide real value to any organization.

As useful as the Balanced Security Scorecard might seem, however, many security organizations—particularly those used to strict taxonomies like the ISO 17799 framework—might find it to be a bit jarring, even radical. That is understandable. In the context of security, Balanced Scorecards go against the prevailing grain. They are disarmingly simple, and they are also necessarily higher-level than framework-focused measures might be (to the extent they exist at all).

Some security organizations might be uncomfortable with the Balanced Security Scorecard concept because it does not give that "old familiar feeling." That is a valid objection. When someone doesn't understand something, it is easy to say no. One way to bridge the gulf between the IT security and business audiences is through a technique called "cascading."

CASCADING SCORECARDS BUILD BRIDGES

Discussed at length by Niven,[32] *cascading* refers to the technique of rolling up scorecards from different parts of the organization. Put simply, departmental scorecards roll up their metrics to higher-level, business-level scorecards. The technique works in reverse too: organizational measures influence and drive the selection and composition of lower-level measures.

Cascading works best when the formula for rolling up measures is clear and transparent. This is an important point. Too often, organizations obscure the formula in such a way that nobody knows how it is calculated. But everyone benefits when the cascading

---

[32] Niven, Chapter 8, "Cascading the Balanced Scorecard to Build Organizational Alignment," pp. 201–221.

formula is dead simple and written in plain language. When each group understands how it can positively (or negatively) affect the overall organizational measures, this helps connect its members' day-to-day activities to the greater good. Niven explains:

> *"An effectively cascaded Balanced Scorecard is not one that simply contains bits and pieces of the highest-level Scorecard. High-level organizational measures could be completely meaningless to the people working at lower rungs of the organizational ladder. A better approach is to carefully examine the high-level Scorecard and determine which objectives and measures you can influence at this level of the organization."[33]*

For example, suppose your organization has identified a high-level objective to maximize the amount of business conducted safely with its suppliers using electronic transaction systems. Two high-level organization measures in the Customer Perspective that support this objective might be

- Dollar volume of transactions conducted electronically, in aggregate and per supplier
- Mean cycle time to provision and initiate transactions, per supplier

From the perspective of security, the second metric "cascades" downward to the security organization. These should be measures that the security organization can influence in a positive or negative way. The cascaded Customer Perspective measures might be

- Mean cycle time to provision partner identities
- Mean cycle time to implement perimeter controls, per partner
- Percentage of electronic transaction messages identified as valid (authenticated and authorized)

These measures could be combined with others from the Sales, Customer Service, and Finance groups to calculate a true "start-to-finish" cycle time that includes all aspects of bringing a new supplier on board. Figure 8-3 depicts our sample cascading process.

This example may seem a bit fanciful—I have deliberately chosen one that is more business-focused than one might typically see in a security context—but it illustrates how the cascading process works. Each department knows how to measure its own performance; each group's results feed the higher-level measures. The combined result provides a complete picture.

---

[33] Niven, pp. 207–208.

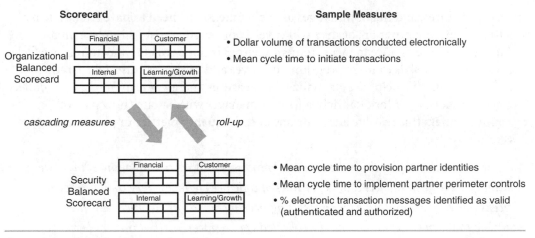

Figure 8-3   Cascading Scorecards

Cascading is a powerful tool that connects the goals and success measures of one organization with those of the organizations above and below it. Cascading benefits not just Balanced Scorecards in the general case, but also Balanced Security Scorecards in particular.

BALANCING ACCOUNTABILITY AND ACCEPTANCE

Breaking down barriers that prevent understanding of the Balanced Security Scorecard is critical to the program's success. Perhaps the most formidable barriers are perceptions and attitudes. What about people who resist scorecard initiatives because it makes them feel threatened?

Ambivalence toward measurement is nothing new. The introduction of Frederick Taylor's principles of "scientific management" in 1911 revolutionized the manufacturing process by providing a systematic way to measure the efficiency of corporations. Many of the industrial productivity gains achieved by society—and the related increases in standards of living—can be traced to the advent of scientific management methods. But at the same time, there has always been an undercurrent of resentment from those under the lens.

Security measurement programs present special difficulty, because many people feel that security is, by its very nature, reactive and unpredictable. The objection goes like this: If we can't measure security, how fair is it to measure *me*?

These objections all stem from a common issue: people like to measure, but they don't like to *be* measured. Scorecards for security metrics are no different. The persons whose successes, failures, and major initiatives are being measured need to have a tangible reason to buy into the program, or they will covertly or overtly resist its implementation.

Surmounting resistance to measurement regimes is not easy. One way to remove feelings of personal risk is to make program objectives and measures *team-based*, rather than individual. This helps depersonalize the measures and gives team members a collective goal to shoot for. Mark Kadrich, a former manager with Sygate (now part of Symantec), offers this real-life anecdote about code-quality metrics implementation at his company:

> *"The interesting thing about the tools and processes that we're employing is that [we attempted to] track defect counts per lines of code per engineer. Very cool for metrics geeks but very intimidating for coders. Engineering hated [it] so much that they insisted that the information not be collected per engineer . . . [but rather] per engineering product team."*[34]

In the end, Kadrich's developers *did* buy into the measurement program, but only after receiving assurance that the scores would be used to further the group's collective objective—writing better code—rather than to finger individual programmers.

SPEEDING ACCEPTANCE USING MOCK-UPS

Organizational and psychological concerns can often derail a measurement program. So, too, can vagueness with respect to results. Many participants in Balanced Scorecard programs want to know what tangible form the scorecard will take when the program is implemented.

Inability to visualize the end product can kill enthusiasm for any effort—not just those of the cancer-curing, globe-spanning, singing-and-dancing, performance-measuring variety. But this issue is particularly important with subjects as new and abstract as a "Balanced Scorecard," something most of the rank and file will not have heard of before. Not knowing what the outcome will be just gives them an excuse to discount the initiative as so much hot air.

In areas other than security, previsualization—prototyping the final result—can be a powerful tool for communicating intent and motivating team members. In the motion picture industry, prototyping techniques like storyboards and computer-generated "previs" movies allow movie directors like Peter Jackson and George Lucas to rough out their ideas before commissioning work to their effects team and studio crews.

---

[34] Message to securitymeterics.org mailing list, August 15, 2005.

Previsualization works in technology, too. A former employer of mine, rapid-application development (RAD) firm Cambridge Technology Partners, perfected a fast-prototyping technique in which consultants built fake application screens overnight to allow customers and prospects to see what the finished application would look like. Cambridge appealed to its customers' need for instant gratification, and in so doing, removed barriers to sale. In the early days, Cambridge won nearly every bid it made using its RAD techniques.

Previsualization works wonders for acceptance of Balanced Scorecards, too. Program managers can, very early on in the program, build a simple set of "mocked-up" Balanced Security Scorecards to show what they might look like.

Creating mock-ups is more of an art than a science. Here are four tips for designing a mock-up for an organization's Balanced Security Scorecard. Effective mock-ups should:

- **Fit on a single sheet of paper.** Scorecards should not be complicated; more than 20 to 25 measures just begs for trouble. If you cannot say what you need to on a single sheet of paper, you are trying to say too much.

- **Convey the program's essence.** Show all four Balanced Security Scorecard perspectives, and include the consensus measures for each perspective. At a glance, readers should be able to get a good perspective on the organization's security program.

- **Sport a clean, uncomplicated design.** Include plenty of white space, and keep the chart junk to a minimum. If you need a model, aspire to the style of *The Economist* or to that of the stocks pages of the *New York Times* or the *Wall Street Journal*.

- **Include a mix of graphics and data.** Too many graphics will confuse the reader's eye, but nonstop columns of numbers aren't good, either. Time series data provides good context; annotations for graphics provide essential narrative support for explaining events.

- **Clearly communicate that the design is *not* final.** Although it may seem like a trivial consideration, it is helpful to prominently label the mock-up as a "draft" or "concept."

When planning a Balanced Scorecard effort, pull in a clever graphics person. Sketch some sample scorecard concepts using your favorite drawing tool, like OmniGraffle, Visio, ConceptDraw, or even PowerPoint. To avoid having team members fixate excessively on a single design—either positively or negatively—create several versions of the mock-up.

Practitioners will find that doing the last things first (mocking up the scorecard exhibit) can powerfully focus the Balanced Scorecard team's attention and stimulate discussion.

SUMMARY

As I mentioned at the start of this chapter, keeping score is a natural human activity. Scorecards help organizations measure their performance by grading their activities against well-understood criteria. To speed acceptance in an organization, security scorecards should be complete, concise, clear, relevant, and transparent.

Scorecards cannot ask too much of viewers. It is tempting to report on everything, even the proverbial kitchen sink. But when constructing a security scorecard, it is wise to scale back the number of selected metrics to the bare minimum. The scorecard should fit on a single side of paper.

Security scorecards work best when they communicate clearly. Clarity implies using plain language and graphics that are easy to understand. Scorecard exhibits should be functional rather than flashy. Annotations are essential for establishing context in scorecards, especially when they include time series graphics. Effective scorecards use quartiles, medians, time series, and cross-sectional measures to provide transparency.

Not all metrics matter to readers. CFOs will want to know about cost and risk, CEOs care about impact on reputation and profit, and CSOs worry about all of these things and a whole lot more. Know your audience; avoid metrics that will cause your audience to shrug their shoulders and say "So what?".

To best align security metrics with senior management, I recommend using an adaptation of the Balanced Scorecard called the "Balanced Security Scorecard." This concept acknowledges that while financial metrics will continue to be used to measure performance, executives need a perspective on nonfinancial metrics that quantify customer expectations and offer insights into the motivation and well-being of employees. The Balanced Security Scorecard, then, contains four perspectives:

- **Financial:** In the traditional Balanced Scorecard, this perspective measures profit and loss, return on invested capital, earnings per share (EPS), and other things. Adapted to the Balanced Security Scorecard, the Financial Perspective should capture metrics that show how security promotes or hinders the ability to generate, and account for, revenues; encourages or retards growth; increases or decreases cost; and increases or decreases risk.

- **Customer:** In the typical Balanced Scorecard, this perspective indicates how effectively the organization serves its customer base. It contains metrics such as customer retention, market share, customer complaints, and profit per customer. The Balanced Security Scorecard's Customer Perspective contains metrics that show how security increases or decreases customers' likelihood of doing business with the organization; enhances or hinders an organization's ability to do business with customers; meets, or fails to live up to, security expectations of customers, partners, and regulators; and burnishes or tarnishes the firm's reputation in the market.

- **Internal Process:** The classic Balanced Scorecard Internal Process Perspective measures how effective the organization's internal processes are at satisfying customers and achieving financial objectives. Typical measures include order-to-cash ratios, product development cycle times, labor utilization, days of sales outstanding, and technology support metrics. The Balanced Security Scorecard's Internal Process Perspective measures how well the security program protects the organization from harm, facilitates granting of access to appropriate resources, maximizes availability of systems, and promotes technological agility in the face of changing threats.

- **Learning and Growth:** In the traditional Balanced Scorecard, the Learning and Growth Perspective measures how well the organization's people are equipped to succeed in the workplace. It contains metrics such as training investment per employee, staff turnover rates, knowledge management metrics, and participation in professional associations. The Balanced Security Scorecard's version of this perspective measures the organization's progress toward spreading responsibility for security, ensures that team members possess the right knowledge and skills, exhibits behaviors conducive to security, and encourages adaptability.

Balanced Security Scorecards should demonstrate strong *cause-and-effect linkages.* When building scorecards, organizations should strive to include metrics that have both lagging measures (historical metrics) and leading measures (which attempt to put numbers around desired behaviors).

The Balanced Security Scorecard might seem radical or jarring to security organizations, particularly those that are used to metrics based on taxonomies like the ISO 17799 framework. That is a valid objection. One way to bridge the gulf between IT security and business audiences is through a technique called "cascading." Departmental scorecards roll up their metrics to higher-level business scorecards, and organizational measures influence and drive the selection and composition of lower-level measures. Cascading works best when the formula for rolling up measures is clear and transparent.

Breaking down barriers, especially perceptual ones, is critical to the success of the Balanced Security Scorecard. Many people feel that security is, by its very nature, reactive and unpredictable, and thus immeasurable. One way to remove feelings of personal risk is to make program objectives and measures *team-based,* rather than individual.

In addition, many participants in Balanced Scorecard programs want to know what tangible form the scorecard will take when the program is implemented. Prototyping the final result can be a powerful tool for communicating intent and motivating team members. Effective mock-ups should fit on a single sheet of paper, have uncomplicated designs, include a mix of graphics and data, and convey the essence of the total program.

Index

Safari®

BOOKS ONLINE

ENABLED

THIS BOOK IS SAFARI ENABLED

INCLUDES FREE 45-DAY ACCESS TO THE ONLINE EDITION

The Safari® Enabled icon on the cover of your favorite technology book means the book is available through Safari Bookshelf. When you buy this book, you get free access to the online edition for 45 days.

Safari Bookshelf is an electronic reference library that lets you easily search thousands of technical books, find code samples, download chapters, and access technical information whenever and wherever you need it.

TO GAIN 45-DAY SAFARI ENABLED ACCESS TO THIS BOOK:

- Go to **http://www.awprofessional.com/safarienabled**

- Complete the brief registration form

- Enter the coupon code found in the front of this book on the "Copyright" page

If you have difficulty registering on Safari Bookshelf or accessing the online edition, please e-mail customer-service@safaribooksonline.com.

Addison
Wesley